W0374192

WHY DOESN'T HE USE A SPOON?

HR

Søren Hilligsøe and Richard Pooley

WHY DOESN'T HE USE A SPOON?

A guide to international business negotiation

April 2016

To Laila

Thanks for your hospitality!

All the best

Søren

Hans Reitzels Forlag

Why doesn't he use a spoon? A guide to international business negotiation

1st edition, 1st printrun

Publishing editor: Lasse Wolsgård
Cover design: Louise Glargaard Perlmutter /Louises Design
Layout and typesetting: Lymi DTP
Type set in: ITC Legacy Sans
Printing: Ednas Print
Printed in Slovenia 2014
ISBN: 978-87-412-5750-1

hansreitzel.dk

MIX
Paper from responsible sources
FSC® C110418
FSC www.fsc.org

Contents

Søren Hilligsøe graduated from the Aarhus School of Business in 1978 with a Masters Degree in English. After graduating he started working as a lecturer at a business college, at the same time using his language skills as an official translator and interpreter.

In the 1980s he worked in export sales in Denmark and the UK, during which time he carried out negotiations with customers in approximately 20 different countries, and in the UK he was involved in numerous negotiations both directly and indirectly as an interpreter.

After his return to Denmark in the 1990s, he started teaching negotiation skills to students, which led to the development of a workshop for businesspeople, which he runs regularly in both English and Danish.

In 2001 he was approved as a trainer of negotiation skills at Management Centre Europe, Brussels. While on the faculty he facilitated both public programmes and in-house programmes for major European companies.

Today he is involved in teaching, lecturing, speaking, writing and training of negotiation skills to students and businesspeople in most of Europe as well as advising and coaching negotiators. For the past eight years he has worked as an Associate Trainer for Canning.

His email is soren@hilligsoe.eu.

Richard Pooley: Richard spent his early years in the UK, Qatar, Zambia, Kenya and Botswana, where he was a Voluntary Service Overseas teacher. After graduating from the University of Exeter in 1974 he worked for the UK's Ministry of Overseas Development in London and, for a short time, at the United Nations in New York.

In 1978, he joined Canning, a UK-based language and management training company. He pioneered the development and delivery of Canning's presentation, negotiation and cross-cultural skills courses through the 1980s and ran their Tokyo office in the early 1990s. During his time at Canning he coached and trained senior managers from major international companies in more than thirty countries on five continents. At various stages since 1986 he has been responsible for Canning's sales in the UK, Japan, South Korea, Brazil, Turkey, Latvia and Estonia.

Richard became a partner of Canning in 1995 and Managing Director in 2005, leading the company to 100% employee ownership in 2009. He retired from the company in 2012 but continues to do specialist training and coaching – e.g. for the Stockholm School of Economics in Riga, Schneider Electric in France, Singapore and the USA, and the University of Exeter in the UK.

Now living in France, Richard focuses on writing, learning French and following the fortunes of Brive's rugby club. He is also a director of Conan Doyle Estate Ltd, which manages the Doyle family's literary, merchandising and advertising rights in Sir Arthur Conan Doyle's works and characters, including Sherlock Holmes.

His email is richard@pooleybath.plus.com.

Acknowledgements

We would like to thank David Lee, Jehad Al-Omari and Chris Fox for their comments on the chapters we asked them to read. David's deep knowledge of Brazilian business culture and Jehad's wealth of stories on negotiating in the Arab world were particularly useful. Chris also gave us permission, on behalf of Richard's former company, Canning, to use the *Negamid* diagram. We hope he does not mind the slight alteration to its labelling. Phillip Lund at Schneider Electric has over the past three years fed Richard an eclectic diet of articles and cartoons on international sales. These informed quite a lot of what we wrote in the first two chapters. We would also like to thank Professor Emeritus Gavin Kennedy for his friendship and inspiration over the years.

We owe a big debt of gratitude to Sarah Pooley, who was our toughest critic. She not only did her best to correct our many errors of grammar, spelling and punctuation, she also made us question a number of our cherished nostrums about negotiating.

The people who have contributed greatly to this book are the hundreds of business people around the world with whom we have negotiated and the thousands of people we have tried to help become better international negotiators. Some of them may recognise themselves in this book, although we hope we have disguised them sufficiently well that others will not be able to identify them.

Vayrac, France and Risskov, Denmark, July 2014

1

What are we on about?

1.1 Why doesn't he use a spoon?
1.2 What do we mean by "negotiation"?
1.3 Is the skilled negotiator made or born?
1.4 Why are international negotiations never quick and easy?
1.5 What result should I want from any negotiation?
1.6 Has the internet fundamentally changed how we buy, sell and negotiate?
1.7 Have you got examples of real business negotiations?
1.8 What happened to David Lloyd George and Eamon de Valera?

1.1 Why doesn't he use a spoon?

It was 11 July 1921. The British Government and the leaders of the self-proclaimed Irish Republic had just agreed to a ceasefire in the brutal guerrilla war which had been going on in Ireland since January 1919. It was time for the two sides to negotiate. The following week the British Prime Minister, David Lloyd George, met the Irish Nationalist leader, Eamon de Valera, in London. They had four meetings that week in which they tried to agree the framework of a treaty that would give most of Ireland her independence. They made little progress and it wasn't until October that the British and Irish started formal negotiations again in London. Although Lloyd George attended these later meetings, de

Valera stayed in Dublin. The Irish leader's absence from the negotiations made it easier for him to repudiate the Anglo-Irish Treaty after it was signed in December 1921. In fact, the terms of the treaty were not that different from those proposed by de Valera himself. Nor were they much different from those proposed by Lloyd George to de Valera at the end of their week of meetings back in July. Hence, many people have asked why the two men could not have reached a tentative agreement at those talks.

Lloyd George made a comment about the Irish leader's negotiating style that was typically colourful and witty:

> Negotiating with de Valera is like trying to pick up mercury with a fork.

But it is de Valera's response that deserves to be remembered and that is the title of this book:

> Why doesn't he use a spoon?

We have often wondered since first hearing of this exchange whether de Valera was just countering one clever remark with an even more amusing one or whether he knew he was making a profound point. Probably the latter. He was not known for his sense of humour.[1]

Historians have long argued about what really happened in the meetings between these two men. Lloyd George had a good idea what he wanted to achieve and how he was going to get it. But he does not appear to have been that interested in what might motivate an Irish patriot like de Valera. Lloyd George was a Welshman, whose first language was Welsh. As a young man, he had campaigned passionately for Welsh autonomy within the UK. So, one would think, here was someone who would understand the emotions that were driving de Valera to demand total independence from the UK for all of Ireland. But instead Lloyd George complained, for example, that the Irishman kept referring to what the British had done to the Irish 300 years earlier under Oliver Cromwell and since. He could not see the relevance of such ancient history to their discussions. He wanted to negotiate with the cerebral Irish leader on an intellectual level whilst de Valera needed to engage with

1 His son, Terry, born in 1922, disagreed: *"Father had an excellent sense of humour, certainly much better than the average"* and cited as proof the fact that de Valera senior would often repeat his rejoinder to Lloyd George "with a chuckle".

the Welshman on an emotional level. The British Prime Minister was a highly experienced and successful negotiator but in this instance he failed badly. He stuck to his predetermined plan and appears to have made little attempt to understand the person he was dealing with, nor adapt his negotiating style nor change his tactics to achieve an agreement. He was not prepared to switch from a fork to a spoon.

This book is a guide to how to negotiate successfully in international business in the 21st century. Yet de Valera's riposte to Lloyd George, made nearly a century ago in the political arena, is a question that is relevant to anyone negotiating a business contract today anywhere from Azerbaijan to Zambia.

Between them over the last 35 years, the authors have been on either the sales or buying side of the negotiating table in more than 30 countries on five continents. For much of that time we have also been trainers of negotiation skills to suppliers and buyers from a wide range of international companies. We have taken part in and heard about numerous negotiations that have concluded with an agreement that proved unsatisfactory or unworkable. And the reasons for such failures have nearly always been the same: lack of flexibility, empathy and creativity by one or both negotiating parties. They came to the negotiations armed only with a fork. In this book we want to tell you why you also need to have a spoon and, yes, a knife and chopsticks too. And we will show you how best to use them.

1.2 What do we mean by "negotiation"?

Gavin Kennedy, a guru to negotiation skills trainers like us, defines negotiation as:

> the process by which we search for terms to obtain what we want from somebody who wants something from us. ... It is an explicit, voluntary traded exchange between people who want something from each other." (Kennedy, 1998)

Negotiation requires movement by everyone involved. If one side does not budge at all and yet an agreement is signed, no negotiation has taken place. As Benjamin Franklin, the US politician and scientist, remarked in 1735:

> Necessity never made a good bargain.

Another US American, President John F. Kennedy, said with reference to the leaders of the Soviet Union:

> You cannot negotiate with people who say what's mine is mine and what's yours is negotiable.

We have settled on the following definition:

> Negotiation is a process of give and take between two or more parties, each with their own needs, targets and world-view, wanting to reach a workable agreement.

Neither Gavin Kennedy's definition nor ours is very catchy. But then negotiations themselves are seldom short and simple. Indeed, if they are, they are unlikely to be effective.

It is worth saying at this stage that "negotiate" comes from the Latin for "business": *negotium*. That word is itself a combination of *nec* (= not) and *otium* (= leisure). The Spanish for both "business" and "deal" is *negocio*. Our Spanish-speaking clients equate doing business with negotiating, which may explain why many of them are puzzled by the readiness of their colleagues elsewhere to compromise when negotiating. Jeswald Salacuse in his 2003 book, *The Global Negotiator,* reveals the results of his survey of over 400 businesspeople from 12 nationalities. A large percentage (74%) of the Spanish claimed their primary goal in a negotiation was a signed contract, whereas 66% of the Indian managers saw their main aim as the creation of a relationship. And 67% of the Spanish saw negotiation as a fight where one side wins and the other loses, unlike all the Japanese who saw it as a collaborative process where both sides win.

So, other than suggesting you take a range of cutlery into the negotiating room, what other questions are we trying to answer in this book?

1.3 Is the skilled negotiator made or born?

No negotiating gene has been discovered. We don't believe there is one. However, it helps if you have certain character traits and abilities: curiosity, creativity, self-control, patience, resilience, a good ear, a sharp eye, a good memory and a head for numbers. And of those attributes, the first three are the most important. Indeed, it could be argued that the rest are included in one of these three. Curiosity can only be useful if you listen and observe. Creativity in a negotiation requires you to remember a lot of things and be adept at swift mental arithmetic. If you can play the waiting game, tolerate ambiguity and handle conflict calmly, you are showing admirable self-control.

A curious person asks questions and listens carefully to the answers. She seeks information and explanation. Armed with this knowledge she can make and then test assumptions. She can begin to understand the real needs and aims that underlie the positions taken by those she is negotiating with. She can also start to formulate creative solutions to mutual problems and find ways around blocks on the way to an agreement. And if she keeps control of her own emotions and is not swayed by any emotional pressure applied by the other side, she will be more respected and more persuasive.

We are sometimes asked where our list of traits and abilities comes from. The answer is from experience and a lot of reading. Whilst there has been a huge amount of research into what type of person makes an effective salesperson and, increasingly, a canny buyer, there has been much less on the qualities needed to be a top-class business negotiator. And even the studies that we have found vary a lot in their findings.

When running a course, Richard will often add "empathy" to the list. According to the Oxford English Dictionary this means "the power of identifying oneself mentally with (and so fully comprehending) a person or object of contemplation." For us it means being able to put yourself in someone else's shoes. We believe it is essential for the effective negotiator to understand the emotional as well as intellectual reasons why the person on the other side of the table is taking a particular position on each issue. The trouble is that so much of the English-speaking world (or, at least, the business part of it) either doesn't understand what empathy means or simply doesn't like the sound of it. Literally, in the latter case. Richard has had serious businesspeople, usually male, opine that empathy sounds weak. Perhaps it is too close in their minds to "pathetic", a word which once was synonymous with "of the emotions" and was not pejorative but to the native English speaker today means "miserably inadequate" (OED). Perhaps curiosity and its attendants, a good ear and a sharp eye, can stand in for empathy.

Clearly, some of the attributes we have listed are largely inherited. But you can still become a better negotiator through practice and learning.

Some learn early because they were brought up in a culture where negotiating was the norm. There is the story of the Vietnamese refugee in the US in the early 1980s who, on reaching the checkout of a small Californian supermarket, insisted on negotiating the price of each item in his full shopping trolley. The bemused checkout staff told him that all prices were fixed. But he was deaf to their explanations and the angry shouts of shoppers queuing behind him. The manager was called and the impatient customers moved to another queue. The Vietnamese man possibly assumed that the boss had arrived because only he had the power to negotiate. So, he kept on demanding hefty discounts. Finally, the manager put all the goods in a bag, handed it to the Vietnamese and told him to take everything - for free - and never darken his store's doors again.

We would contend that many, perhaps most, people in the advanced economies of the West, who are now in their 30s or older, were not brought up to negotiate. In the developed world of the second half of the 20th century, a world of stable careers, supermarkets and fixed prices, children did not observe much negotiating outside the home. Previous generations, like children in less economically-developed countries today, were used to the haggling of street market traders and door-to-door salesmen and entered the world of business much earlier in life. The result was that when young Westerners in the 1960s and later were first faced with the opportunity to negotiate - buying a second-hand guitar or a car perhaps - they didn't realise that they were in such a position. And if they did try to negotiate, they didn't know how to do it. Many found it embarrassing, even frightening. This put them at a disadvantage when negotiating on behalf of their companies in the international arena with people who learned their bargaining skills much earlier in life. Perhaps this explains why we have seen the demand for negotiation skills training in the West grow so fast in the past 30 years.

Søren admits that he knew nothing of negotiating when he first started selling internationally in the 1980s. He'd been brought up by his Danish parents to be nice and pay the asking price. Export sales soon taught him otherwise. He found negotiating both challenging and fascinating. Eventually he tried his hand at negotiating outside the business world, just to see if it could be done. He has never forgotten his first time.

A friend had given him a DVD for his birthday. But he had no DVD player. So, he went in search of one and was soon standing in the electrical goods section of a high-street shop in Denmark listening to a young salesman explaining the virtues of a range of DVD players. Søren had liked the look of a Korean model, retailing at the Krone equivalent of €40. However, the young man dismissed it as "not very good" and, after a quick tour of other, increasingly expensive machines, suggested Søren buy the "state of the art" model at €240.

"What makes it better than all the other ones?" Søren asked.

"Well, it is a well-known brand with high-quality components built to last."

Søren pondered in silence. The salesman then added:

"But it's last year's model and it's the last one we've got."

Presumably he was suggesting that if Søren did not buy it now, someone else might beat him to it. Søren was simply grateful for the extra information. He wondered if he could use it to lower the price. So, he probed further:

"Last year's model, you say. What does that mean?"

"It means that it cannot play all the new formats that have been developed over the last year."

"Such as...?"

The young man mentioned a lot of things that Søren had never even heard of and certainly did not feel that he needed.

"I see. So, this model is **not** 'state of the art' then?"

"Er...that's true," the salesman replied.

"You said that it is the last one you have got?"

"Yes."

"So, it is taking up space on your shelf and stops you displaying the new model?"

"Yes, you could say that."

"Okay, if you make me a good offer, I'll take it off your hands."

"It's €240"

"Come on," Søren countered. "I said a good offer. You have just told me that its use is somewhat limited and you want to get rid of it, but I'm still willing to buy it from you provided the price is right." He supported this by taking out his wallet. "Look, I have brought the cash to pay for it. Make me a proper offer."

Five minutes later Søren walked out of the shop with the €240 DVD-player, having paid just €130. And the salesman "threw in" the cable to connect the player to the TV, which would normally have cost about €25.

The salesman was right about the DVD player. It was very good quality and worked really well for more than ten years. But Søren has often wondered whether the young man reflected on how poorly he had handled the sale. He had asked no questions to find out Søren's needs. He had been pressurised both by Søren's silence and by his questions to say things that weakened his position. He had given things away for free simply because Søren asked him to. It was clear he had never met such behaviour from a customer before.

Since then Søren has seldom missed an opportunity to negotiate, and not just when shopping. If, for instance, a company inconveniences him in any way, he will negotiate compensation. The simple question "How are you going to compensate me for this?" still works well in a world that is unused to negotiating.

Perhaps though "the times they are a'changin'". The arrival of the internet has enabled younger people in the West to learn how to negotiate earlier than their parents did. Price comparison sites and online trading abound. And the harsh economic climate has forced many Westerners – young and not so young – to learn the art of negotiation.

When it comes to learning about negotiation early, Richard was luckier than Søren. Though British, he spent much of his childhood and early adulthood in South America, the Arabian Gulf, and eastern and southern Africa. He has good memories of watching the curio sellers of Lusaka, Livingstone, Nairobi, Mombasa and many a dusty rural African market deal with Western tourists. These salesmen were master negotiators. They were very happy, of course, when the crazy *Wazungu*[2] accepted their vastly inflated "best prices". But, as they confided to the teenage Richard, they were just as happy when they had to haggle, even if they got less money. It was a Zambian who taught Richard the importance of never accepting the other side's first offer:

> If he says yes to my first price, I feel bad. Maybe he would have paid me more. If he wants another thing, I will make an even higher price.

To these Africans negotiating was, and still is, a game to be enjoyed and to be discussed endlessly afterwards. We too love negotiating and hope that comes through in this book.

1.4 Why are international negotiations never quick and easy?

Both of us have been in business negotiations in our own countries – the UK and Denmark – where a satisfactory agreement has been reached in less than an hour. The people in the room spoke the same language, knew each other well and had a deep knowledge of the business being discussed and the companies involved. But as soon as you start negotiating with people you don't know from organisations or sectors you are not familiar with, the road to an agreement becomes longer and less smooth. And if those people are from a different culture and speak a different language, that road to a lasting and workable agreement becomes yet longer, rougher and more hazardous.

We remain astonished at how little serious attention is given to cultural and linguistic differences by so many writers and researchers on negotiation. Much of the research on negotiation has been done in the USA. The work done originally at Harvard Law School has been hugely

2 *Wazungu* means "aimless wanderers" in Swahili, and was used to describe the first European explorers of East Africa. Later, this word was applied to the rich, white colonial rulers and visitors. Today, wealthy black Africans can also be called this, although *wabenzi* – drivers of Mercedes Benz cars – still seems the preferred label for them.

influential and important. It is the basis of most of the negotiation skills courses we know of. But a lot of this research assumes that what has been observed at negotiation tables in the USA applies throughout the world. It doesn't. Talk to seasoned negotiators who have haggled their way across the planet and they will tell you how important it is to understand the very different values, attitudes and behaviour that exist between even neighbouring societies and ethnic groups. We are not talking about cultural etiquette here. Yes, if you blow your nose on a handkerchief in Japan and put it back in your pocket, they will think your behaviour disgusting. If you keep handing documents to your Arab negotiating partner with your left hand, he will feel uncomfortable. But what matters is how and why people around the world interpret so differently other people's behaviour and communication during a negotiation. We have devoted a whole chapter to culture.

It is well known that mistranslation and misinterpretation can bedevil international negotiations. But how many native English speakers realise that they are losing business because they cannot speak or write their own language in a way that can be understood by their negotiating partners? This is one of the things we look at in our chapter on communication. Before we change the subject, let's test you. If you are a non-native English reader, how easy was it for you to understand the title of this opening chapter? If you are a native English reader, try explaining "What are we on about?"[3] to the next non-native English speaker you meet.

Some writers on negotiation give great prominence to different personality types and how best to handle someone who scores high or low on a psychometric test scale. We agree that it is important to understand how your personality can affect your behaviour when negotiating. So, we have written a chapter on personality types. However, we are sceptical as to how quickly you can judge correctly the character of the person you are dealing with, especially if he or she is from another country and speaks a different language. It is even trickier to do so if the negotiation is being conducted online between people sitting in different parts of the world.

We believe it is very important to know your own strengths and weaknesses as a negotiator. You can't become a better negotiator if you

3 It means: "What are we talking about?" Or "What do we mean?" Or "What are our main messages to you?" It can be pejorative.

don't know what needs improving. Hence, you need to learn what type of negotiator your personality has made you become. Not only will this enable you to become more skilled at negotiating, it will also make you more aware of how you may appear to those with whom you are negotiating. The process of analysing your own personality will undoubtedly make you better able to analyse the character of your negotiating partner. If the negotiation process allows you the time and opportunity to assess the personalities you are dealing with, this will certainly help you. But your focus should be on your own negotiation behaviour and communication style and how to improve them.

Cultures are different and have different rules for negotiations; people have different characters and negotiate in different ways. *Vive la différence!* Deal with it – literally.

1.5 What result should I want from any negotiation?

The standard answer to this question in North America and much of Europe is: Win-Win. Unfortunately, this term has become a cliché and often a totally misunderstood one. Too many people think it means you should be nice, open and fair with the other side and aim for a 50-50 compromise. We have seen advertisements for negotiation courses that say: "The most important trip you may take in life is meeting people half way."

This is nonsense. No competent negotiator should be aiming for a 50-50 compromise. You should be trying to get the best possible deal for your side. That could mean that you get 80% of what was available and the other side only gets 20%. If the other side walks away feeling that they still got the things that they really wanted, they will feel they have won too. The point is that it is in your own interests to make the other side reckon they have got a good deal. It is usual in business to want to have a long-term relationship with your suppliers and customers. It is expensive to keep changing suppliers and you go out of business if you keep losing customers. But that is what will happen if they believe you screwed them in the negotiation.

Anyway, a negotiator should not be thinking that there is a fixed amount available to be negotiated. It is rare in business for one side's aims and wants to be a mirror image of those of the other side. A variation on the old story[4] of the two sisters arguing over who should have the one remaining orange in the fruit basket makes this point well. They finally agree that the older sister should cut the orange in half; the younger sister will then choose which half to take. The older sister makes sure she cuts the orange exactly in two. She then takes her half, cuts off the rind and throws the flesh in the bin...at the same time as her sister throws the rind from her half of the orange into the bin and starts eating the flesh. It turns out that the older sister wanted to use the orange rind to make a cake and her sibling wanted it for its juicy flesh. "Why didn't you tell me?" they ask each other. To which the unspoken answer is, "Because you didn't ask." By not finding out the other sister's needs, each ends up with exactly half of what they could have got.

The key message of Follett's story - find out what the other side needs - is central to the original Win-Win concept - often called either *principled* or *integrative* negotiation. If during a business negotiation the two sides manage to create a deal that is bigger and better than both were originally aiming for, then both sides have "won". But this still doesn't mean that they have won equal amounts.

Unfortunately, we have noticed some writers on negotiation have used the widespread misinterpretation of Win-Win to rubbish the concept and sell their books. It appears they have not looked at what the original proponents of the Win-Win approach actually wrote.

We mentioned Harvard Law School earlier. They set up the Harvard Negotiation Project in 1979 to find out what happens when people try to resolve conflicts and negotiate agreements. This research led to what has become known as the Win-Win approach to negotiation.

The original aim of the Harvard Negotiation Project was to answer the question, "What is the best way for people to deal with their differences?" They wanted to find a more productive way of resolving conflict than, say, resorting to a battle between lawyers outside or inside a courtroom. They did so by observing and interviewing professional negotiators.

They found that negotiators tended either to be too "soft" or too "hard". The soft ones tried to create a good relationship with the people on the other side, whom they saw as partners. But, by avoiding

4 Told by the US management theorist, Mary Parker Follett, in 1940

personal conflict, they made too many concessions. They were soft on the people and soft on the points at issue. The hard negotiators were not interested in establishing a strong relationship with people they saw as opponents. They sought to get as much as they could even if it left the other side resentful and hence uncommitted to fulfilling their side of the deal once it had been signed. They were hard on the people and hard on the points.

The people running the Harvard Negotiation Project came up with the concept of *Principled Negotiation,* which argued for a negotiator who was soft on people he was negotiating with but hard on the points they were negotiating about.

This new approach had four guidelines:

PEOPLE	Separate the people from the problem
INTERESTS	Focus on interests, not positions
OPTIONS	Create options for mutual gain
CRITERIA	Insist on objective criteria

The description of the ideal negotiator - soft on people, hard on points - we have reduced to the acronym *SOPHOP.* And the approach itself has become better known as Win-Win.

The lazy writers who rubbish *Principled Negotiation* also state that the Win-Win approach will stop people walking away from a deal when it's in their interests to do so. It is not clear where they get this idea from. Nobody should go into a negotiation without knowing what is ultimately unacceptable to them. You must always know when to say "No" and be ready to leave the negotiation table, temporarily or permanently. It helps a lot if you have worked out what alternatives are available to you if you don't sign the agreement. This is called your "Best Alternative to a Negotiated Agreement" or BATNA. And this idea was developed by the same people at Harvard who gave us Win-Win.

Neither of us like facile slogans for tricky processes, especially one as complicated as negotiating. But if asked to give a label to our approach, we go for "Big Win - Little Win". If pushed to explain this, we add: "Let the other side win just enough."

1.6 Has the internet fundamentally changed how we buy, sell and negotiate?

The development of the internet should have been a boon to business negotiators. People can communicate and do business with each other much more quickly and cheaply. But it has actually made it harder for people to negotiate.

The good news first: it is far easier to be better prepared for a negotiation. Useful information about a company, its products and culture, other suppliers, and even the personalities of the people you are going to negotiate with can be found far more quickly than was possible just a few years ago. But quantity, of course, is not the same as quality. In the new world of Big Data you need to spot the signals relevant to you amid the noise of all that information.

Surely then, with both sides better informed, negotiations should go more smoothly? Not so. The internet has altered the balance of power between buyers and sellers. The ease with which buyers can now compare companies, products, services and prices around the world has made life tougher for negotiators on the sales side. Suppliers are increasingly faced with Requests for Proposals (RfP) from purchasing departments who have trawled the net for information and are confident they know what they want. They appear only interested in finding the cheapest supplier. The RfP process can all be done online and sometimes without any real negotiation taking place.

Recent research by Corporate Executive Board, a major US-based advisory company (Adamson & Dixon, 2011; Adamson et al., 2012), shows that the best performing salespeople are no longer winning business by selling a solution to a problem perceived and defined by their clients. They win by making the client aware of problems that they will face in the medium to long-term and suggesting solutions to those. The CEB researchers call this Insight-Based Selling. "Relationship Builders", who simply try to meet their customers' wishes, are not winning the big business-to-business contracts. "Challengers", who offer customers fresh insights and challenge their assumptions as to what they need, are today's top sales performers. This research looks solid to us. Not only did the CEB people survey over 6,000 sales representatives from 83 companies, they also looked at what was happening on the other side of the table: they studied the purchasing process in nearly 600 companies.

However, we are not convinced that "Relationship Builders", as defined by CEB, were ever the best salespeople. Professor Neil Rackham is one of the world's top authorities on selling, marketing and negotiating. His research on negotiation (Rackham & Carlyle, 1980), even though it was based on observations of trades union-management negotiations in the UK and is over 30 years old, has proved valuable to business negotiators and negotiation skills trainers. We refer to this research several times in our chapters on tactics and communication. Rackham's book, *SPIN Selling*, published in 1988, has been a best-seller ever since and forms the basis of the sales training delivered by Huthwaite Inc., the UK-based research and training company he founded. *SPIN Selling* was the result of a study of 35,000 sales calls made in over 20 countries. Rackham was sufficiently impressed by CEB's research to agree to write the foreword to their 2011 book. He makes this point in it:

> Surveys of customers consistently show that they put the highest value on salespeople who make them think, who bring new ideas, who find creative and innovative ways to help the customer's business.

Richard has been running an advanced sales course with the global account managers at one major international company since 2011. Many of them, from a wide range of countries and selling in many different sectors, have told him that there is nothing fundamentally new in what the CEB people are saying. The best salespeople are those who know their customer's business well enough and are trusted by the customer sufficiently that they are listened to when they challenge their client's current thinking. In other words, the best sales people are what we like to call "Challenging Relationship Builders"... and they always have been.

Even so, as we have said, the world in which salespeople operate has undoubtedly changed because of the internet. They now have to sell to well-trained purchasing managers who are far-better informed than they used to be. To bring such buyers to the negotiation table requires salespeople to challenge the assumptions underlying the buyers' RfPs. They have to make buyers doubt whether they really do know what their companies need. They then have to come up with solutions to problems the buyers may not have realised they had. Hence, negotiators on the sales side have had to become more assertive, more creative and more persuasive.

By far the biggest change that the internet has brought to negotiation is in the use of email and other online methods to negotiate deals. Researchers give a wide range of figures for the percentage of business negotiations that are conducted by email. Everyone agrees that at least a part of all international negotiations is done by email. A significant proportion of such deal-making is done entirely online and by phone with no face-to-face meeting in the same room. We use the phrase "at the table" in this book but, in fact, it is increasingly a figurative term. The negotiators may meet face-to-face on the web using Skype or some other VoIP. But even that is not quite the same as being in the room together. All this has changed the nature of negotiations. We look at the consequences in our chapters on communication and culture.

One of the many unforeseen results of the development of online communication and the increased sophistication of telephonic hardware is that it has become difficult to keep negotiation confined to the workplace or normal working hours. Emails are viewed on smartphones and tablets and few people can resist the siren calls of those electronic alerts even if they are officially on holiday. This has made it difficult to separate the preparation part of the negotiation process from the negotiation itself. Yet the skilled negotiator should still give time to preparation and not allow herself to be hurried into reacting to every incoming call, text message or email.

1.7 Have you got examples of real business negotiations?

We have. We will refer throughout this book to real negotiations that we have been involved in or heard about from our clients. In a number of cases, we have had to disguise the real companies involved to protect the guilty (and to save our publishers from negotiations with expensive corporate lawyers).

At various points in the book we try to make our points easier to understand by referring to a realistic but fictional negotiation between a couple of fictional companies. GerMedica GmbH is an international pharmaceutical company based in Stuttgart, Germany. Balança Tecnologia do Brasil (BTB) is a producer of weighing equipment based in São Paolo, Brazil.

GerMedica GmbH started life in 1886 in Stuttgart. The founders were Dr Maximilian von Niederstein and Dr Friedhelm Ackermann. In the early years, the company only supplied local German hospitals and pharmacies; but during the last century it established subsidiaries in the UK, France, Italy, Spain, Switzerland, Austria and the USA. It is still owned by descendants of the founders, and now specialises in therapeutic agents for the treatment of oncological diseases and their related symptoms. GerMedica's annual turnover is close to €1 billion. Over 10% of this is spent on Research and Development, done at its laboratories in Stuttgart and Pompton Lakes, New Jersey. It employed 2,443 people last year.

Ulrike Fröhlich heads up the laboratory equipment department of GerMedica's Global Procurement Division. She is a 46-year-old married woman from Augsburg in southern Germany. She has two sons. She has a PhD in Chemistry and has worked for GerMedica for 16 years. She has never lived abroad but her job requires her to travel about six times a year to visit overseas suppliers and attend fairs and exhibitions. She speaks high-intermediate-level English and tourist Spanish.

BTB was founded in 1952 in the state of Pernambuco by Adolfo Cunha, grandfather of the current chairman and owner, Vitor Cunha. Its first products were heavy-duty industrial scales and weighbridges for the mining and construction industries. The company later moved into other, smaller types of weighing equipment. Three years ago they launched their first analytical scales for use in research laboratories. BTB's main plant and offices are all on one beautifully-landscaped campus in the wealthy São Paulo suburb of Morumbi, bordered on one side by the *favela* (slum) of Paraisópolis. The company's annual revenue is $180 million and it employs over 1,500 people. Brazil accounts for 80% of its income and the rest of Latin America for 10%. Europe (Spain and Portugal) and Canada each contribute 5%.

BTB's International Sales Manager is Anselmo Oliveira, a 37-year-old married man from Recife in north-east Brazil. He has three children. He graduated in Mechanical Engineering from the Federal University of Pernambuco. Unusually among Brazilians his Spanish is almost as fluent as his native Portuguese. But his English is, at best, intermediate level. He moved from Recife to São Paulo five years ago when he was offered a job by Senhor Cunha.

1.8 What happened to David Lloyd George and Eamon de Valera?

Fifteen months after Lloyd George met de Valera in London he was no longer the British Prime Minister. He never regained power. De Valera became Prime Minster of the Irish Free State in 1932 and eventually President of the Irish Republic from 1959 to 1973. The immediate consequence of Lloyd George's failure to use a spoon in 1921 was a bloody civil war in Ireland. We'll return to this at the end of the book.

2

Is it worth negotiating and, if so, what planning should I do?

2.1 Why negotiate at all?
2.2 Be prepared!
2.3 The Negamid
- **a.** What is it?
- **b.** The Four Constants
  - Culture
  - Company
  - Competition
  - Character

2.4 The law

2.1 Why negotiate at all?

Anecdotal evidence indicates that a lot of commercial transactions between businesses involve no negotiation. A buyer in company A gets quotes from suppliers B, C and D, compares them and chooses supplier C, probably because C's bid is the cheapest. This seems particularly common in the developed world between small companies inside the same country. Yet negotiating is in both sides' interests. If the only benefit from negotiating was for the buyer – by getting a lower price – then the seller would indeed be wise to avoid haggling. But there are several reasons why it is advantageous for a seller to negotiate.

First and most importantly, it is only through discussion between the two parties that each side can find out if the solution to the buyer's problem is the optimal one. For example, it may be that a different model in the seller's product range will meet the buyer's needs better than his first choice. This may or may not improve the seller's profit on the deal but it at least ensures a more satisfied customer who will probably want to buy from the same seller in future. The point is that getting the best deal is not synonymous with getting the best price. What may seem to the buyer to be a minor and inexpensive change to the seller's original proposal may in fact be the difference between a good profit and just breaking even to the seller. Richard saw this often when negotiating training contracts with his company's clients. It made a significant difference to the profitability of a long-running training programme if, say, instead of delivering a two-day course once a week on Wednesday-Thursday, the client would accept having two courses back-to-back from Tuesday to Friday every other week. The latter arrangement was a far more cost-effective use of the trainers' time. It also, for other reasons, often improved the quality of the training itself. Even if Richard passed on some of the cost-saving to the client by lowering his price, his profit would still be greater than under the original arrangement. Yet it wasn't until the clients were negotiating with Richard or his colleagues that they fully understood why a relatively minor change for them could result in both a lower price and better courses.

Another reason to negotiate is that it makes it much clearer to the seller what the buyer is expecting from him and much clearer to the buyer what the seller can really provide. The risk of cost overruns, missed deadlines and sub-standard service or products is significantly reduced. So many business-to-business relationships have soured simply because the client was not absolutely clear in his own mind about the amount of work he wanted the supplier to do. This seems to be a particular problem in the IT field where the scope of work is not specified in sufficient detail before contracts are signed and the client then tries to widen the scope post-signature ("Oh, we need to have this field in the database too..." "We have decided to involve our Spanish and Portuguese offices in this project as well..."). A thorough negotiation process makes such nightmares less likely.

Finally, a business relationship that starts with a negotiation is more likely to be a long-lasting one. It is in the seller's interests to have a negotiation. Both sides invest expensive time, energy and thought to arrive at a mutually-acceptable agreement. Why would a buyer want to go through all that again to arrive at another agreement with a different company, especially if the seller's product or service has met his needs?

If you are selling, you should always ask yourself before embarking on any negotiation whether the final deal is likely to be worth all the hassle of quoting, pitching and haggling. You also need to decide how good your chances are of winning the business. Is your company perhaps being asked to tender solely to satisfy the buyer's purchasing policy? For example, the buyer has already decided to make a choice between two existing suppliers but his policy requires him to get at least three quotes. So, he asks you to make up the numbers but doesn't tell you that you have no chance of getting his business.

We know of at least one case where suppliers were asked to submit detailed technical proposals and drawings as part of their quotes. All this information was then used by the prospective customer to manufacture the product in-house.

You may also be encouraged to bid for work so that the buyer can put pressure on his current supplier to improve their offer. This is a common and legitimate ploy, though it can backfire on the buyer. When Søren worked in export sales, he was invited by a British pharmacy group to tender for some business. But he did not get it. He subsequently discovered that the British purchasing manager had told his current British supplier that Søren's Danish company had quoted similar prices to theirs despite having to ship goods from Denmark to the UK. Surely, the British supplier was asked, you must be able to reduce your price? And they did. Søren did not stop visiting the client. However, he signalled to the buyer that he knew what had happened. A few months later the buyer rang Søren: "Can you help? Our usual supplier is having production problems and can't deliver." Søren offered to send his products at the price he had first quoted in return for a long-term contract. The relieved purchasing manager agreed.

Even if you think the purchasing process is a sham, our advice is to go through the first stage. There is always the chance that your proposal is sufficiently interesting that it makes the buyer question the wisdom of continuing with whatever game he is playing. And, of course, he may not be playing games anyway.

The buyer too sometimes needs to decide if it is worth negotiating. He may be forced to deal with a monopoly supplier - for example, of a rare commodity or of a unique product that has been patented. We can all think of examples in the energy sector where a whole industry, or even a country's economy, is beholden to a single supplier of oil, gas or electricity. We would argue again that it is still worth trying to get the best deal you can. Negotiating with a supplier who knows you have to buy from him is galling and even humiliating. But the negotiation gives you an opportunity to get more information about the supplier and his plans. For instance, what will he do once the seam is mined out, the patent expires or a second gas pipeline is built from a different supplier?

Let us return to the two fictional companies and people we introduced you to at the end of the last chapter. What sparked the business discussions between GerMedica and BTB? What made Ulrike Fröhlich and Anselmo Oliveira decide it was worth trying to negotiate a deal across an ocean and between two continents?

BTB's Brazilian owner, Vitor Cunha, decided last year that the company needed to expand its export business. He told his International Sales Manager, Anselmo Oliveira, to concentrate on winning business in Europe beyond the Iberian Peninsula, and in south-east Asia. This is why Anselmo found himself manning a small stand at the world's largest trade show for the weighing industry, the InterWeighing Fair, held this year in Shanghai. He and his assistant had a lot of interest in BTB's large-scale weighing equipment, mostly from Asian and Australian companies. On the last day he had met a prospective German buyer, Ulrike Fröhlich of GerMedica. She was looking for a new supplier of analytical scales for use in their research laboratories in Germany and the USA. They had had a good meeting. It helped that his assistant speaks a little German as well as excellent English (she comes from Santa Catarina in southern Brazil where a lot of German immigrants settled). Ulrike[1] had fired lots of questions at them. She was particularly keen to assess the reliability and accuracy of BTB's scales and to

1 We shall switch to calling them Ulrike and Anselmo from now on. However, if they were real and were talking to each other, they would continue to use each other's surnames -Ms Fröhlich and Mr Oliveira. In our experience, Brazilians prefer to remain formal in their business dealings with each other and foreigners until the relationship is well established. Germans do the same; though seem happy to switch to using first names with each other when on our courses.

know more about BTB's production process and quality control system. Fortunately, Anselmo's technical background made it easy for him to answer her queries. He, in turn, had asked her questions about their current suppliers, their budget for this equipment and the reasons they were looking for a new supplier.

But, once back in São Paulo, Anselmo wondered if it was worth pursuing the GerMedica lead. He had found out that the Germans currently bought their lab scales from two of the most reputable manufacturers in the industry – Labal Corp. in Basel, Switzerland, and Becker AG in Munich, Germany. Quality was obviously very important to GerMedica. And Ulrike had made it clear that a key issue in deciding which supplier to use was how swiftly the manufacturer could repair or replace a broken-down machine. If a breakdown is not solved quickly enough – inside four hours in some cases – a timed research process at GerMedica's labs may have to be re-run, costing tens of thousands of Euros. So, why would GerMedica even consider a company like BTB? The quality of sophisticated bought-in equipment is much easier to control when your suppliers are only down the road from your head office. And there is no way that BTB could repair or replace their machines inside four hours, unless they were prepared either to have two technicians permanently available in GerMedica's US and German laboratories or to supply one back-up machine for every one they delivered. Both Labal and Becker have US subsidiaries close enough to GerMedica's New Jersey site for this issue not to be a problem for them.

Anselmo had probed a little to see whether Ulrike was playing games with BTB. But she had seemed open and honest. The recent bankruptcies of two major European suppliers and the damage caused to supply lines by natural disasters had made GerMedica's board decide that no company should be allowed to supply more than 35% of any one product or service. Any exception had to have approval from the board. So, GerMedica's annual expenditure of about €1 million on laboratory scales had to be split between Labal, Becker and a third and, possibly, fourth supplier. However, the contracts with Labal and Becker were due for renewal this year. So, how the €1 million was divided between the three or four suppliers had yet to be negotiated.

Anselmo decided to get Senhor Cunha's advice. Was it worth trying to get the GerMedica business – no more than €100,000 in the first year? Even if the Germans were prepared to have a Brazilian supplier, they surely would not risk more than 10% of their annual spend on a far-away, unknown company that had only recently moved into this highly-specialised market. And what prices should he quote if he did bid for GerMedica's business? He had calculated that BTB's standard model scales were about 25% cheaper than those of Labal and Becker, though he had no idea what discounts they offered GerMedica.

Meanwhile, back in Stuttgart, Ulrike had been wondering whether to ask BTB to tender formally for the scales contract. She had liked the way Anselmo had answered her many questions during their meeting; he was not like the typical mouthy salespeople she so often had to deal with. She had also liked the fact that he quizzed her a lot too. He genuinely seemed to want to know more about GerMedica and, in particular, their quality standards.

However, she had met several weighing equipment companies in Shanghai who offered what GerMedica needed. Two of them were Latin American competitors of BTB. She had been impressed by the quality of their products and systems. Their ex-works prices were similar to BTB's – 30% less than Labal and Becker's pre-discount prices for standard models (though their quotes were in US dollars, so she needed to take the volatility of the US dollar:Euro exchange rate into account). Also, unlike BTB, these Latin American firms had been making precision scales for research use far longer than BTB.

Everything she had told Anselmo in Shanghai had been true but she had not told him the whole truth. There was an extra reason why GerMedica might want to work with a company like BTB. It was confidential and, anyway, if she had told him, she would have weakened her bargaining position considerably. She gave herself another week to make up her mind about whether or not to invite BTB to bid.

Back in Brazil, BTB's owner took little time to tell Anselmo what to do. His intuition and his 30 years of experience in buying and selling in Brazil pointed only one way: *Go for it!* If these Germans were playing games, the negotiation would still teach Anselmo and BTB a lot about Europe's biggest market. Anyway, he suspected this Fröhlich woman had not told Anselmo the real reason they were prepared to consider a non-European supplier. Aim high on prices but be prepared to come down a lot. And if they got the business, even if it was small and unprofitable, having a prestigious company like GerMedica as a client would open other doors.

Anselmo had already started to arrange a sales trip to Spain and Portugal. He emailed Ulrike to ask if he could take the opportunity of being in Europe to see her in Stuttgart. His email made up her mind for her. She emailed back and said she looked forward to meeting him at 15.00 on Friday 5 June.

We shall be coming back to the negotiation between Anselmo and Ulrike at various points later. But why spend so much time setting the scene and explaining each person's thinking? Because in our experience not enough businesspeople ask themselves the question: Is it worth trying to do business with company X? As we hope you can see from this simple story, the question forces you to do more than estimate the true value of any contract you might negotiate, important though that is. It also helps you in deciding your aims, targets, strategy and tactics. These are subjects we will be returning to in the next two chapters. Finally, it also pushes you into finding out at an early stage what the other side is really trying to achieve. How? By asking questions. Note how both salesman and buyer appreciated the number of questions each asked the other at that first meeting in China. We shall return to look in detail at this vital negotiation skill in Chapter 5.

2.2 Be prepared!

It is normal to begin a negotiation skills course by asking the participants what they think ensures a successful negotiation. No matter where we are in the world, one of the first words we hear is "preparation". And nearly always someone will quote a proverb or saying. Two of the most popular are Robert Baden-Powell's Scouting motto – be prepared – and Benjamin Franklin's memorable antithesis:

> By failing to prepare, you are preparing to fail.

And, of course, these worthies and our participants are right. You need to be as fully prepared as possible before starting any negotiation. But when we ask the same participants how and what they should prepare, we get a wide range of answers. These will always include variations on the following:

- Decide on our aims and strategy
- Agree on what would be the best overall result for us and what is the minimum that is acceptable

- Calculate the minimum acceptable/maximum achievable on each variable – e.g. price, volume, delivery method and schedule, payment terms
- Fix our opening position
- Figure out what the other side want to achieve and what their priorities are
- (Supplier) Find out who we are in competition with for the contract and work out how our offer is better than theirs
- (Buyer) Compare this prospective supplier's offer with those of their competitors
- (Supplier) Consult with other departments in my company to make sure I don't overpromise and underprice
- (Buyer) Consult with other departments in my company to make sure the supplier doesn't underprovide and I don't overpay
- Work out our tactics

Other, less frequent, answers are:

- Find out about the personalities of the people we are going to be dealing with
- Decide who will be negotiating on our side and the roles we will take
- Agree a process and agenda with the other side
- Consult our lawyers about which country's system of law we want to govern the contract

The answers, of course, often depend on the jobs our course participants have, the businesses they are in, the size and type of deals they negotiate, the countries they come from, their sex, their age and their experience of negotiating internationally.

All buyers tell us that they do a thorough background check on the financial health of the supplier they are about to negotiate with. They will also usually have a long checklist covering such matters as quality standards and systems, employment policy, staff training and qualifications, safety procedures and environmental policy. This is hardly surprising. *Caveat emptor* (*Let the buyer beware*) is a legal warning known to even the most callow purchasing manager. What does surprise us is how few negotiators on the supplier side take equal care to get under the bonnet of their prospective customer. Few have heard of *caveat venditor (let the seller beware*). Yet it is just as important for them to know whether they will get paid on time (or at all) for the goods or services they will be supplying.

However, suppliers seem to be better than buyers at the preparation stage in assessing less quantifiable matters. They spend more time than buyers working out who the real decision makers and influencers are on the other side. They will then do their best to make sure that any negotiation is with such people. As we said in chapter one, the best negotiators on the sales side try to assess what the customer really needs rather than just accept what the customer has said he wants. This makes it easier for the supplier to suggest persuasive solutions to overcome the buyer's resistance once the negotiations are under way.

However much preparation you do, you can't know everything about the other side's needs, interests or possible behaviour. This will lead you to make assumptions about the other side's likely position - its strengths and weaknesses - and their targets. Assumptions though, whilst necessary, must be tested throughout a negotiation. The novice negotiator will base his strategy on such assumptions and be unwilling, often unconsciously, to check whether his assumptions are correct. He is reluctant to change his strategy mid-negotiation. The skilled negotiator, on the other hand, knows that even the best initial strategy will have to be adapted to take account of new information learned during the negotiation.

Field Marshal Helmuth von Moltke (the Elder), the great Prussian general of the late 19th century, knew this too:

> No plan of operations extends with certainty beyond the first encounter with the enemy's main strength. (Translation from German)

This is often translated into English as the simpler "No plan survives contact with the enemy", which seems to suggest that there is no point in making a plan. But this was not von Moltke's message. He was a meticulous planner and highly successful as a result. The key words in the quote are "extends with certainty". He knew that his battle plan would have to adapt continually in response to many new factors - switches in the enemy's lines of attack, deployment of new weaponry, shifts in alliances, changes in the weather.

Another distinguished general, Dwight Eisenhower, Supreme Commander of Allied Forces in the Second World War (and future US President), made a similar point to Moltke's:

> In preparing for battle I have always found that plans are useless but planning is indispensable.

What are both men telling us? Plan your negotiation and keep planning but don't stick to "The Plan".

2.3 The Negamid

a. What is it?

So, how should you plan for any international negotiation?

When Richard and some of his colleagues at Canning were given the task of producing a course on international negotiation skills back in the 1980s, they pooled their own varied experience of negotiating as salespeople in different countries. They then interviewed business clients to check if the current negotiation theory tallied with reality. The few books on negotiation at that time were mostly written from the sales point of view. So the Canning team spoke to buyers to learn how they managed negotiations with suppliers.

One of the main results of this research was the *Negamid* – see Figure 2.1. At first, this was an attempt to visualise the process one might expect to go through in order to reach a deal. You (= *Us*) and the other side (= *Them*) start a long way apart, both in what you want to achieve and how much each side knows about the other. As each side prepares and then negotiates, each learns more about the other's culture and market, about the people involved in the negotiation and about the other company's real needs and goals. Both sides come closer together until a deal is agreed. Inevitably it was, and remains, a very simplistic visualisation of a complicated, multifaceted and, often, tortuous process. Even so, it struck a chord with many highly-experienced negotiators and still forms the core of Canning's and our negotiation skills training. What the course participants particularly like is that it gives them a simple and logical check-list at the preparation stage. This has become its main use.

Figure 2.1 The Negamid (© Canning) adapted with permission from the Canning School Ltd.

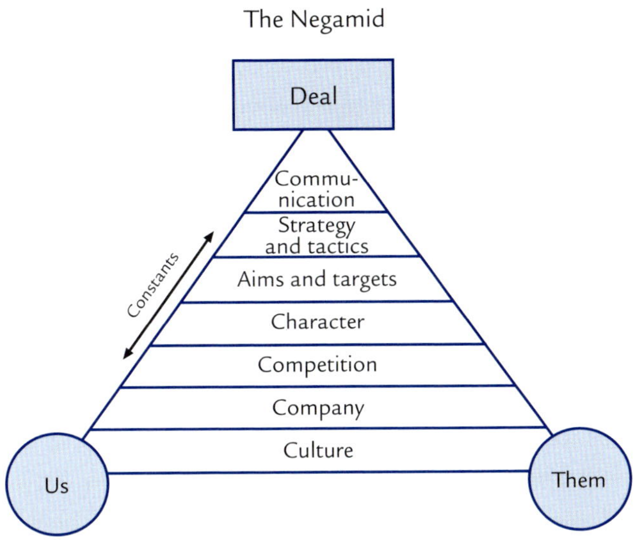

b. The Four Constants

There is nothing in this world constant, but inconstancy.

Jonathan Swift, Anglo-Irish author of that great satire on 18th century political life, *Gulliver's Travels*, was right. But in the short life of any negotiation, four things do, almost always, remain constant: the values of the culture you are dealing with, the condition of the company you are hoping to sell to or buy from, the nature of the market you are working in, and the personalities of the people you are talking to. These form the bottom four layers of the *Negamid*: *culture, company, competition* and *character*. Before you think about what you want to achieve in the negotiation and how you are going to do it, you need to arm yourself with as much data as possible on these four subjects.

We often do an exercise on our courses where we ask people to imagine that they are on a plane, going to negotiate a contract with a foreign company. As they make themselves comfortable in their business class seat they spot that the person next to them works for this company. Perhaps they have seen the company's name on the person's bag as they stowed it in the locker above or maybe it was the logo stuck on the back of the person's tablet or phone.

We ask our participants to write down those questions that they would ask their flight companion, which might help them be better prepared for the coming negotiation. While they are doing this, the trainer draws four squares on the flip chart or white board with a "C" at the top of each one. The students then read out their questions. Three of the four squares fill up with queries such as "Do you know Mr or Ms X?", "Does your company spend a lot on R & D?" and "Who would you say are your main competitors in the Y field?"

These three examples are good questions and could lead to valuable information. The trainer completes the "C" word in the squares - *Culture, Company, Competition, Character* – and puts the questions in the relevant square. However, the answers to many of the questions we are offered could be found easily online or by reading the company's annual report. And the *Culture* box stays empty or nearly so.

Yet the questions that go in the *Culture* box are the easiest to ask your neighbour on the plane. Everyone feels they are experts on their own countries and are happy to talk about their culture without feeling threatened. And these are the questions that can lead people to lower their guard and give you information about the company you are about to do business with, about your competitors, and even about the people you will soon be meeting.

Let's suppose, like Anselmo of BTB, you are flying to Germany to meet a prospective client (in his case, Ulrike of GerMedica). You could try: "It's my first trip to Germany. What things do I need to be careful about when meeting people for the first time?"

Now, we hope that you or Anselmo will have already done your homework and know the answer to that question. And, as you will see later, knowing the correct cultural etiquette when doing business in another country is not as vital as some make it out to be. What is important for you to know before you go into any negotiation with people from another culture is how they see the world, what behaviour they consider normal and positive, and what communication style makes them like and trust you. And those are just the kind of insights a simple question like the one above can elicit. At first, your neighbour on the plane will probably tell you that Germany is little different from your own country even though you both know that this can't be true. He's just being polite. But then he will start telling you about the small differences, which seem to get bigger the more he speaks. He'll start giving you advice and before long he will be telling you what it is like working in his company... the company you are about to visit.

Okay, the probability of finding yourself sitting on a plane next to someone from the company you are about to do business with is very low indeed. But most people who do this exercise learn three things from it about preparing for a negotiation across borders:

- Ask questions that give you qualitative answers on people and their behaviour, as well as ones that give you hard facts and figures
- Seek information about a country, a market, a company or a person in places where opinions are rife and unguarded – e.g. blogs, social media
- Don't underestimate the importance of culture

Culture

Homo Economicus, or Economic Man, may be a useful model for economists but he or she does not exist. Nobody acts wholly rationally with complete knowledge, aiming to make as much money as possible for themselves at minimal cost. If we all did, there would be no need to negotiate anything. We would all know both the price and the value of everything. Negotiation is made complex (and fascinating) because people are emotional, ill-informed and guided by a range of forces, most of which they are not even conscious of.

Each person is a product of the genes they were born with and the environment in which they were raised. Their values, attitudes and behaviour are heavily influenced by the society in which they have been living and the organisational and functional culture in which they work. A young French mechanical engineer working for Renault in Paris won't negotiate in the same way as a middle-aged Indian woman working as a finance manager in the state-owned Indian Bank in Chennai. Homo Negotiatus does not exist either.

We have used the word "culture" in relation to cross-cultural differences several times already. It's time to define it. Here is what Geert Hofstede, the self-styled "founder of comparative intercultural research", had to say in 1991:

> Culture is the collective programming of the mind which distinguishes the members of one human group from another.

Another Dutch researcher and writer in this field, Fons Trompenaars, defined culture in 1993 as:

> the way a group works together to solve its problems ... and reconcile its dilemmas.

The great Chinese philosopher, Kong Qiu, known to Westerners as K'ung Fu-tzu or Confucius, wrote:

> Men's natures are alike; it's their habits that carry them apart.

For us, culture is:

> the way **different groups** of people around the world **solve the same problems** – e.g. how to make decisions, how to communicate, how to live and work in harmony with others, how to learn, how to lead, how to negotiate ...

Note that nobody has equated "culture" with "country". The nation state is a modern construct and a very unstable one too. The world map of 1872 (see Figure 2.2) shows how much national boundaries have changed in the past 140 years. Empires have risen and fallen. Countries in Africa and Asia have been created by colonial officials in far-away cities such as London, Paris, Lisbon and Berlin. Others have emerged from revolution and war, and disappeared, re-emerged, shrunk or grown as a result of further revolution and war. Go back just ten years from 1872 and ask yourself how you would have drawn the boundaries of what we now call the United States of America. Go a little further back to 1800 and you would see that the boundaries in Latin America and Europe are radically different from what they were to become 15 years later.

Figure 2.2 Map of the World 1872 (Wikimedia Commons).

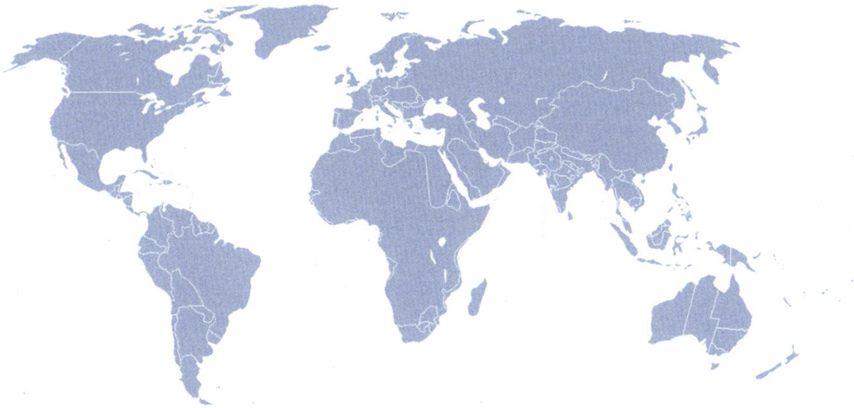

Millions of people fought to create all these nation states. They declared that they were prepared to die for their "country", "nation" or "fatherland". Yet, more often than not, the nation they were creating or defending included several groups of people of different ancestry and history, who spoke different languages or dialects, followed different religions or belonged to different sects, and had different customs and rituals.

Cross-cultural researchers such as Hofstede and Trompenaars have been criticised by anthropologists and sociologists for equating culture with country. Hofstede based his original findings on two separate sets of questionnaires completed by 117,000 employees at IBM's offices around the world in the late 1960s and early 1970s. He had to compare the attitudes and behaviour of people from one country with those of another. The questionnaires did not have the necessary information to enable him to compare one ethnic or regional group of people within a country to other groups within the same country.

We go into detail on culture in Chapter 6 but we will look now at the results of one of Hofstede's "cultural dimensions" – *Power Distance*. It is the most useful one for negotiators preparing for an international negotiation. It is a good guide to the likely decision-making process inside the company you are dealing with.

Hofstede defined *Power Distance* as "the extent to which the less powerful members of institutions and organisations within a country expect and accept that power is distributed unequally." The Hofstede Centre has encouraged people to complete their questionnaire online, enabling it to keep updating the results on this and other dimensions.[2] There has been relatively little change in those results over the past 40 years, despite the disappearance and reappearance of many nation states. A "0" score means that the less powerful people of that country find the notion that power should be distributed unequally totally unacceptable. A "100" score shows that the less powerful see such unequal distribution of power as normal and acceptable.

Figure 2.3 Relationships – Power Distance (Hofstede, 1973, updated 2014).

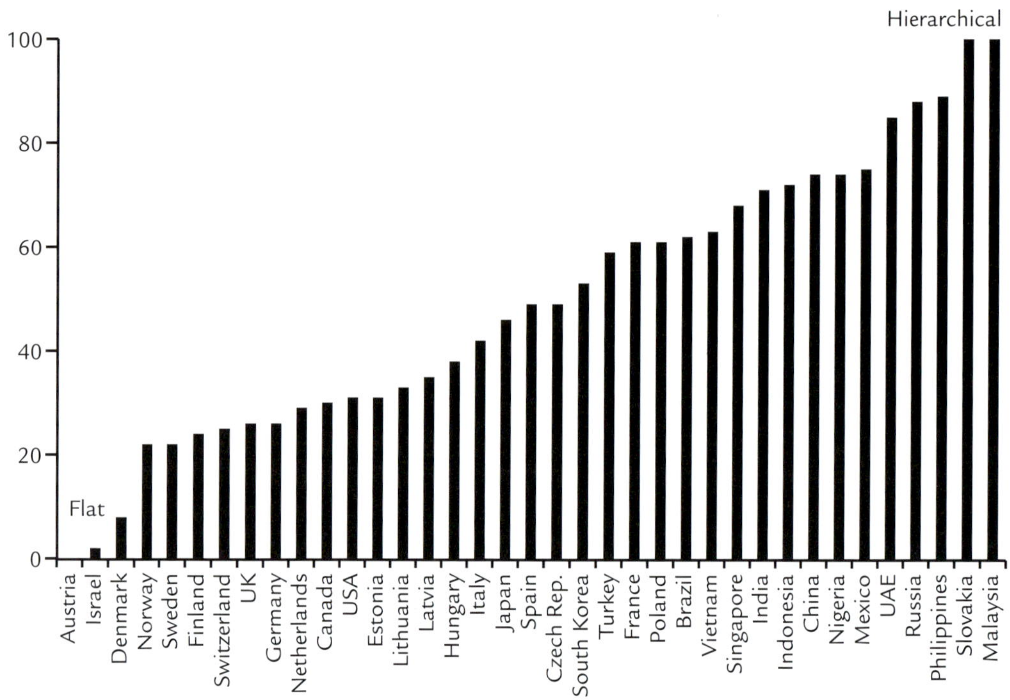

Readers of Hofstede's books and these updated results have said things like:

> Ah, so the Austrians are non-hierarchical, whilst Malaysians are extremely hierarchical.

2 The Hofstede Centre and itim International have developed the *Culture Compass™*. This is a useful tool for negotiators who want to compare their values and attitudes with those of the culture they are dealing with.

Those were the exact words of a Russian businessman on one of Richard's seminars. Such interpretation is very common. It makes life so much easier if we can put each nationality into a clearly-labelled behavioural box and then work out how we are going to do deal with them. Yet, as their definitions of culture show, neither Hofstede nor Trompenaars does in fact say that "culture" and "country" are the same. Their research and that of others such as ourselves, show that a significant number of people of one country tend to think and behave in a certain way. The important words are "significant" and "tend".

Not all Austrians are non-hierarchical. Indeed our own experience of working and negotiating with Austrian businesspeople made us question this particular result of Hofstede's. One of Søren's Danish students spent a semester at an Austrian university and was reprimanded by one of her Austrian professors for only addressing him as "Doctor". She should, he told her, have called him "Doctor, Doctor".

We are not alone in questioning Hofstede's score for Austria. Many have assumed, wrongly, that his "AUS" stands for Australia, which is widely regarded as one of the most non-hierarchical countries in the world. But "AUS" does stand for Austria. Hofstede found, among those 1,247 Austrians in his original study, a majority who would not accept that power should "be distributed unequally in their country". In other words, he found that a significant number of Austrians tended to wish to live in a society where power was spread evenly. His research was done only 25 years after the end of the Second World War; most of IBM's Austrian employees were fairly young. Their views on hierarchy and the nature of leadership must surely have been influenced by their country's recent history. Most of their parents and grandparents had welcomed their fellow countryman, Adolf Hitler, into Austria with great enthusiasm in 1938.[3] In fact, as Figure 2.3 shows, Hofstede's findings continue to be updated and Austrians continue to score very low on this scale.

At the very least, Hofstede's findings could be a starting point for a discussion as to what they might mean for you when negotiating with Austrians. In other words, all this cross-cultural research should be seen as a useful tool with which you can start digging into the culture of the person or people you are negotiating with. But just like all the other

3 For more on Hofstede's Austrian results we recommend you read the article *Austria's Power Orientation – Ending a Controversy on Hofstede* by German cross-cultural trainer, Dr Michael Buchmann. It can be found at www.europublications.com/downloads/austriaspowerorientation.pdf

assumptions you have to make about the other side, you must test the cultural ones too.

In the rest of this book, we shall use national labels – e.g. the Italians, the Danes, the Chinese – just as we have done earlier. This is for convenience. We will assume that you will understand that we are generalising. When we say "the Chinese", for example, we know full well that even though 92% of the population of the People's Republic of China is Han Chinese, this does not mean they will all behave the same way when negotiating with you. There are huge differences within this ethnic group, the world's largest. But even so, there are also significant similarities in values and attitudes that make many generalisations about the Chinese valid and useful for the non-Chinese negotiator.

Some say to us that cultures are changing so rapidly in these days of globalisation and the World Wide Web that one can no longer be sure that what was true only a few years ago is correct today when negotiating across borders. It is certainly true that cultures change, as Theodore Zeldin noted in his book on the French:

> There are two gestures now considered typically French: kissing as a form of greeting, and frequent handshaking. Both were once typically English, and caused much wonder to French visitors [to England]. Kissing was the normal form of English greeting in the reign of Elizabeth I [1558-1603]. In the nineteenth century 'le handshake' was imported from England by dandies; there even used to be professors who gave lessons in Paris on how to shake hands. (Zeldin, The French, first published 1983, latest edition 2012)

Many of the facts about France and some of the descriptions of French etiquette in Richard's well-thumbed 1984 copy of Dr Zeldin's book are now outdated. But the book remains an excellent guide for anyone wishing to understand French values, attitudes and behaviour. These only change slowly over decades or centuries in almost every culture and are what matter to the international negotiator.

So, how can you best prepare to negotiate with people from a particular culture?

First, read our chapter on culture in this book so that you know what you should be trying to find out. Then start exploring in your local bookshop or library or online. There are plenty of excellent books on the market that can answer your questions about the values and norms of business behaviour in all but the smallest country. We have listed at the back of this book the ones we think useful. There are also a few websites that can give you valuable cross-cultural information. We have listed these too. Indeed, go online and type in, say, "Nigerian culture" and you will be overwhelmed with advice on how best to survive and thrive in Lagos, Ibadan or Kano.

If the negotiation is important enough, book yourself on a culture-specific cross-culture course. But check the programme and trainer before signing on. Many of these courses will tell you much about cultural etiquette and very little about what makes people tick in the target culture. The former can be found online for free and is not very important anyway. It's the latter that you need to know. And there are a lot of so-called cross-cultural experts who have gained their knowledge of a country by spending a few months teaching English in some small town in the back of beyond. Ideally, you need advice from someone who has worked in business in the country for several years.

You may be lucky and have colleagues who know the culture you are about to negotiate with. Buy them a drink and pick their brains. If, of course, the negotiation is taking place in a country where your company has an office, you will almost certainly be going into battle alongside local colleagues. Arrive a day early and let them be your cultural advisers.

Company

When Anselmo was preparing for his meeting with Ulrike in Stuttgart he would have found out a lot about GerMedica's structure, financial state, products and purchasing process before leaving Brazil. Indeed, as we have said, he should have learned this before deciding whether to follow up on his meeting with Ulrike at the trade show in China. Such preparation will have told him how many and what type of his products GerMedica could be interested in buying, at what price and on what terms.

But, vital though this information is for the forthcoming negotiation, it is not enough. Anselmo should also spend time trying to figure out GerMedica's organisational culture. This will tell him how decisions in the company are made and by whom. It will tell him what is likely to impress Ulrike and what isn't. That can make all the difference between success and failure at the negotiation table. In fact, if you look back to our description of the meeting in China and Ulrike's feelings about it, you can see that she was impressed by the way Anselmo answered her many technical questions. He gave detailed and accurate answers based on his qualifications and first-hand experience of BTB's manufacturing process. Many of the salespeople she meets don't have such deep knowledge of the products they are selling. Her positive reaction is, of course, a reflection of her own values and background. She has a PhD in Chemistry. She buys highly sophisticated kit for use by her research colleagues. But her reaction is also influenced by her company's organisational values. It is not hard to imagine that a German company with a 130-year history in the pharmaceutical industry, which is still run by descendants of the scientifically-minded founders, will have a strong cultural preference for dealing with well-informed technical people.

There are other clues to GerMedica's and BTB's corporate cultures in our descriptions, which you have, no doubt, noticed. The differences between them could have caused one or two problems in the later stages of the negotiation between the two companies. But, as you shall see, Ulrike took advice from a colleague and managed to avoid them.

So, what is "organisational culture" and how can you get to know what it is in a big international company?

Edgar Schein, a US psychologist and management theorist, described organisational culture as:

> a pattern of basic assumptions invented, discovered or developed by a given group, as it learns to cope with its problems of external adaptation and internal integration... taught to new members as the correct way to perceive, think and feel in relation to these problems.

More succinctly, Bill Ouchi, another US management theorist, defined it as:

> How things are done around here.

These are very similar to the definitions of "culture" we gave you earlier. You can easily find a lot of useful information on the culture of a country online. However, you won't find much about a company's organisational culture when you search its name, unless the company is known to have a distinctive culture – e.g. Google, Procter & Gamble or 3M. The "About Us" section of many companies' websites will proudly tell you what their values are. They will give you their "Vision" and "Mission Statement". US companies, in particular, will do this. However, many Asian and Latin American companies, for example, tend not to tell you their values so openly. Even so, the facts about itself that a company puts on its website can give you an idea of what is important for the people working in the company. Its annual report can give you a few clues if you are good at reading between the lines. The way a company's organisation chart is designed can tell you something about its attitude to hierarchy.

Best of all is to talk to people who have worked for or with the company. And when you go for your first meeting at a company, arrive early so that you can get a feel for what it is like to work there. It's amazing what you can learn about a company's culture by skimming through the latest staff newsletter in the reception area, observing how employees behave or listening to bits of conversation.

A British colleague has had over 35 years' sales experience in various parts of Europe. Here is what he has to say about the importance of understanding the corporate culture of your clients:

> When you go into a prospect's company for the first time, you're going into a new world. It's like conducting an anthropological survey. From the minute you walk in the door, you've got to start building a picture of this unknown tribe's symbols and totems. Individuals take on the colours of what's around them. The guy you're meeting may well, by nature, be open, gregarious and easy-going, but if he's surrounded day-in day-out by a load of uncommunicative introverts, he could appear that way himself. I've got one client company where, regardless of individual personality, everyone is extremely pernickety and anxious about bureaucratic details. In another – a state-owned industry – all the people I meet seem perpetually confused and never quite able to get on top of what is happening.
>
> The tiniest detail can give you insight, so that you've got to be constantly alert and observant. I went into one of Italy's biggest companies many years ago and the first thing I saw – and heard – was a security guard loudly and angrily reprimanding someone who appeared to be a senior manager. What did this tell me?

> Well, of course, there was no way I could be sure at the time. But it was an important impression. The first tiny piece of a huge jigsaw. And that's what you have to do: pick up hundreds of tiny jigsaw pieces and try gradually to fit them together to form a picture.

Competition

Whether you are a buyer or a seller you should know what others in the same market are doing. If you are a buyer, you need to know who your company's competitors are buying from and what exactly they are buying and, if you can, what they are paying. You need to be able to assess the pros and cons of all the products or services that compete with those offered by the seller in front of you.

And, in the same ideal world, if you are the seller, you should have exactly the same information. How else can you respond effectively to the buyer who says he can purchase a better product for less on more favourable terms from one of your competitors?

We don't live in an ideal world though. We have already said that one of the qualities that can help you be a skilled negotiator is to have a good memory. But few people have such a phenomenal memory that they can recall all those facts, figures and arguments in the heat of a negotiation. Even if you can slow the negotiation down to give yourself time to access the data (in your head or on a computer), you will still find it very hard to get hold of exactly the piece of information you need at that moment.

So, be selective. If you are a seller, do all you can to find out who you are in competition with. If the buyer won't tell you, you will have to make some educated guesses. If you are totally in the dark, assume you are up against the competitor you respect or fear most. Then work out how your offer is better than theirs. Be selective here too. Decide what factor is most important for the buyer. Is it price, discount, currency, volume, speed of delivery or implementation, reliability, warranty, design, payment terms, financing, length of contract, exclusivity ... or some combination of a few of these? Then focus on showing how your company beats the others on this issue.

Likewise for the buyer. Decide on your priorities: what must the seller's product or service be able to do for you to even consider buying from them? Then find out what their competitors can offer on those key matters.

One tip for sellers: never rubbish the competition when negotiating with a prospective client. There is a chance that the buyer has bought from that competitor in the past. He may regret doing so but if you say how bad your rival is, you are reminding the buyer of his mistake. You make him feel bad about himself. And he will start to feel bad about you as a result. And if he has not bought from your competitor before? He will still feel bad about you. People simply don't like to hear self-serving criticism and will transfer their negative feelings on to you. Stick to the facts and show how you are better than the competition, not how they are worse than you.

Anselmo of BTB is lucky. He knows who his main competitors are; Labal and Becker are GerMedica's current suppliers and clearly highly thought of by the client. Ulrike has indicated that BTB will be judged on the reliability and accuracy of their products, though price will still be important. He must ensure he knows all he can about his competitors' production process and quality control system. He knows their list prices for standard models. He needs, if he can, to find out what they charge for bespoke models, and whether BTB have the necessary expertise to produce such tailored equipment. GerMedica may invite others to bid for this contract. Ulrike would not have gone all the way to Shanghai to his industry's main trade show unless she had a real need to find additional suppliers. But Anselmo has no idea who these other competitors might be. His best course of action is to focus on learning more about GerMedica's current suppliers.

Ulrike knows all she needs to know about her current suppliers. However, she badly needs to get more information about BTB's competitors, especially in Latin America. Quality is indeed her priority. So, she needs to be sure that a new supplier's production process meets her company's very high standards. She also requires assurance that a supplier can always deliver on time and at very short notice. She may have to go to Latin America to check out several companies, including BTB.

Character

We'll hand back to our sales colleague for this section:

> If a prospect offers me a coffee, I always say: yes. Ordering the coffee distracts his attention from me for a few moments. That

> means I can observe him as he speaks to his colleagues. I can look round his office, and glance at what's on his desk. When I first joined the Sales Department, the guy who was training me asked whether I could read upside down. I thought it was rather an odd question at the time. But I soon found out why he thought this was such an important skill. You can find out a lot from the papers and scribbled notes on someone's desk. In fact, the whole office and everything in it can give you valuable clues about the company and the person you're meeting.

He then tells some stories about people he has done business with. We particularly like this one:

> Then there was the lady whose office felt more like a meditation room. When I walked in – at 10.00 in the morning – there were candles burning on her desk. We spent a very pleasant hour together talking about life and business in general. But I left without any clear idea of what she really needed. I later discovered – from one of her colleagues – that she had recently converted to Buddhism. Whenever I was in her town, I made a point of dropping in to see her for an informal chat. Round about the fourth of fifth visit, we finally got down to business. Contrary to my initial expectations, she turned out to be one of my best clients: efficient, practical, well-organised, extremely open and very straightforward.

Both sides in any negotiation should take time to find out about the people they are about to deal with. Sites such as LinkedIn can be a mine of information.

Like us, our sales colleague is sceptical about the value of personality type theories in analysing a prospective customer, though he found them useful in analysing his own sales and negotiating style:

> I don't consciously try and fit a customer into any particular category. You know, this guy seems to be an intuitive type, so I'd better appeal to his imagination. Or, this one's obviously a visualiser, so I'll paint plenty of word pictures. You simply don't have the time or the brainspace. You've got to keep an open mind. Initial impressions can be very misleading. All you can do is keep your eyes and ears open; pick up and try and interpret as many pieces of the jigsaw as you can; respond positively; try

and mirror or match your prospect's way of doing things; and constantly adapt to what you are perceiving. You've got to make sure the customer enjoys meeting you. He's more likely to do that if he feels you understand something about him.

2.4 The law

If you are going to do business with a company in another country, it is essential that the contract states clearly and unambiguously what will happen if something should go wrong. If there is a problem between two companies based in the same country, any dispute that cannot be solved through further negotiation will be settled within the legal system of that country. However, what happens if, say, a Danish supplier is battling with a Chinese buyer over the interpretation of their contract? If that contract does not state explicitly and accurately what legal system governs the contract ("governing law") or in which place the dispute will be arbitrated ("the dispute resolution forum"), both companies could end up spending a fortune in legal fees in what lawyers call "conflict of laws disputes". Not only will resolving such conflicts be very expensive, they drag on for a long time and make it almost impossible for an equable business relationship between the two companies to be restored.

There is no point in drawing up a contract between companies in different countries if there are no clauses stating the governing law and the dispute resolution forum. The contract really won't be worth the paper it is written on. The governing law is usually that of the buyer's country but can be that of the seller, or of an entirely different country. English law is the one most commonly used to govern international commercial contracts. Within Europe, French, German and Swiss law are commonly used. In the USA, it is New York law. In Asia, Japanese, Hong Kong and Singaporean law are the most favoured. Likewise, any litigation to settle disputes does not have to be in the same country as that of the governing law.

If we take the Danish-Chinese example, the Chinese buyer will probably try to insist during the negotiations that the governing law is Chinese and that any litigation takes place in China. The Danes should not allow themselves to be pushed into accepting this. If they suspect that as a non-Chinese company they may not get a fair hearing in a Chinese court (and, there is, sadly, a mass of evidence that they will not), they should counter by proposing that a different governing law be agreed –

e.g. English law – with, say, Hong Kong as the dispute resolution forum. They may be surprised at how readily the Chinese client agrees to this (after showing a suitable amount of apparent distress at the implied insult to China's legal system).

One reason why English and American law are so popular when choosing the governing law in international contracts is that they are common-law systems. Cases are decided by precedent: what decisions were made in similar cases over the past centuries? Companies who go for these systems can have a good idea what the judgement is likely to be should they go to court. On the other hand, in civil-law systems – e.g. those operating in France, Spain and Portugal and in the countries of their former empires, judges can interpret laws in many different and surprising ways. Companies are much less sure what will happen if they end up in court.

Going to court is costly and time-consuming. So more and more companies are choosing private arbitration rather than trying to solve disputes in court. The International Chamber of Commerce in Paris and the Singapore International Arbitration Centre are both growing in popularity.

Why mention all this at this point? If the international deal you hope to sign is a significant size and at all complex, you must decide which governing law and dispute resolution forum is best for you. This will mean consulting lawyers who know what the advantages and disadvantages are of choosing one law rather than another when doing business with a foreign company. This will take time (and money!). So, get the advice before you step on the plane. And be ready to negotiate on both the law and the forum.

There is an extra matter to watch out for when drawing up an international contract. If the two parties speak different languages, it makes sense to have the contract in both languages. Make sure that you get a professional translator to check the wording in the version that is in the other side's language. It is common for smaller companies to keep their costs down by using part or all of standard foreign language documents when drawing up bilingual contracts. This is risky. We have come across several cases where the wording in the contract, whilst correct in one language, has been mistranslated. For example, in one recent case, "English law" in the English version of the contract was translated into Russian as "law of Great Britain". There is no such legal system and so the Ukrainian arbitration tribunal decided that it could not establish the true wishes of both parties as to which governing law prevailed. This may seem a strange decision to any neutral observer; surely it is pretty obvious what the wishes of both parties were. It was just a translation mistake. Yes, it was, but one that proved very useful to the eastern Ukrainian company when they wanted to wriggle out of their obligations under the contract.

Different cultures around the world have very different attitudes to contracts. Developed countries in the West tend to have great respect for the law and place considerable importance on having water-tight contracts. But in a country like China, for example, contracts are often viewed with suspicion and as attempts by foreign companies to trick them. The Chinese see litigation in resolving disputes as a sign of shameful failure; the two sides should be able to bridge their differences quietly and privately. The well-known and very costly legal war between the French company, Danone, and its Chinese joint venture partner, Wahaha, between 2007 and 2009 shows what can happen if these different attitudes are not understood and discussed during an international commercial negotiation. We will come back to these differences in greater detail in Chapter 6.

What about BTB and GerMedica? The German buyers would expect the Brazilians to agree to have German law governing the contract between them and for any dispute to be dealt with in Germany. After all, they are the buyers and they have little experience of working with Latin American companies and no in-house knowledge of Brazilian law. If, however, GerMedica plan to build their market in Latin America, they might find that their new Brazilian customers, for example, will insist that their country's law govern their contract with the Germans. Moreover, Brazil has a new and effective local arbitration system which has the force of law. Many foreign companies working in Brazil have accepted the country as their dispute resolution forum when negotiating with local companies. Could GerMedica's legal department use any contract with BTB as a means to learn about the Brazilian legal system? Unlikely perhaps but Ulrike should have a word with her legal colleagues.

Anselmo has a relaxed attitude to contracts. In Brazil, if there is a problem in a business relationship, you don't call in the lawyers. You sit down with your supplier or client and find a solution together, preferably over a very cold beer or a *caipirinha*.[4] Anselmo calls this *jeitinho*. Literally, this means *a little way*. In practice it means *there has to be a way around this problem*. So, he is probably not intending to argue over which country's law should govern the contract with GerMedica. In fact, he has probably not even realised that this is something that is negotiable. When selling in Latin America and Iberia, he has just assumed that the buyer decides. It would be a good idea if he took this particular issue and contracts in general a bit more seriously when negotiating with Ulrike. She will lose confidence in a person who does not seem to take care that every clause in a contract is clear and unambiguous.

4 A potent alcoholic drink made with sugar-cane juice, sugar and limes.

3

What do I want to get out of this?

3.1 Aims

In the previous chapter we introduced you to the Negamid and discussed how to start preparing for your next international negotiation. Now, we will move up the model to the next stage in the preparation process: deciding on your aims and targets.

These two words are often thought to be synonymous. We believe there is a subtle yet important difference between them. An aim is more general than a target. Perhaps your aim is to reach a deal with a large customer in a new market. Making a large profit is not a priority. More important is to begin establishing a reputation for high quality and reliability. By contrast, your targets are specific and many. For example, you may want to sell at least 100 machines a year over a three-year period at a price per unit of no less than $2000 ex works, payment within

60 days, quoting in US dollars, and with staggered delivery every six months. You can accept a profit margin as low as 2%.

An aim is often qualitative, whereas a target usually has a number attached to it.

When Ulrike of GerMedica visited the InterWeighing Fair in Shanghai, she wanted to identify additional suppliers of analytical scales for use in her company's research laboratories in Germany and the USA. She already has two suppliers – Labal in Switzerland and Becker in Germany. But the board of GerMedica has decided that no company should be allowed to supply more than 35% of any product or service. So, she must find at least one more supplier of these sophisticated products. She is also under constant pressure to reduce costs. She has discovered that BTB and other Latin American producers are up to 30% cheaper than Labal and Becker, even after transport costs are taken into account. Should she cut the number of machines she buys from her existing suppliers? It's convenient that their contracts are up for renewal later this year. However, there is an extra reason why she is particularly interested in sourcing from Latin America: GerMedica is planning to establish a Research & Development facility in São Paulo, Brazil, within the next two years. Everyone in the Purchasing Division has been told to take this into account when looking for new suppliers or renegotiating contracts. And like all her colleagues, Ulrike has been told not to reveal this information in negotiations until absolutely necessary. There is a danger that she would weaken her bargaining power if she were to tell a Brazilian supplier about this, especially if this company were the only specialist producer in the country. There is another reason why she mustn't show her full hand too early but we shall come to that later in this chapter. So, what is Ulrike's aim? To find at least one Latin American, preferably Brazilian, supplier to provide very reliable, high-quality analytical scales at a lower cost than her current Europe-based suppliers.

And what is Anselmo's aim? BTB's owner wants to increase their export business, especially outside the Spanish and Portuguese-speaking world. Senhor Cunha worries that too many of their eggs – four out of five – are in the Brazilian basket. So, Anselmo wants to reach a deal with a company like GerMedica at almost any price above break-even. With a German pharmaceutical company like them on BTB's client list, doors at bigger European companies such as Bayer, Sanofi and Roche, would surely open for him.

3.2 Targets

Negotiating involves movement. In order to reach an agreement both parties must be willing to move towards each other on most issues. The assumption at the beginning of most negotiations is that there is some distance between the targets of the two parties. "We're still a long way apart on price," or "We're getting a little closer to agreeing on the delivery schedule," are typical ways of describing this distance.

If you were trying to buy a silk scarf in Yeşilköy market or the Grand Bazaar in Istanbul, you would normally haggle over the price and nothing else. You would have an idea of what is a reasonable price for the scarf and would have worked out what is the most you are willing to pay. The latter would be your *exit point*; a centime, penny or kuru more and you would head for the exit. If you wanted to start the negotiation yourself, you might suggest a price to the stallholder which is less than the price you consider reasonable. This is your *entry point*. In reality, of course, the stallholder will have told you the price of the scarf as soon as he saw you glance at it. This will be his *entry point* and, this being Turkey, his opening price will probably be higher than your *exit point*! But you have haggled in many markets and know that sellers often quote an absurdly high price at first. So, you tell him that you saw a similar scarf at half his price at the other end of the market and start to walk away. He calls you back and after much bad acting by both of you a price is agreed which is a bit closer to his *entry point* than yours (he has sold thousands of scarves in the past 30 years; you have only bought three in your life). But the final price is within both your *exit points*. There has been movement along a single line of possible prices and all you had to do was work out a target - the reasonable price, the minimum you think it is worth - your *entry point*, and the maximum you are prepared to pay - your *exit point*. You were calculating your negotiating or bargaining range.

Determining your negotiating range

A typical commercial negotiation is far more complex than the bargaining in a Turkish market. Many issues other than price have to be agreed. And on each matter, each side should have worked out its target, its *entry point* and its *exit point* - i.e. their negotiating ranges. Nor are the issues independent of each other. The better made a product is, the higher its price is likely to be. The longer a buyer extends the payment period, the more a seller will demand a higher price to compensate him for having to wait for payment. So, you have to bundle all the variables into a package and prioritise each one before even getting to the negotiating table.

You must have a clear understanding of what you want to get out of any negotiation before you get into it. What is the best deal that you can realistically hope for? How much are you willing to concede on some issues? If you do not have a negotiating range on at least some matters, you have no flexibility in the negotiation and it is likely to end in deadlock.

Your Most Desirable Outcome (MDO)

When you were haggling over that silk scarf in Istanbul, your *entry point* was the minimum that you thought it was worth (having assessed that it was real silk rather than fake). The best deal you could have got was to pay that *entry point* price. If the stallholder had agreed to sell the scarf at that price, then you would have achieved your most desirable outcome (although we hope you might have revised your belief that the scarf was made of real silk).

In the much more complicated negotiations of international business, you still need to establish the most desirable outcome (MDO) for your company, however hard it may be to calculate exactly. Look at all the different targets that are in the package you are negotiating and decide what you simply MUST achieve (high priority), what you WOULD LIKE to get (medium priority) and what would be NICE TO HAVE (low priority).

In Ulrike's case, the most desirable outcome of her negotiation with Anselmo includes getting a price for the analytical scales that is 30% below the amount GerMedica is paying its two current suppliers. But this is a medium priority and her negotiating range is quite wide - between 10% and 30% below the current price.

Her biggest concern is quality. Her top priorities are to have a supplier who can meet the necessary DIN (Deutsches Institut für Normung) standards for such precision instruments and can repair or replace any malfunctioning machines within a very limited time period. She is all too aware that if just one machine fails to work during a timed research process in GerMedica's labs and is not fixed or replaced, the whole procedure may have to be repeated at a cost of tens of thousands of Euros. So, no matter how low BTB's price, if they are not able to offer a solution that guarantees that GerMedica's research projects are not disrupted, Ulrike cannot do a deal with Anselmo. Whilst a satisfactory solution to this swift repair or replacement issue is a non-negotiable target for her, the various ways of achieving it are negotiable. If BTB offer to train GerMedica's laboratory maintenance staff to repair a broken-down machine, using components and software supplied by BTB, what will it cost and who will pay for it?

Another high priority for Ulrike is to have a small order of five standard machines to be tested in the first six months. GerMedica needs to be sure BTB's products are reliable and accurate before they will place a much bigger order.

Payment terms are a low priority for her. GerMedica gets negligible benefit by taking, say, 90 days rather than 60 to pay $10,000. Even on an annual order of $100,000, payment terms remain a low priority. However, she knows that they could be a higher priority for BTB. If Brazil's inflation rate continues to rise, suppliers like BTB will want to be paid as quickly as possible.

Your Least Desirable Outcome (LDO)

Back to that market in Istanbul. You really like the scarf and are convinced that it is indeed made of real silk. But the stallholder has hardly moved from his ridiculously high opening price. In fact, he has only come down to your *exit point* – the highest price you are willing to pay. It's getting late and the traffic to the airport will be building up. You mustn't miss your plane. You pay up, consoling yourself with the thought that the Turkish seller would have accepted a much lower price if the scarf had not been made of silk. It was the least desirable outcome of the negotiation but at least there was a positive outcome: you are the proud possessor of a beautiful silk scarf.

Just as you must work out the most desirable outcome to any negotiation, so you must look at the other end of the negotiation range and decide what is the minimum you can accept in order to close a deal – your least desirable outcome (LDO)

And Ulrike's least desirable outcome in the negotiation with Anselmo? She has to find a new supplier, even if GerMedica do not set up an R & D facility in Sao Paolo. Her top priority is quality. So, she will be satisfied if she signs a contract with BTB that guarantees no disruption to her pharmaceutical company's research process, wherever that takes place. If this means accepting a price that is only 10% lower than the price charged by GerMedica's current suppliers, she won't be especially happy but it will be better than any other deal she is likely to negotiate.

NEGOTIATING RANGES

Example 1: A DEAL IS POSSIBLE

(seller) MDO ———————————— LDO

LDO ———————————— MDO (buyer)

Example 2: A DEAL WOULD NOT MAKE SENSE

(seller) MDO —————— LDO

LDO —————— MDO (buyer)

In example 1 above, there is a generous overlap between the ranges of the two negotiators; so, in principle, they should be able to reach an agreement.

However, in example 2 there is no overlap between their respective ranges, so from a business perspective it would not make sense to close a deal. Indeed, if both sides do their homework, at least one of them will realise that the negotiating ranges do not overlap and will pull out of the negotiations at an early stage. This may, however, depend on whether one or both parties have a strong *BATNA*.

3.3 The best alternative to a negotiated agreement (BATNA)

BATNA is a concept that was introduced by Roger Fisher & William Ury of the Harvard Negotiation Project in their book *Getting to Yes: Negotiating Without Giving In* (1981). In the book they recommend that a negotiator should "avoid having a bottom line" (what we have called a least desirable outcome) but instead "have a BATNA". As is evident from what we have said above, we firmly believe that it is important to have identified the least desirable outcome to a negotiation, to know how far it makes sense for you to go before pulling out of the negotation. So, we disagree with Fisher and Ury when they say you should not have a "bottom line". But we very much like their notion of a BATNA. Their acronym stands for:

BEST ALTERNATIVE TO A NEGOTIATED AGREEMENT

We prefer:

BEST ALTERNATIVE TO NO AGREEMENT

What does this mean? If you are negotiating, you need to know what you will do if you can't reach a satisfactory agreement. It's not enough to say to yourself: "Well, I'll see if I can find another supplier/customer/ joint venture partner." When deciding whether it is worth negotiating with a company, you will have thought of all the alternative options available to you. A buyer is unlikely to seek quotes from only one seller. A seller is always on the lookout for new, more profitable clients. A company about to enter into a joint venture, alliance or merger will, as a matter of course, have looked to see who else they might get into bed with. Look at these alternatives, do your calculations and choose the one which is the best option, should you fail to reach an agreement with the people you are about to negotiate with. This option is your BATNA. It becomes a psychologically important benchmark for you in the negotiation.

Figure 3.1 shows a road that ends in a fork. Think of the road as the negotiation process. The fork illustrates the situation you find yourself in if you are pushed to the limit in the negotiation. You have arrived at your least desirable outcome, your planned *exit point.* At this point you will need to make a decision. If what is being offered in the negotiation is still better than your BATNA, then accept their final offer and sign the contract. On the other hand, if your BATNA is now more attractive than the agreement the other side is proposing, then politely bid your negotiating partners "Goodbye" and pick up the phone to that other potential supplier/customer/partner: your best alternative to no agreement.

Figure 3.1 The BATNA Concept (Ury, 2007 ©)

D. Develop Your BATNA

(**B**est **A**lternative **T**o a **N**egotiated **A**greement)

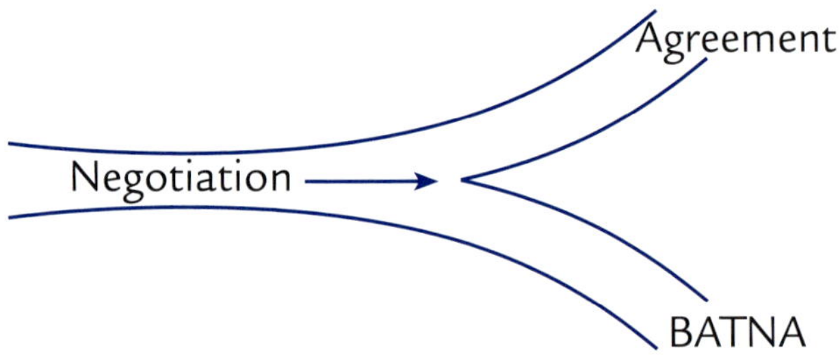

Best course of action
if you cannot reach agreement

The biggest benefit to you of identifying your BATNA is that it gives you the power to say "No" to an unsatisfactory deal. The more options you have should the negotiation fail, the more strength you have to influence the terms and conditions of the agreement in your favour. You will feel more confident at the negotiation table.

A few words of warning though: be as objective as possible about the pros and cons of this alternative option. We have noticed that negotiators, ourselves included, can overestimate the pluses and underestimate the minuses of their BATNAs. If you make this mistake, you may end up rejecting a good offer. Have you ever found yourself saying: "I probably have some other options, but this seems like a good deal"? If you have, then you will understand that knowing you have a good alternative is better than assuming you have one.

Choosing and improving your BATNA

The BATNA concept is useful but not always realistic. Fisher and Ury and many of those who have since taken up their "Have a BATNA" cry do not seem to have appreciated that in business-to-business negotiations between sellers and buyers, only buyers can normally find a solid BATNA.

We have searched far and wide – on the internet, in books, among our colleagues, from our own negotiating experience – for instances of where a seller has been able to employ a strong BATNA in a negotiation. Time and again people will tell you how important it is to have a BATNA, give you a good example for a typical buyer (often it is the competitor the seller fears most) and then draw on people's private lives to instance a strong BATNA for a seller.

It's not difficult to identify BATNAs when negotiating in your private life. If you are selling a car, you might get a written offer from a car dealer for, say, €9,000 and then see if you can sell the car privately for more. The €9,000 offer is your BATNA should you be unable to do a deal with anyone else. It also serves as your benchmark against which you can do your calculations when negotiating with others. Suppose a neighbour offers you €9,500 in cash but says he can't pay you until the end of next month. Has the offer from the car dealer got a time limit? Will you accept the extra €500 and risk your BATNA dropping to €8,800 after next month?

A job-seeker would like to have several job offers before he goes to his first interview; it puts him in a stronger negotiating position with any potential new employer. But he may not be in that fortunate position when economic times are hard. If he already has a job, he would be wise to have a firm job offer in place before he jumps ship. He may even use this offer to negotiate a better deal with his current employer.

If you live in a city where house prices are rising, it probably means there are more buyers than sellers. So, a prospective buyer, especially if she is choosy about the house she wants to live in, may find it hard to argue with the seller of her dream home that she could buy a less expensive property in the next street. A seller in this market has little problem identifying and using his BATNA. He won't stop showing his house as soon as he has the first serious bid; he'll wait and see if there is another potential buyer.

In the world of business-to-business negotiation, it is usually much easier for buyers than sellers to identify their BATNAs. Sure, buyers have to buy from someone; but they normally have a choice of suppliers. No purchasing manager will walk into the negotiation room without having one or two well-researched alternative options sitting on his desktop.

Or so we both thought until Søren was asked by a major client to comment on the new preparation manual they had just produced for use by their global procurement people. Søren received the short version of this manual, which ran to a total of 28 PowerPoint slides. A lot of the slides were concerned with technical matters, which were outside the scope of Søren's negotiation skills training. But he was astonished to discover that nowhere had the designers of this manual mentioned the need for a buyer to investigate thoroughly his other options should he fail to reach an agreement with a supplier. Søren urged them to include "Find your BATNA" in the list of things the purchasing managers had to do before starting to negotiate. They did so and, the buyers soon realised how much extra power a well-worked out BATNA gave them.

What BATNA can a company salesperson find and use when negotiating? The obvious answer is another customer. But we find many sellers at the negotiating table have not actively looked for and researched such a customer. It's more a case of "If this guy doesn't buy, I'll see who else there is who will." As salespeople ourselves, we sympathise with this reaction. It is sometimes possible to play one customer off against another. Your products or services may be of such superb quality or have such a strong brand identity that buyers are falling over themselves to do a deal with you. But, as we have said, this is rare, although we will look at a couple of cases later where the seller is either a monopoly supplier or is operating in a market where there are more buyers than sellers. If you can easily find another customer who can serve as your alternative option should negotiations break down, you have got a BATNA of sorts. But it will hardly ever be as strong as the buyer's one. So what should you do? Weaken the buyer's BATNA. Make him doubt that he has got one.

Weakening the other side's BATNA

You may recall what we said in chapter one:

> The best salespeople are those who know their customer's business well enough and are trusted by the customer sufficiently that they are listened to when they challenge their client's current thinking. ...They have to make buyers doubt whether they really do know what their companies need. They have to then come up with solutions to problems the buyers may not have realised they had.

A seller should try to show during the negotiation that the other options available to the buyer are not as good as he thinks they are. As we said in Chapter 2, this does not mean saying how poor the competition is. Instead, make the buyer doubt that his alternative supplier understands his business and the problems he faces as well as you do. Find the weak points in your competitors' offer that he may not have thought of and that make your package so much more attractive. Suggest some plausible but worrying scenarios:

> What would happen if you needed a machine to be produced to a different spec. and delivered at, say, two weeks' notice? We could guarantee that because we are on your doorstep.

The implication in this example is that the buyer's BATNA cannot both produce and deliver in such a short time, presumably because this other supplier is based far away.

Or:

> What would you do if there was a natural disaster that made it impossible for your Chinese or Korean suppliers to ship this equipment to you? There is far less danger of something like that happening here.

This is a natural line for a domestic supplier to take to try and undermine the buyer's confidence in his overseas suppliers. Notice how he does not have to say anything negative about his foreign competitors. He just adds to the worry lines on the buyer's forehead by reminding him of the disruption to supply chains caused by earthquakes, tsunamis, volcanic eruptions, hurricanes and floods.

Or:

> Don't forget that all our software developers are employees of the company. We don't need to outsource. This gives us much greater control of the process and means we can make promises to you that we can keep.

Again there is no direct attack on the buyer's BATNA. The seller's competitor is not even mentioned but the implication and message is clear: you are safer with us than with them.

And that is the key message that a seller should be trying to deliver whenever he is attempting to weaken the buyer's BATNA. A buyer wants to get the best deal he can for his company but he doesn't want to take too many risks. He is answerable to his colleagues, for example, if the component he has bought is faulty and causes delays and stoppages in the production process or, worse, only comes to light once the final product is in the hands of the consumer.

Let's return to the world of BTB and GerMedica. How did Anselmo and Ulrike find, improve and use their BATNAs?

On the face of it, Anselmo was in a weak position at first. He thought he was being offered the chance to supply analytical scales to GerMedica's R & D sites in Stuttgart and New Jersey – new markets a long way from BTB's Brazilian base. He assumed that he would be asked to provide a small number of these so that GerMedica could evaluate their quality. He hoped then to get a larger order of up to 100 machines, although he didn't know how many of these would be bespoke scales, which would cost much more than the standard model price of $2,000. He knew he was competing against two European companies who could beat BTB on everything but price. He thought he might also be up against some non-European suppliers with a longer track record than BTB had in the high-tech end of the weighing industry.

What then was Anselmo's BATNA in the first round of discussions with Ulrike? He had been researching the pharmaceutical market ever since BTB started producing analytical scales. In their home market, BTB initially targeted the government-owned research labs in Brazil. Meanwhile, Anselmo, responsible for export sales, first went after the pharmaceutical companies in Spain and Portugal. He speaks their languages. There are strong cultural and business links between the two countries and their old colonies.

However, on his latest trip to Europe he decided not only to see old friends in the Iberian Peninsula and to meet Ulrike at GerMedica in Stuttgart. He also tried to get a meeting with any European drugs company with a production or R & D facility in Brazil. And he succeeded in getting a meeting with someone in purchasing in the French pharmaceutical company, Sanofi, in Paris before he went on to Stuttgart. Okay, it was just an introductory meeting with a junior manager and no negotiation took place. But the French were interested to know more about this Brazilian supplier. After all, Sanofi's biggest factory is in Brazil. Sanofi became Anselmo's BATNA. It was not a strong one but he went into his meeting with Ulrike feeling much more confident that he had at least one other option should their discussions go no further.

Then he got an email from Ulrike, after their meeting in Stuttgart, telling him that GerMedica was planning to open an R & D laboratory on his doorstep in São Paulo. She wanted BTB to bid to supply this new facility. But first they would need to provide five standard scales to their Stuttgart laboratories to undergo a six-month trial. She finished the email by saying that she would be visiting Brazil the following month to see BTB and "other companies in the region". She asked if she could have a tour of BTB's factory, meet the top management and discuss the new proposal she hoped Anselmo would send her in the next 10 days.

Anselmo still had Sanofi as his BATNA. But, at first sight, Ulrike's BATNA had become a lot weaker: neither of BTB's European competitors have a factory in Brazil, able to deliver high-quality scales at a moment's notice. Anselmo knew of only one other Brazilian company that could supply analytical scales to the specification demanded by GerMedica. And they were in Curitiba, 400 km to the south of São Paulo. But Ulrike did mention that she was going to visit other companies "in the region", whatever that meant. Was she being deliberately vague? Was she trying to make Anselmo think she had other options apart from BTB? Anselmo might have been tempted to conclude that he didn't need a BATNA anymore. GerMedica would surely have to buy from BTB.

Anselmo and Senhor Cunha are no fools though. Anselmo debriefed his boss as soon as he had got back from Europe and received Ulrike's email. They admired her negotiating skills. It was clear now why she had not told Anselmo about the planned R & D lab in São Paulo. It was not just that telling him too early would weaken her bargaining position. By making him believe that BTB would be delivering scales to their sites in Germany and USA, she had forced him to think of creative solutions to the problem of instant repair or replacement of these fragile machines. And she had made him give her information she could use to strengthen her BATNA.

She had made it clear at the meeting in Shanghai that the repair and replacement issue was a problem that BTB had to resolve to her satisfaction. At the meeting in Stuttgart she had grilled him on this. Could BTB have a technician permanently on-site to maintain BTB's scales? What would this cost BTB or was this extra to the price? How about training GerMedica's staff to maintain the kit? What would that cost? Or maybe BTB could deliver a spare machine with each batch of five? What would that cost? And what would it cost to design, produce and deliver bespoke machines? How easy would it be for GerMedica staff to repair such equipment? Anselmo's technical knowledge meant he was able to answer all these questions well, though he had needed a double whisky once Ulrike released him to go back to his Stuttgart hotel.

Anselmo had smiled ruefully when he got Ulrike's email and recalled her endless questioning at the meeting. Thanks to him she now has all the information she needs to negotiate with her current suppliers, Labal and Becker, BTB's European competitors, and any other non-Brazilian supplier. She has a good idea as to how much extra it will cost them to deliver their analytical scales to GerMedica's planned R & D site in São Paulo. Anselmo wishes he had asked Ulrike a few more questions when they met in Shanghai. He had not tested his assumption that BTB were being asked to supply GerMedica's existing labs in Germany and the USA.

Anselmo has several jobs to do before he and Senhor Cunha sit down with Ulrike at BTB's offices next month (and in the next chapter). He will send her a revised proposal, of course, and brief all his colleagues about her forthcoming visit and its importance to the company. He will also arrange a visit to Sanofi's production facility and development lab in Brazil, as recommended by the young Jean-Francois Lefevre at Sanofi's head office in Paris. He still needs to have a BATNA.

So, here are the steps to follow in arriving at your BATNA:

1. List all your alternatives should you fail to get an agreement within your negotiating range.
2. Look for the less obvious ones - be creative!
3. Evaluate each alternative:
    - Is it realistic? Could it be used?
    - How valuable is it?
4. Select your best alternative (BATNA) as your benchmark in the negotiation. If what is being offered at the table is less attractive than your best alternative, then go for the best alternative.

And, if you haven't got a BATNA? Find a way to weaken the other side's one.

Talking about BATNAs

- If you have a strong BATNA, then use it to influence the other party. Think of the timing. If you reveal your BATNA too early, you may close down the discussion and exploration of a workable solution
- If you don't have a strong BATNA, don't tell them
- If a negotiation is going badly, then consider revealing that you have a BATNA. It may increase your leverage
- If you think they have a poor BATNA, try to get them to talk about it
- If they have a good BATNA, you don't want to talk about it. Unfortunately, they probably will. This is a signal to you that it might be a difficult negotiation for you

Special cases

a. Dealing with a monopolist seller

No negotiator is in a weaker position than one with no alternative to a deal. If this is the case for you, then there is a risk that the other party may try to dictate the terms to you rather than negotiate them. This is typical in situations where a supplier has a monopoly on a product, raw material or service. They may decide that they can afford to abuse their power and charge extortionate prices. Unless you can come up with a workable alternative, then you will have to dance to their tune. However, this abuse of power can backfire, although seldom as quickly as the buyer would like.

A supplier of raw materials to one of Søren's clients, a manufacturing company, found himself in such a powerful position. When the two sides met for their annual contract negotiations, he took full advantage of this. In fact, he even made fun of his customer by saying things like: "Well, let's see. How much money should I be making off you guys next year?"

This contempt for the customer infuriated the procurement director of the manufacturing company. So he decided to do something about it. He explained the situation to his fellow directors and concluded by saying, "Not only are we vulnerable by not having any alternative, but also this is not a very nice guy. He seems to get a special kick out of humiliating us." The group discussed the situation at great length and a question was put to their R&D director: "Can we research our way to a substitute for this?" The answer was: "Probably, but it will take time and be costly."

The Board of Directors decided to allocate the necessary funds. The R&D director was right; it took seven years and the total cost ran to over $20m. But, at last, they were able to do without the monopolist supplier.

Now, one would think that a professional procurement director would simply inform the supplier that his products were no longer needed. But, oh no; they wanted to see him suffer. When the man came to the annual contract negotiations, they let him go through his usual little spiel. When he assumed that his customer was just about to renew the contract, they pulled their rabbit out of the hat – their BATNA: "We have developed this in-house. We don't need you anymore."

Søren has often wondered if the supplier ever reflected on why this happened to him. If he had, and if he had been truly honest with himself, then he would have realised that his arrogant behaviour had, in the end, cost him a lucrative contract.

b. Handling being a buyer in a sellers' market

At some times and in some industries there are more buyers than sellers. So, the sellers have the BATNA-power. Søren came across just such a situation recently in Scandinavia in a fairly new industry. His client was competing with a lot of other companies to buy a number of specific types of production plant across Europe. The owner of a single plant in, say, Spain might be approached by Søren's client one day, having received an offer from a German company the day before and a Swedish one a week earlier. The Spanish company may not have had any intention of selling but this did not stop them playing one bidder off against another in order to find out what price they might get should they, one day, wish to sell. This was a useful exercise for them but an expensive waste of time for Søren's client.

What advice did Søren offer his client? The first thing was to get them to see if they could find a BATNA in this sellers' market. Actually, the first thing was to get them to understand what a BATNA was and who in their market had one! It soon became clear that they didn't really have a BATNA and that they would be better employed in weakening the BATNA of the sellers. But before they did that, they needed to identify the "time wasters" such as the Spanish firm mentioned above. In other words they asked themselves what we said you should ask yourself before embarking on any negotiation: is it worth it? Having reduced the field of feasible candidates by about 80%, they next had to get the sellers to think about more than just price. They played on the fears that many sellers can have, especially when dealing with strangers from another country: "Will these people actually pay up?" Søren's client made much of the fact that their backers had deep pockets with no holes in them. Their credit rating was excellent. The message to the potential seller was "You are safer with us than with them." Result? Whereas before they were buying very few of the plants they bid for, their success rate shot upwards. And they were not wasting precious time chasing after castles in the air ... or in Spain.

Steps in the preparation process:

1. Analyse your situation in case you do NOT get an agreement with the other party. What options have you got? Choose the best one of these as your BATNA.
2. Think about what the other party may do if you can't come to an agreement. What is their likely BATNA? This will tell you who needs who the most.
3. Identify your own needs and interests. Prioritise them to identify what you MUST get from the negotiation. Establish your MDO (Most Desirable Outcome).
4. Based on your BATNA-power, if any, decide how far you are willing to go in the negotiation. Establish your LDO (Least Desirable Outcome).
5. If their BATNA is far stronger than yours, prepare to undermine their confidence in theirs during the negotiation.

3.4 Relationship power

In addition to BATNA power, some writers on negotiation highlight the importance of what they call *role power,* something you would normally find in hierarchical cultures. We came across an example of this thinking in an edition of Harvard Law School's *Negotiation Newsletter* (Vol. 9, no. 7, July 2006). The writer claimed that using a BATNA was characteristic of negotiations only in more individualistic *Western* cultures. *Eastern* cultures, he argued, are more interdependent and more inclined to be influenced by interpersonal obligation and authority relationships. In these *Eastern* cultures, hierarchy, or *role power*, dominates negotiations. He then gave some examples to support this contention.

The first one was hypothetical. A young Japanese accountant is considering whether to bid for an apartment that one of his firm's senior managers is selling. However, he has already found three other apartments that he would be happy to buy. The senior manager has already bought a new house and as yet nobody has made a bid for his apartment. But even though the younger man has a strong BATNA – the best of the other three apartments – he does not use it to drive down the price that he will pay the senior manager for his apartment. Why? Because the senior manager will have some influence on the young accountant's future career and his *role power* has a strong impact on the negotiation.

The second story was a real one from the life of the writer of the Harvard newsletter. When he was an assistant professor at an American university, he bought an apartment from a full professor in his department under the same conditions as the Japanese accountant hypothetically did. Thanks to his strong BATNA, the writer, despite being a subordinate employee, was the more powerful party in the negotiation and so negotiated the price downwards. Apparently, he had not worried that the full professor might use his *role power* to punish him for this. In fact, he thought that it might have influenced his career prospects negatively if he had not used his BATNA-power. The full professor knew the market conditions as well as he did, and might view him as being too soft if he had not wielded it to get the best deal for himself.

The writer was wrong on at least three counts. First, we feel bad at having to generalise at the country level when we comment on the cultural differences and similarities between, say, the French and the Chinese. But to talk about *Western* and *Eastern* cultures is taking generalisation too far.

Secondly, Japan is not nearly as hierarchical as many people think. The writer may be right in saying that the Japanese accountant would not use his strong BATNA to negotiate a lower price for his senior manager's apartment. But this has little to do with the fact that one man is more senior than the other. What matters is what kind of obligations the two men feel they have towards each other. Richard knows from first-hand experience that a Japanese subordinate would use a BATNA, if he had one, with his boss just as much as any US American subordinate would.

Thirdly, people all over the world find and use BATNAs, not just individualistic "Westerners". Japanese buyers would never dream of going into a negotiation with a supplier without having several alternatives up their sleeve. They use their BATNAs as a weapon with which to beat their suppliers, however long and strong the relationship with those suppliers has been. And so, in our experience and that of many of our clients, do the Chinese and the Koreans.

However, that writer in Harvard's *Negotiation Newsletter* was right about one thing. There is something else that many business people from, for example, the USA, the UK and Germany tend to ignore when negotiating. It is the power that existing relationships have in determining who wins a contract. We call this *relationship power*; it is much more important than role power. Much of the world would prefer to do business with people and companies they know and trust. Many contracts are signed because of the strength of the relationship between the parties, not because the deal is objectively better than the alternatives. We look in considerable detail at the power of relationships in Chapter 6 but we would like to finish this chapter with a story that illustrates just how strong this power can be in influencing the course of negotiations. Our story is also from Japan but has the merit of being a real one.

Richard had moved to Japan to run his company's subsidiary there. One of his first decisions was to tell his sales staff to focus on the foreign subsidiaries of Canning's existing European clients and to try to book meetings with either the foreign boss or the Japanese HR manager. One of the obvious targets was the Japanese subsidiary of a German car manufacturer – a long-standing client of Canning in Europe but not in Japan. Canning's Tokyo office had had plenty of nice meetings with the HR people at this subsidiary over the previous five years. There had been lots of flattering comments about the quality of Canning's training courses and vague promises of future business but also assurances that they were very happy with their existing, Japanese supplier. No business had ever materialised. In his first meeting with Ikeda-san, the 53-year-old Japanese HR director, Richard got the usual *tatemae*[1] treatment – nice language for the stranger. Still no business. Six months later Richard and one of his Japanese salesmen, Kawabe-san, were into their third meeting with this company; there was no sign they were making any progress. Then Richard inadvertently struck gold. As he had done

1 *Tatemae* is best translated as *façade*; lots of very polite and often flattering words to ensure harmony within the group. Its opposite is *honne*, meaning *to say what you really think*, which is best done one to one.

before, he listed the many highly-reputable foreign companies Canning worked with in Japan and included one name that he had forgotten to mention at the previous meeting. It was the Japanese subsidiary of a British chemical company. Ikeda-san's eyebrows shot up one millimetre (body language in Japan is nothing if not controlled) and asked Richard to repeat the British company's name. When Richard did so, Ikeda-san asked rather aggressively who had attended Canning's courses from this company's Japanese office.

Richard sought Kawabe-san's help. Then he remembered something...

"Actually, I myself coached the head of the Human Relations Department last month. Hashimoto-san and ..."

Ikeda-san interrupted him – one of the rudest things you can do in Japan.

"You were teacher of Hashimoto-san?!"

Ikeda-san started sucking his teeth and looked as if he had been hit by something. Richard noticed that Kawabe-san was beaming. Ikeda-san muttered something to the young salesman, which Richard didn't catch. Kawabe's beam reached his ears. He bowed until his head almost hit the table.

The HR director nodded for a long time and then took a deep breath.

"So, Pooley-san, tell me what training you did with Hashimoto-san."

Richard did so in great detail until Ikeda-san appeared satisfied he knew enough.

As soon as they had left Ikeda-san's office, Kawabe-san told Richard the good news: Hashimoto-san was Ikeda-san's *sempai*[2]. This meant that Canning could expect at least some business from Ikeda-san's company in the near future. Back in Canning's office Kawabe-san spent a few minutes on the phone talking to his other contacts in the two men's companies and explained to a baffled Richard a little of what was going on.

---

2 *Sempai* means *"mentor"* or *"senior"*; a *sempai* is usually a few years older than his *kohai* or *"protégé"*.

Hashimoto-san, now 56 years old, had joined a Japanese company after graduating. Ikeda-san joined the same firm three years later. As was then normal in Japan, Ikeda-san had asked his senior colleague if he would give him the honour of being his mentor. Hashimoto-san had agreed and the two men established a strong bond. Hashimoto-san guided Ikeda-san through the highly-factionalised world of Japanese business; the younger man gave his support to the older one whenever he could. Over 30 years later each man was an HR boss but in different companies. The relationship was still one of mentor and protégé.

Richard had been the *sensei* (teacher) of Ikeda-san's *sempai*. This posed a problem for Ikeda-san. His company had a long-standing relationship with a local training company. He knew the Japanese boss very well and felt a strong obligation to continue using his company. But the man wasn't his *sempai*. His *sempai* had been taught by this young *gaijin* (foreigner); so Hashimoto-san must think the foreigner's company was a good one, despite not being Japanese. And as Hashimoto's *kohai*, he felt obliged to use Canning too.

Sure enough, Richard's company was asked by Ikeda-san to bid for a share of his company's training budget in the following financial year. Ikeda-san tested the quality beforehand by sending some junior staff on various courses and, despite underhand attempts by the existing training provider to block Canning, awarded the bulk of the training contract to Richard's company. Ikeda-san still felt an obligation to the existing provider, however, and gave him some work – mostly technical training, which Canning didn't do.

You may be wondering how Kawabe-san got all this information in the space of a few minutes on the phone. He didn't. He just got the basic details. Enough for Richard to ring Hashimoto-san and invite him to dinner. Hashimoto-san was delighted to accept; how could he refuse his *sensei*? And you don't need to be told what the two men discussed over their *sashimi* and *sake*.

This is but one example of the power that relationships can have in determining the outcome of a business negotiation. We could give you many more. Indeed we describe one or two more in Chapter 6, when we look at the effect culture has on negotiation behaviour.

It is time to move to the negotiation table. After a brief look at the different strategies that are employed when negotiating, we will turn to what works and what doesn't when you are actually negotiating: the tactics – the effective ones and the ones used by the other side, which only work if you allow them to.

4

How do I get what I want?

4.1 Strategy and tactics – definitions

Just as people can confuse aims with targets, so also can strategy and tactics be seen as synonymous. They are not. A strategy is a plan of action that will enable you to achieve your aims. Tactics are the many ways and means that the strategy is put into effect so that you can reach these aims.

The word strategy derives from the Greek word for military leader. One of the most important jobs of a general at war is to work out how best to win that war: e.g. where and who to attack first and with what. This is his strategy. He will also have a strategy for how best to win a major battle: e.g. which troops do I use where and how and with which weapons? Meanwhile, the officers in the field are working out their tactics: e.g. do we stay in this strong defensive position or do we move at night and attack the enemy from the rear? The word tactic comes from the Greek for "the art of making arrangements".

Figure 4.1. Strategy and Tactics

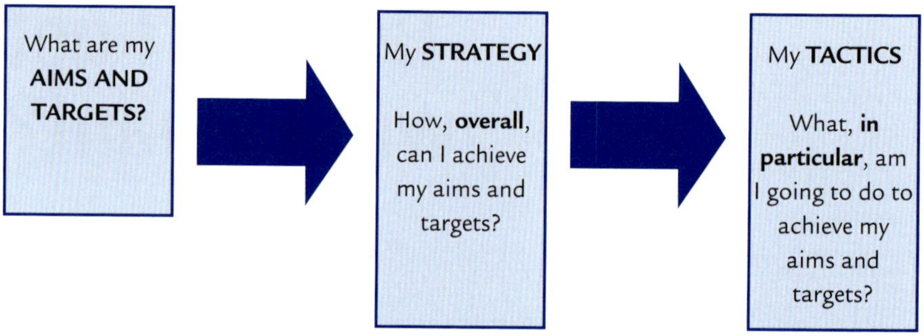

Figure 4.1 illustrates the link between what you want to achieve from the negotiation (your aims and targets) and how you are planning to achieve them in detail. So, your strategy will have an effect on your behaviour when you negotiate - your tactical moves.

What do we mean by these words in commercial negotiations? A strategy for a particular negotiation between a buyer and a seller will usually be heavily influenced by their current purchasing or sales policy. Ulrike of GerMedica has been told that there is a new purchasing policy: no supplier should be allowed to supply more than 35% of any one product or service. So, her aim is to divide the supply of every product she is responsible for between at least three suppliers. She has another aim: to find top-quality suppliers to service the new research laboratory in São Paulo. And she continues, like all buyers, to aim to keep costs down. What then is her overall strategy to achieve these three main aims? To get as much information as possible on all potential suppliers (especially Latin American ones), compare this data with what she knows about her existing suppliers and then, and only then, negotiate deals with at least three candidate companies for each product category in the next twelve months. *Get information, compare* and *negotiate*: these are how, overall, she can achieve her aims and targets.

Ulrike did not just develop a general strategy to meet her three main aims as a purchasing manager. She also worked out a strategy for each negotiation, including the one with Anselmo of BTB. She has had two meetings with him and there have been several emails between them. It is this type of strategy, the one that you should adopt for the negotiation itself, which we shall be looking at in more detail in the next part of this chapter. We shall then move on to the tactics that you may wish to employ during the negotiation and also examine the so-called *dirty tricks* that are most widely used in international negotiations.

This does not mean that having an overall strategy is not important; far from it. But this general strategy will depend on many factors outside the scope of a book on negotiation. We have listed where you can find descriptions of these general strategic models in the bibliography.

4.2 Strategy

a. What strategy should I employ in a negotiation?

The choice of strategy is not an easy one, as most negotiators are torn between on the one hand wanting to compete to get all of the value they can and on the other wishing to cooperate enough to make sure that they get the deal. However, the right strategic mix at the table can even enhance the deal.

To help you identify your strategy for a negotiation, you can start by asking: "Who needs whom most?" If the answer is that you think you need the other party more than they need you, the balance of power between you and them is in their favour. This will have an impact on your choice of strategy; and theirs.

Another powerful influence on your choice of strategy is what alternative, if any, you have in case the negotiation is not concluded successfully. The better your alternative - you will remember BATNA from the previous chapter - the more power you have to say no to an unsatisfactory outcome.

In Figure 4.2 is a model to help you decide which strategy to adopt when negotiating.

Figure 4.2 The Dual Concern Model

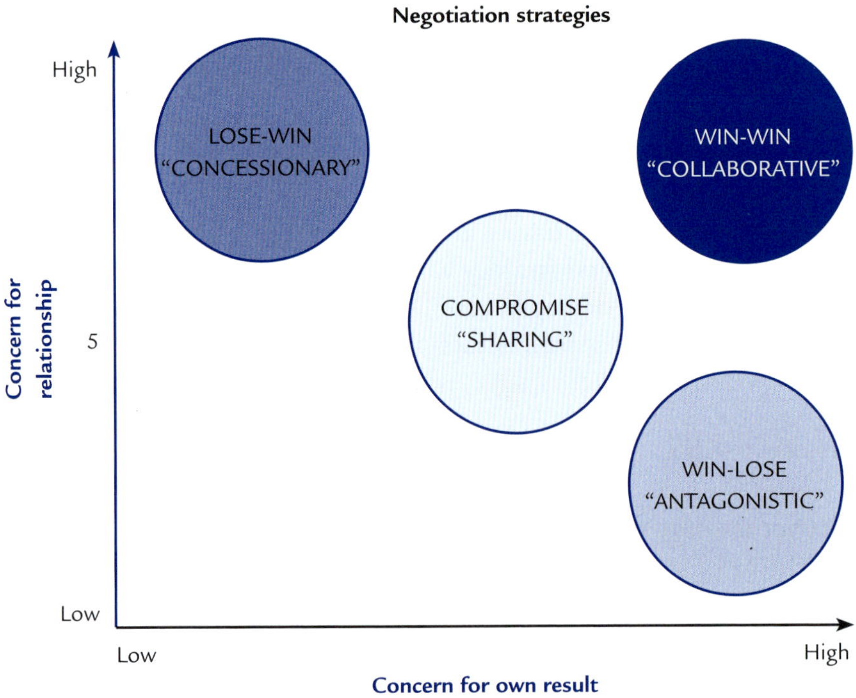

This model is our adaptation of the dual concern model.[1] It describes the two related concerns that all negotiators have to consider when they plan and prepare for a negotiation:

1. How much concern do I have for getting a good result for myself?
2. How much concern do I have for my relationship with the other side?

Your answers to these questions will help you decide which of four strategies you should adopt during the negotiation. Your negotiation strategy can be:

- **Concessionary** – your main concern is to build a good and long-lasting relationship with the other side
- **Antagonistic** – you are not interested in a long-term relationship; you just want to get the best deal you can
- **Sharing** – you are keen to get an agreement between both sides as quickly as possible

1 The Dual Concern Model is also known as the Managerial Grid. It was developed by two American psychologists, Robert Blake and Jane Mouton, in the 1960s. Originally, it was intended for leadership development, but it was later redesigned for use in conflict resolution.

- **Collaborative** – you are keen to create, with the other side, the best possible deal by spending time finding out what extra value is available

b. When and how do I apply each strategy?

The *concessionary* strategy is applied by negotiators whose main aim is to build, maintain or strengthen a relationship with the other side. They decide to be very friendly and accommodating in their dealings with their negotiation partners and will avoid a confrontation at all costs. Literally. They make concessions without trying to get something in return. They don't trade. Its most extreme form is a lose-win strategy: they come away with a deal that makes no money for their company and the other side gets all it wants. Such an extreme version of the strategy is not as rare as you might think. A company that wants to spin off a loss-making subsidiary or division that no longer fits in with its strategic vision may even pay another company to take it off its hands. A buyer may be forced to rely on one supplier for a key raw material and have to accept whatever terms the seller imposes. He has to grin and bear it, knowing that upsetting the supplier could result in delivery delays or further price increases.

More common though is the case where a seller is trying to break into a new market or wants to get a client who will act as a reference. These are exactly the twin aims of Anselmo of BTB. His strategy during the first part of his discussions with Ulrike of GerMedica was a concessionary one. He was prepared to accept making very little money on the deal so that BTB could get a foothold in the northern European pharmaceutical market. It was a loss-leader. So, he decided to give all the information Ulrike asked for, tried to build a warm personal relationship with her and made a business proposal that was much less profitable than the ones he had negotiated with his other foreign customers. Now, though, BTB are in a much stronger position. GerMedica need local suppliers to equip their planned laboratory in São Paolo and BTB is one of only two producers of analytical scales in Brazil. Will he adopt a different strategy for the negotiation that is about to take place with Ulrike in São Paulo?

The concessionary strategy is not one we would recommend unless you are in a similar situation to that described above. It tends to lead to a zero-sum outcome: one side's loss is the other side's gain, and no extra value is created in the process. This outcome is sometimes called a distributive agreement: the existing value has only been redistributed between the parties.

Furthermore, the negotiator using this strategy is often seen as submissive, the kind of negotiator who likes to give something for nothing. We shall look at the mind-set of the different types of negotiator in Chapter 7. Suffice to say now that someone who concedes too readily and does not trade one thing for another not only loses money for his company, he also loses the respect of the person he is negotiating with.

The *antagonistic* strategy is used by negotiators for whom the only important thing is to get the best possible deal for their company. They adopt a confrontational style and will try hard to extract concessions from the other side without giving anything in return. A lot of people flinch at the thought of such behaviour and it is not unusual to find academic articles and books that say that this approach is never acceptable. However, this uncompromising strategy is common and more successful than the academics tend to admit. For example, it may be the right strategy to adopt if you are negotiating a one-off contract with a company with whom you do not expect to have any future relationship. If you are sure that you will never see or hear from the other side again, why spend time cultivating a strong relationship? The disadvantages of this strategy are many though. How certain are you that you will never want to do business with these people again? And if they also perceive this as a one-night stand (the metaphor used by the Managing Director of one of Søren's clients), surely they will have an antagonistic strategy as well. If neither side is prepared to concede, there will be no agreement. Neither side wins. Finally, like its opposite – the concessionary strategy – the antagonistic approach results in a distributive agreement. No extra value has been found.

An antagonistic negotiator likes to get something for nothing. In the short-term he will often make a lot of money for his company. But in the process he will make a lot of enemies, who will take every opportunity to punish him and his company in the longer term.

The *sharing* strategy is very commonly used by negotiators and often with good reason. Many deals have to be concluded quickly to meet a deadline imposed by the seasons (think of the food and clothing industries), by governments (the end of the financial year or the introduction of a new tariff barrier) and by companies (quarterly sales targets, the start of a new purchasing policy, the end of the budget year). Neither side has time to explore new options and "add value". The fastest way to reach an agreement is one where there is minimal confrontation and both sides feel they have got what they want by not conceding too much and only giving way on matters of low priority. If the two sides already have a good working relationship, the pressure is on to close the deal in a way that seems fair to both sides. "I give a little and you give a little. How difficult can it be? Let's split the difference." These are the unspoken feelings of both sides.

The sharing strategy is also regularly adopted by those who think that their negotiations are simple ones. There are few issues beyond price that have to be discussed. It will be difficult to find extra value.

Our problem with this strategy is that it invariably does end up leaving potential value on the table. If time really is short, then we can understand why negotiators decide to go half way and compromise. But so often we come across people who sign in haste and repent at leisure. They realise that they could have got a better deal if only they had spent time asking far more questions of themselves and of the other side.

One of the reasons why negotiated agreements are so often less successful than they could have been is because neither side has tested their assumptions about what each variable being negotiated actually costs. Let's take an example from our own world – the provision of management training and consultancy. Most of the negotiations we take part in are fairly simple ones. A negotiation with a company and its subsidiaries to supply trainers to deliver a range of courses in several different countries is relatively simple (though a logistical nightmare) when we compare it with the highly complex negotiations many of our corporate clients have to conduct. Even so, a long-standing client for whom we ran a series of courses throughout the year only realised after a few years that he could get an extra day of training at half-price if he switched from having one three-day course to two two-day courses. He had not realised that the cost to us of adding another weekday was not pro-rata. If he had known this at the beginning, he might have changed his request and opted for two-day courses rather than three-day ones. He would have saved himself a lot of money. Who was at fault here? Both sides. He should have tested his assumption that our daily cost did not vary. We should have tested our assumption that he only wanted three-day courses. Neither side had asked each other enough questions.

It will not surprise you to learn that the *collaborative* strategy is the one that we believe works best most often. This is the one where both sides aim to win. This is only possible if extra value is found in the course of the negotiation. In the example we gave you in the previous paragraph, we are ashamed to admit that we adopted a sharing and not a collaborative strategy. If we had really explored all the possible ways of supplying a training programme to our client, we would have come up with a better deal for both sides.

This strategy involves identifying the concerns and interests of the other side and exploring ways of meeting them by trading value for value. Unlike the concessionary and antagonistic strategies, this strategy will lead to integrative outcomes – it tries to integrate the concerns and interests of the two parties – and always involves an exchange of value – something for something.

It is not an easy strategy to implement. You want to concede as little as possible when negotiating those things that really matter to you. You may have to pretend that those things which are less important to you are, in fact, a high priority. You must trade on every issue. At the same time you are trying to keep the relationship with the other side as warm and respectful as possible.

We often us the acronym SOPHOP to describe this tricky process: Soft on People, Hard on Points. If we look at the dual concern model diagram again and substitute "People" for "Concern for relationships" and "Points" for "Concern for own result", as in figure 4.3, you will begin to see how this acronym was formed. Unfortunately, "Hard" and "Soft" cannot be substitutes for "High" and "Low" on both axes, which can make this confusing. However, we like the other acronyms this labelling produces: someone who is Soft on People and Soft on Points is, well, a bit soppy. And a person who is Hard on People and Hard on Points can make the other side hopping mad!

Figure 4.3 Are you SOPHOP?

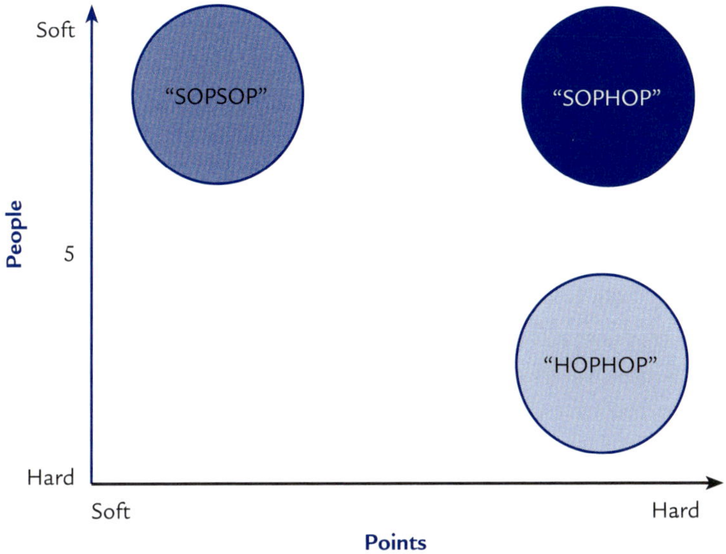

SOPHOP sits in the same place as the collaborative strategy. However, this does not mean that someone who adopts such a Win-Win strategy is, by nature, a SOPHOP person. We will return to this in Chapter 7 when we look at personality types and how these affect people's behaviour and choice of strategy.

So, you have chosen the appropriate strategy for the negotiation you are about to start. What tactics should you employ at the table? We will look at this next - the heart of any negotiation. And in Chapter 5 we will look at the words to use while negotiating - the *Communication* at the top of the *Negamid*.

4.3 Tactics

As we have said, tactics are the more specific, step-by-step moves and behaviours adopted during the negotiation process to support your overall strategy. We shall assume that you have decided to go for a collaborative strategy - getting the best deal you possibly can for your company while, at the same time, developing a strong and sustainable long-term relationship with the other side. We will take you through the process and recommend some appropriate tactics.

Of course, there are inappropriate tactics too. Such tactics are commonly referred to as *dirty tricks*. However, just as one man's terrorist is another man's freedom fighter, so what you may think of as a dirty trick, the other side may consider an appropriate tactic. And what you may judge to be unfair or unacceptable behaviour when used against you in one negotiation, you may think reasonable for you to use in another negotiation, especially when employing a different strategy. Indeed, as you will see, we are doubtful that many so-called *dirty tricks* really are dirty at all, whatever strategy is being used.

In this section we will stick with the labels *appropriate tactics* and *dirty tricks*. We will describe both and give you guidance on how best to deal with the latter. But you need to remember throughout that our definitions of *appropriate* and *dirty* are based on the assumption that your strategy is a collaborative one.

a. Appropriate tactics

One of the first things you need to think about when working out your tactics is how you would like the meetings or series of meetings, to flow. For a collaborative strategy, we would recommend the *3 Es* –

Exchange → Expand → Eliminate.

During the first part of any negotiation you should be aiming to get as much information as possible from the people you are negotiating with. There will be a proposal on the table and perhaps a counter-proposal. You want to know what lies behind these proposals: what is important to the other side, what is not? This is the *exchange* stage.

Once you have a better idea of the other side's position, you can start trying to find creative ways not only of closing the gaps between you but also adding to the value of the whole package you are negotiating. You are now in the *expand* part of the negotiation.

Finally, you have to reject the unworkable or unacceptable solutions and agree together on what is feasible and acceptable: the *eliminate* end-game.

No negotiation, however simple, ever runs in such a straight line. Inevitably, for example, you will find yourself suggesting ideas while probing for the other side's real interests. The other side may not want to follow the path you are trying to take them on, especially if they are not as willing as you are to adopt a collaborative approach. But it is still worth trying to keep to this three-stage structure yourself: it makes it easier for you to keep control of the negotiation process.

Throughout the negotiation you want to maintain a cordial and constructive relationship with the other side (*Soft on People*) whilst getting all you possibly can for your side (*Hard on Points*). We describe below how you can achieve this during each stage of the negotiation.

Exchange

Build Rapport by *Asking Questions* and *Testing Assumptions*

Knowledge is power

Thomas Hobbes, English philosopher (1588-1679)

One of the most important sources of power in a negotiation is information. As soon as you start preparing for a negotiation you should try to discover as much as possible about the other side's needs and interests. This is not only to make sure you are better prepared; it is a way of building rapport. A tactic both of us have often used when negotiating as salesmen is to email or ring the client before the negotiation starts and ask a string of questions. We might already know the answers. It doesn't matter. We are showing how seriously we are taking the negotiation and how much we want to ensure that our initial proposal meets their needs. It is flattering to receive such attention. It makes them feel better about us.

Never assume, because when you ASSUME, you make an ASS out of U and ME.

Jerry Benson, US American TV and Film writer (1938-2006), from the script of the *Odd Couple*, 1973

Benson's quip is amusing and oft-quoted.[2] However, you have to make assumptions about what the other side want before you start negotiating with them. You don't have complete knowledge. The key is to test your assumptions. Asking questions before and at the beginning of a negotiation will enable you to do so before getting into the de-

2 Apparently he picked it up years earlier from a teacher in a typewriter repair class. We'd love to know why s/he used it.

tail of the negotiation proper. Once in the nitty-gritty of the negotiation, emotions can run high and patience can wear thin. Irritation can swiftly grow if, late on in a negotiation, you make a proposal based on a wrong assumption.

We talked about the importance of testing assumptions when we were describing the shortcomings of the *sharing* strategy. The client we mentioned earlier could have cut the overall price of a multi-course training programme by 13% (and trained many more people) if he had tested his assumptions about our pricing structure:

Client: "Am I right in thinking that your daily course fee is the same whether it is two days or three?"

Salesman: "Yes, it is."

Client: "What if we do two two-day courses back-to-back?"

Salesman: "Well, if they can be run Tuesday to Friday, the daily rate drops to £XXXX.[3] But I understood you wanted each course to run for three days."

Client: "Not if you can convince me that we'd get almost the same result in two days. I hadn't realised it would be cheaper."

Salesman: "Only if you do them Tuesday to Friday."

Client: "Fair enough but..."

You may think that it would not have benefited us to test our assumption that the client was wedded to three-day courses. But it really is more cost effective for us to run courses over a Tuesday-Friday period; so we wouldn't have lost out. And how do you think the client felt about us when he discovered that he could have made a big saving, without sacrificing quality, by changing the length and timing of the courses? Did he blame himself for not testing his assumptions? Of course not; he blamed us: "I wish you had told me that at the beginning." It made the contract renewal very tricky. Ask yourself how he reacted when told

3 You didn't think we were going to tell you what our courses cost, did you? Contact one of us if you are interested in negotiation skills training and we can give you a price. Then we can negotiate.

that we could no longer hold the price at the level he had had for a few years.

Anselmo had been struck by the number of questions Ulrike had asked him in their meetings and knew that he had impressed her with his detailed answers. The rapport between the two of them had grown as a result. But he subsequently realised that he should have asked more questions himself and tested his assumption that she was only looking for a third supplier for GerMedica's existing operations. Had he asked, she might not have told him the whole truth but a probing question could possibly have revealed more than she intended:

Anselmo: "Am I right in assuming that you want us to deliver just to the two research labs?"

Ulrike: "For the moment, yes."

Anselmo: "I see. So, this may change?"

Ulrike: "Possibly. But first we need to know whether you can supply scales of sufficiently high standard to our existing labs."

If you ask a question, it's a good idea to listen to the answer. Negotiation trainers often promote the virtues of active listening. When asked what this means, they will tell their students that they must say things such as "I see", "really?" and "interesting" to show the other side that they really are listening. There is merit in this advice; silence is interpreted negatively by many people. But for us, active listening is so much more than demonstrating that you have heard what the other side has said. You should try to pick up the signals, often unintended, which tell you what people are really thinking.

If Anselmo had had the conversation with Ulrike that we gave you just now, what would he have deduced from Ulrike's "For the moment"? That his company might be asked in future to deliver to other GerMedica sites? That GerMedica might open a new R & D lab? This information could be good news for him and BTB. So, he instantly tries to learn more: "So, this may change?"

Ulrike, perhaps realising that she has said more than she should have done, tries to steer the conversation back to her biggest worry about

BTB (and Anselmo's, if he is honest): are their products of high enough quality? But in doing so, she sends two more verbal signals to Anselmo: "Possibly" and "first". If he really had had this discussion with her, he might have come back to these signals later (to do so now might just irritate her):

"Can I take us back to something you said earlier? You mentioned that you may want us to deliver to more than just the two existing labs..."

(She didn't but now she will find it a bit more difficult to fob him off with a vague answer.)

"Which other sites would you want us to deliver to?"

Note that his question assumes that he has already got the contract to deliver to the existing sites!

Ulrike could, and probably would, tell him that all this is irrelevant to their discussion and that he should concentrate on how BTB could deliver their products to her company's current sites. But there is a chance that she would come clean and tell him that they are considering opening a new lab. The chance of getting such valuable information would have been worth the risk of annoying her. In fact, far from being annoyed, she would probably have admired his negotiating skills.

There are plenty of other "signals" that you can turn to your advantage:

"That is our standard price" →	"I see. So, what qualifies for a non-standard price?"
"We can give a 5% to 7% discount." →	"7%? Well, we can think about that."
"We normally charge for that." →	"Do you? Are we a normal customer?"

Richard has been hit by that last response more than once in the UK. British purchasing managers do not wish to be considered "normal". For them the opposite of "normal" is not "abnormal" but "privileged" or "superior".

If you are dealing with people from a culture where "small talk" at the beginning of a meeting is considered the norm, take advantage of this and ask questions about matters outside work. Often such conversations turn towards topics related to business. You can learn a lot, much of it of direct relevance to the negotiation itself. Small talk is an opportunity to fish for information at a time when people are sometimes less careful about what they say. At the same time, small talk is a means to learn more about the characters and personal interests of the people you are about to negotiate with. Finally, small talk has one benefit in international negotiations that is sometimes overlooked: it enables the participants to tune into the different accents and ways of speaking around the table before they start talking about serious matters. In many business cultures small talk is a deliberate tactic to develop and build working relationships.

We shall look at the many types of questions you can ask in the next chapter (*Communication*) and show you in greater detail why questioning is such a vital negotiating tactic.

Develop Trust by *Agreeing an Agenda* and *Summarising Often*

You want the negotiation meeting to start positively. What better way than to agree on something as early as possible: the agenda? Even if an agenda was agreed and circulated before the meeting started, it's a good idea to check that everyone is happy with it. Does the order need to be changed? Is there something missing? How much time do we have? Will anyone else be joining us? Shall we agree to take regular breaks? Start as you mean to go on: by reaching an agreement.

If no agenda was proposed beforehand, take the initiative and propose one yourself. The *exchange-expand-eliminate* structure is a good starting point. Proposing an agenda and inviting input from the other party are good ways of taking control of the process. They also demonstrate your openness to the other side's wishes.

Many people find negotiating stressful. An agenda can make this difficult process easier for them to manage. Provide a logical structure and you will earn their gratitude and trust.

Richard often finds it useful at this stage to ask the other side to sign up to the mantra of *Nothing is agreed until everything is agreed.* He will go on to explain why he thinks it is important for both sides to adopt this approach: people feel more inclined to suggest and consider new ideas and solutions; they don't feel they have to agree on one issue before they can move on to another; they don't get stuck haggling over minor details. If the other side accepts, it is a sign that they also have a collaborative strategy. The atmosphere in the meeting becomes just that little bit warmer. People relax; it will be tough to reach an agreement but it's not going to be a fight. If they don't agree or they respond with implicit rejections – "Let's see how it goes" or "That's an interesting idea", then Richard knows that he is probably dealing with people who do see negotiation as a fight. Forewarned is forearmed.

Summarising is another useful tactic to engender trust. Taking the time to recap will enable the other side to check that they have the same understanding as you do of what has been discussed or agreed. They will appreciate, albeit subconsciously, that you are keen to avoid confusion. Do it frequently: at the start of a meeting to recall what has been discussed before the meeting, at the moment when a point has been provisionally agreed, at a time when both sides appear deadlocked and need reminding of what has been agreed so far, after a break to keep everyone focused and, of course, at the end of each negotiation meeting.

Keep Things Open by *Not Closing Doors*

It's all too easy when negotiating to be too categorical. When you have to make it crystal clear that you cannot agree to something, you may be tempted to say: "That's not acceptable" or "We can't do that." Such responses are certainly clear but they will not make the negotiation go any easier or faster. Better to reject in way that is clear but enables the negotiation to continue.

Suppose you are a buyer. A supplier has asked you to accept a price that is beyond the maximum you are prepared to consider. You must reject it but in such a way that the seller does not feel that every door he is trying to open is being slammed shut in his face. The tactic is to express disagreement or rejection in a relative rather than absolute way. "That's not acceptable" does not take either side any further forward in the negotiation. All the supplier knows in this case is that you won't accept his price. But if you say, "That's far too high", he at least knows that there is a price – a much lower one – that would be acceptable to you. He can then ask the question, "What price would not be too high?" or "What price were you expecting to pay?" You, of course, will name a figure that makes the seller shake his head. If he is a good negotiator, he will respond with another relative statement along the lines of, "That's well below cost for us". He could have said, "Sorry, I can't agree to that." But whilst the first response keeps things open and helps both sides move along their negotiation range, the second is static.

It's a good idea early on in a negotiation to indicate which things you are prepared to trade. You can do this best by not overtly rejecting proposals from the other side. Keep things open: "We would only be prepared to consider pricing in dollars, if we can put an exchange rate clause in the contract" or "My answer to that depends on what protection you can offer us should the exchange rate go against us."

Build Rapport by *Never Accepting the First Offer*

One of the most difficult things to explain to a novice negotiator is why one should never accept the other side's first offer, even if it seems a good one. It seems counter-intuitive: surely, if he is giving me what I want, I should gratefully accept it?

Put yourself in the other person's shoes. Let's imagine that he is trying to sell you his car. You have had a good look at it and reckon it's worth €9,000. You ask him what his price is. He says €8,000. Probably, your first reaction is to wonder if you really did check the car thoroughly enough. So, you have another look inside and out. You still reckon it's worth €1,000 more than his quote. You agree to pay €8,000. How does he feel? If you could hear the thoughts in his head, they might go something like this:

> Hell. He didn't even try to beat me down. That means he reckons he's got a good deal. Damn it! I could have named a much higher price and let him beat me down a bit. But I would still have got more than €8,000.

He feels an idiot (especially if he is a "he"). Who has made him feel an idiot? You have. You bastard! Now, he asks himself: "How can I get back some of that money that I gave away?"

He will try his best to claw back that "lost" money. Maybe he will tell you that you have to pay for the six months left on the car's licence or the vehicle roadworthiness test that he had done last month; and that the price he quoted did not include the toolkit or detachable GPS system. You may end up paying closer to €9,000 than €8,000.

And yet, if you had sucked your teeth and shaken your head when he first said €8,000 and offered €7,500, he would have smiled, asked you if you were joking and said that he could not go below €7,800. And, with a heavy sigh, you would have shaken his hand on €7,800. Result? Not only would you have saved yourself a further €200, you would probably have got the toolkit, GPS system, six-months licence and roadworthiness test all thrown in for free. Instead of effectively paying, say, €8,800, you would have paid €1,000 less.

Meanwhile, the seller is congratulating himself on his negotiating skills too. His first price was above what he was expecting to sell it for. He had started at €8,000 but had thought he would get €7,500. So, he had "gained" €300. Everybody is happy; everybody is a winner...in their own minds.

Negotiating an international business deal is a lot more complicated than haggling over the purchase of a car. There are many more variables to be negotiated. Even so, if you agree too readily to one part of the other side's proposal, they are likely to have the same reaction as the seller of that car. They will try and compensate for their perceived generosity and resist conceding on other variables, even if it makes sense for them to do so. Moreover, they will subconsciously blame you for their "mistake". Above all, just as with the car purchase, you will probably get a better overall deal if you firmly and politely reject the other side's first offers (whilst, of course, making it clear that you might accept something a little bit further towards your end of the negotiating range).

Give Room for Movement by *Aiming High*

You will meet a Kuwaiti businessman called Abdul Latif in the next two chapters. He is one of the shrewdest negotiators Richard has ever met. He attended one of Richard's first negotiation skills courses back in the mid-1980s. It soon became clear that he had little to learn from either his trainer or his fellow participants. He was there because he wanted a break from his business and wished to improve his English by coming to the UK. He came for dinner at Richard's London flat and kept Richard, his fiancée and the other guests entertained all evening with stories of doing business in the Arabian Gulf. Although Richard probably learned more about negotiation in those few hours than he has before or since, there was one particular piece of advice that has stayed with him more than any other: *aim high*.

Abdul Latif said that he would always make ridiculous opening offers. He was in import-export; so one day he might be a seller, the next a buyer. It didn't matter what side of the table he was on; he would decide on his aims, his negotiating ranges and his targets and then open the negotiation with a proposal that was way beyond what he expected to get. Admittedly, as we shall see in Chapter 6, negotiating ranges in the Arab world tend to be very wide. But Abdul Latif would work hard to find arguments justifying his opening bids. And he would only start moving away from his entry point after a lot of arguing and if he was getting some genuine concessions from the other side in return for moving. Sometimes he would end up with an overall deal that was better than his most optimistic forecast. And yet, nearly always the other side felt they had got a good deal. His contacts around the Gulf would tell him of customers and suppliers boasting of how they had got the better of him.

His explanation of why this tactic worked so well for him did not require a degree in psychology. His absurd opening offer would immediately and emphatically be rejected by his negotiating partner. Abdul Latif could see that this made the man feel good about himself: he was being allowed to show how tough he was. And then the man felt even better as he demolished every one of Abdul Latif's justifications of his extreme position. Finally, as Abdul Latif slowly began to move away from his first offer, always in return for something from the other side, the man could take pleasure from watching the way his tough talking was forcing Abdul Latif to make concessions. All the time, Abdul Latif would show through his gestures and manner how much pain he was having to bear. In the end the two men would embrace and agree that whilst it had been a tough meeting, a good deal had been reached. And indeed it had...in the minds of both men.

In one way, Abdul Latif was obeying two old bargaining rules: give yourself enough room to move, have enough in your pocket to give away a bit. But he was doing more than that. He was using his negotiating partner's wish to be seen as tough and persuasive to his own, considerable, advantage. Richard has called this the *Abdul Latif* tactic in his honour ever since.

Expand

Widen the Scope by *Searching for New Options* and *Linking Ideas, Proposals and Facts*

Once both sides have shared as much information as they are willing to and tested each other's assumptions, it is natural to see what other options are available – a different method of delivery, outsourcing part of the production, sharing design costs... In reality, this exploratory stage can start as soon as the first proposal has been made. But even if it has, it is worth explicitly stating that you would like to spend some time seeing if there is anything neither side has thought of. Such discussion creates a positive atmosphere: both sides are trying to find mutually beneficial solutions. At the same time, it creates opportunities to find out what really matters to both sides. We gave you an example of this when discussing the need to test assumptions:

Client: "What if we do two two-day courses back-to-back?"

Salesman: "...But I understood you wanted each course to run for three days."

By using one of the most common openers to an exploratory question – "What if..." – the client is finding out if there are cheaper solutions to his training problem. And the salesman, in testing his own assumption that the client wants 3-day courses, discovers that price is perhaps more important than quality to his client.

This exploratory process usually makes you connect individual aspects of the whole package with each other. In this last example, price and quality were being linked. As you discuss the various options available to you, such issues as volume, quality, design, delivery methods and schedules, packaging, payment terms and, of course, price are linked together. Do you remember how the conversation between our salesman and his client continued?

Client: "Not if you can convince me that we'd get almost the same result in two days. I hadn't realised it would be cheaper."

Salesman: "Only if you do them Tuesday to Friday."

By making connections you are automatically doing what every skilled negotiator must do: trade.

Create a Provisional Agreement* by *Trading, Not Giving

This is the most important tactic of all.

Søren is fond of telling his course participants that "generosity is not contagious". He goes on: "Many things are contagious, but generosity is not one of them. People think that if they make a concession, the other side will automatically reciprocate. Why should they? Moreover, if you give something for nothing, then you are signalling to the other side that there may be more to be had. You are inviting them to play hardball."

There are some people who will reciprocate but they are few and tend not to be commercial negotiators. Not only is it not normal for someone automatically to give you something in return for your concession, it is not in your interests for them to do so. If the other side gives you something simply because you gave them something, it is usually because they don't value very much what they have given you. Don't forget that they have chosen what to give you in return. You have not linked your offer to something of equal value that you want from them. Why would they voluntarily offer you something of equal value to what you gave them?

Let's imagine that you are a seller and have conceded a cut in price worth €5,000 to the buyer without asking for anything in return. But the buyer apparently decides to be nice to you and gives you, perhaps, a reduction in the payment period that only costs her €200. It's not an equal trade. It might be the case that going from 60 days to 30 days' payment is worth far more than €200 to you. But is it really worth €5,000 to you?

By giving, you are ceding control of the negotiation to the other side. You have changed from a collaborative strategy to a concessionary one – *lose-win*

Some people use the term *bargaining chip* to describe something they can use to trade for something they want. No matter how insignificant a concession may seem, you should consider trading it for something, rather than giving it. Even if what they want has very low or perhaps zero value to you, try to look at it through their eyes. There must be a reason why they want it, so why not get something in return? Most negotiators find that they have something that does not cost them a lot, at the same time as it has a higher value for the other side – such as the payment period for the buyer in the earlier example. We call this a *cheap chip*. Decide what your *cheap chips* are during the preparation stage and try to work out what the other side's priorities are. Test your assumptions early on in the negotiation meeting. You then know what you can trade for what.

So, how exactly do you trade? Through conditional bargaining: you make the other side an offer and tell them what you want in return:

> We could give you a discount of 5%, if you can increase the annual order to 110 standard machines.

Some people[4] think that it is best to say first what you want the other side to give you, and then what you are prepared to offer in return, which is why this tactic is sometimes called *If-Then*:

> If you can increase the annual order to 110 standard machines, then we could give you a discount of 5%.

In section 5 - *Speaking conditionally* – of Chapter 5 we give advice on how best to structure your conditional sentences when bargaining.

> Man has almost constant occasion for the help of his brethren, and it is in vain for him to expect it from their benevolence only. He will be more likely to prevail if he can interest their self-love in his favour, and show them that it is for their own advantage to do for him what he requires of them. Whoever offers to another a bargain of any kind, proposes to do this. Give me that which I want, and you shall have this which you want, is the meaning of every such offer; and it is in this manner that we obtain from one another the far greater part of those good offices which we stand in need of. (Adam Smith, The Wealth of Nations, 1776)[5]

Adam Smith's 18th century English is not that easy for today's native English speaker to understand. But his message is still clear: "(**If** you) give me that which I want, (**then**) you shall have this which you want." Yet, 240 years later, too many negotiators still don't get it.

---

4 Gavin Kennedy is one; he is a passionate exponent of *If-Then*

5 Our thanks to Gavin Kennedy for pointing out this advocacy of conditional bargaining by the father of modern Economics. We also love Smith's simple definition of Man: "an animal that makes bargains."

Eliminate

Reach an Agreement by *Closing*

Among the questions we get asked most frequently are "When is the right time to close a negotiation?" and "What is the best way of doing it?" A lot of people get very anxious about this. There is no need. If you have used the tactics in the ways we have described above, especially the trading one, it is not hard to get to the magic words: "That's it. We have agreed everything."

Type "closing techniques" in your search engine and you will find websites that list over 100 different types of closing. Most of these methods are not just useless; they could badly damage your chances of reaching an agreement. Several of these sites will urge you to follow that old sales tip: It's as simple as ABC: Always Be Closing. No, you should not. The lists of closing techniques and the advice that comes with them are nearly all provided by salespeople for salespeople. You should ignore them, especially if you are a salesperson.

As we said in the first chapter, purchasing managers have become much more sophisticated and well-trained in the last 20 years or so. They can spot a typical close almost before a salesperson utters it. They have been trained to spot closes. And they do not like them. How do we know? Because many of our clients are from big purchasing departments and have told us so. We have also noticed a welcome change in some of the advice provided online. Look again at that first page of sites under *closing techniques* and you may find one or two who agree with us.[6]

So, how do you get to *Yes*? You said at the beginning of the negotiation that nothing is agreed until everything is agreed. At least, we hope you did and that the other side accepted this. You have explored all the options that you have been able to think of. You have linked ideas and issues. You have traded and traded. All the time, we trust, you or a colleague have been noting and regularly summarising what has been provisionally agreed. You think you have exhausted every subject (and

---

6 We particularly like the advice provided by Geoffrey James of Salesforce. We haven't read his latest book – *Business Without the Bullsh*t* – for the simple reason that it only came out as we were putting the finishing touches to our one. But if it contains some of the commonsense advice that he gives on his blog, it must be good. Richard particularly likes the fact that Geoffrey says that empathy is one of the five characteristics of successful salespeople. And successful negotiators.

yourselves). What more is there to do? Use the one closing technique that upsets nobody and unites everybody: the *summary close*.

What is the summary close? A summary...of all the summaries that you have noted and both sides have provisionally agreed. Suggest that one or other side does this. If you do it, take it slowly. Watch the body language of the other side. If you see a shake of the head (and you are not in India, where this might signal agreement rather than disagreement), stop and wait to see if the person says he disagrees. If he doesn't, move on. If he does, ask him to say what his objection is, clearly make a note of it and suggest that you all come back to it later. Start with those things that you are most confident will not be objected to. Build a feeling of joint agreement: "we have achieved something here". Price is the issue that triggers the most objections even if it has been linked to almost every other issue. People somehow feel they are obliged to object to the price. So, it is best to come to it towards the end of your list of provisionally agreed points. And best too to deal with the objections then and there. Often, once the price objections are dealt with, the other disagreements disappear.

And that's it. The summary close requires a lot of patience from everyone, not least the person doing the summarising. As we discuss when we look at team negotiations, you need to decide who will do the summarising on your side if you are not negotiating on your own. It's a key role.

b. Dirty tricks

We said that we would stick with the term *dirty tricks* in describing inappropriate tactics. It's a catchy label. Observe someone reading a book on negotiation skills at an airport bookstall and, often as not, they will flip to the pages that describe these nefarious practices. Perhaps you are one of those people and this is the first bit in this book you have read. In that case: welcome, read on and please buy the book.

Participants on our negotiation skills programmes are always eager to learn about the dirty tricks used by others, but not, of course, themselves. They all claim that they don't intend to employ them. Far from it; they just want to know how best to deal with them, should they be used against them. Of course they do.

A colleague of ours once grouped dirty tricks into what he called "The Dirty Dozen". He was inspired by the film of the same name from 1967 in which 12 men are selected for a dangerous mission behind enemy lines in World War Two. They are all prisoners serving very long sentences or destined to be executed. They are given the opportunity of participating in what is considered an impossible suicide mission. If they survive the mission, they are free. They know the chance of survival is very slim, but the chance of freedom means more to them than the risk of dying. We believe our colleague compared dirty tricks to this suicide mission because if the other side in a negotiation does not realise you are tricking them, you will survive. But if they do spot what you are doing, the deal may be doomed.

Chester Karrass, one of the pioneers of negotiation skills training for businesspeople[7], describes in his book *Give & Take* (1974), two hundred strategies and tactics that he claims have been successfully applied for thousands of years by men who learned them by intuition or from father-to-son.[8] Most of these, apparently, are what his readers would consider inappropriate or dirty. Other writers have described tricks and ploys that are not included in Karass's book.

This talk of dirty tricks is all great fun. But how many genuinely *dirty* tricks are there? The only truly unprincipled ones are those where a negotiator deliberately does or says something that puts the person on the other side in a weak position from which he or she finds it very difficult to escape. In most cases though, a negotiator who accuses the other side of playing dirty should blame himself instead. He has allowed the other side to put pressure on him by putting himself in a vulnerable or weak position in the first place. Before we explain what we mean by this, let's look at some real dirty tricks. They all involve putting the negotiator on the other side under physical pressure.

i. Feeling tired and emotional? – Physical pressure

The British satirical magazine, *Private Eye*, uses the euphemism *tired and emotional* to describe someone who is drunk. Getting the people on the other side of the negotiating table exhausted and hung-over before starting to negotiate with them is one of the oldest dirty tricks in the world. And it is a genuine dirty trick. Don't let those cross-cultural experts persuade you that in, say, Russia or South Korea it is the norm to ply your negotiating partner with spicy food and lots of alcohol the

---

7 The seminar he launched in 1968, entitled *Effective Negotiating*, is described by Dr Karrass as "the most successful seminar in the US". He says he has created "a negotiating arsenal no other negotiator in the country can match".

8 So, there is a negotiation gene and women never negotiate?

night before negotiations begin. No self-respecting Russian or Korean business negotiator would negotiate with a compatriot who tried such a dirty tactic. Yes, socialising and lots of small talk is expected in order to build the relationship. But the time to get blind drunk is at the party or banquet to celebrate the signing of the contract.

You have just endured a 13-hour long Economy class flight to Seoul. It is late in the afternoon by the time you get to your 3-star hotel. You are expecting to meet the Korean company you are negotiating with at 9.00 the next morning. Three days of negotiations have been scheduled, including a factory visit. You are on your own. The hotel receptionist hands you a message from the Koreans welcoming you to South Korea and informing you will be picked up at 19.00 and driven to a restaurant for a "welcome dinner". How very considerate of them, you think. And it is possible that you may have a couple of pleasant hours drinking tea and tasting *kimchee* for the first time, after which you are allowed to collapse alone into your hotel bed. Possibly. But it may be that you will experience what the top management of a British insurance company once endured in Seoul: a "welcome dinner" that ended after midnight, included many alcohol-fuelled toasts to the new relationship, and where every man had a young Korean woman next to him to provide certain manual services while he ate.

If you are not sure you are the victim of a deliberate underhand tactic, have a look through your half-open eyes the next morning and see if you will be negotiating with the same people you were partying with the night before. If they are all or mostly different, you have indeed been tricked.

Before we are accused of being anti-Korean, let us assure you that this kind of dirty trick can be and has been used all over the world. Richard once watched a party of clearly tired Japanese businessmen being wined and dined by their German hosts in a Dusseldorf restaurant while he was at a nearby table with some course participants. He managed to speak to one of the Japanese when collecting his coat. This was the first night of their visit; they were due to go on to a nightclub; the interpreter they had brought with them had already been sick after eating pork knuckle and dumplings. Perhaps those Germans were just being friendly though.

How can you avoid getting into such a situation? First of all, treat your body and mind with more respect. It's a false economy to fly Economy and stay in a cheap hotel if you are going to do any serious negotiating on the other side of the world. And go a day early, not just so that you can catch up on sleep and begin to get over the jet-lag, but also so that you can tune in to the local culture. If this isn't possible, propose starting the first meeting in the afternoon the day after your arrival. Don't rush into the negotiation. Secondly, consider negotiating with at least one other person alongside you. International negotiations can be particularly exhausting; lighten the burden by sharing it. We have more to say about team negotiations in Chapter 8. Finally, politely refuse any welcoming party of any kind in advance. Warn your host that you always go straight to bed after a long-haul flight so that you are fully refreshed when you finally meet them. This gives you the licence to refuse any invitation that you receive on arrival: "It's very kind of you but I did say that I am not able to attend any event the night before we meet." They will get the message: this is not someone we can play games with.

Other forms of physical pressure that some unscrupulous negotiators can apply include putting you in a chair that is lower than theirs, making you face the sun coming through a window, and keeping the room at a temperature they are used to but you are not.

In all cases where you feel the other side is playing dirty, you should make it clear as early as possible that you are not willing to be treated in such a fashion. Take the situation described in the last paragraph: stand up, walk to the window, open it if you feel the room is too hot, and turn and face your hosts. Take command of the situation. Show that you are not going to be bullied. At the same time, ask yourself if you really want to do business with people who behave like this. If not, catch the next flight home.

So, what about all the other so-called *dirty tricks*? These are tactics that are used by the skilled negotiator to put pressure on you to make concessions. But it is usually you (or your company or your boss) who has made it possible for that pressure to be applied. We have put these tactics into six more categories of pressure. We then advise how you can avoid being a target for each tactic and how to respond if you find yourself facing it.

ii. Flying tonight? – Time pressure

Most of us when negotiating are under some sort of time pressure. Maybe a salesman needs to bring in €45,000 of new business by the end of the month, if he is to reach his quarterly sales target. A buyer has to place an order for some raw materials in the next fortnight, if his colleagues in the factory are to increase production by 40% for the Christmas season. A project manager has to get his haulier to allocate another three trucks a day for the 450 km trip from port to project location from the beginning of next week, if his company is to avoid paying a large penalty for missing a contract milestone. A promoter must sell at least half of the remaining 1,500 tickets for tomorrow night's rock concert, if he is to have enough money to pay the bands, let alone himself.

Is it unfair or immoral for a buyer, a seller, a haulier, or a ticket agent to try to get the best deal they can in the situations we have described above? We don't think so. If the seller, buyer, project manager or promoter have been foolish enough to reveal what time pressure they are under, we have little sympathy. Maybe we have some for the promoter: he got his pricing wrong, the bands were not as good or as popular as he expected. Even so, if a ticket agent interested in buying 50 tickets innocently asks whether there are any tickets left, surely it is better to say that there are "just a few" than admit the venue will only be two-thirds full?

We reckon there are at least six time-pressure tactics.

When are you flying home?

This is a common question, especially when put to someone who is negotiating an international deal far from their own country. If you tell the other side when you have booked to fly back, your hosts may be tempted to delay negotiating on the things that matter most to them until you are almost in the taxi on the way to the airport. They assume that you will make concessions rather than board the plane without a signed contract.

It's not difficult to deal with this: have an open ticket (or pretend you have one). You can then adjust your departure date if you need to. Indeed, it is probably best to anticipate the question and state as early as possible that you have the authority to stay on if necessary. If you really do have to catch that booked flight, say that you are willing to come out again to complete the negotiation or that you will be happy to host another round of negotiations, if it is required. The most important thing is not to get yourself in the position where you really do have to have a signed contract when you board the plane.

A variation of this tactic is when the other party tries to impose a time limit. "I must have your decision on this by 4 p.m. tomorrow". If this deadline does not suit you, try to determine why it is so important to them: "Can I ask, why 4 p.m. specifically?" Such questioning may reveal the time pressures they are under, which you can then use to your advantage! Go on to explain why their deadline does not work for you and propose your own one.

We are pulling out

Just when you seem to be close to an agreement, the other side says they cannot continue with the negotiation. They may claim that you have been unreasonable with your demands or that they have had a better offer elsewhere (another type of pressure tactic we discuss later). We have seen this tactic variously entitled – *Left at the altar*, *Cold feet* or *Second thoughts*. Whatever the title, it's not a clever move. If they don't really mean to pull out of the negotiations and you call their bluff by saying "Okay, the deal's off", they will find it difficult to restart the negotiation. They will have lost face and undermined the trust that has been established. And they certainly won't get any further concessions from you. If you don't call their bluff, but instead probe carefully and politely as to why they want to cancel the negotiation, they will probably reveal something which you can use to trade further with them. In such situations always ask yourself why anyone would invest so much time, money and energy in a negotiation if they are intending to pull out at the last moment. It doesn't make sense.

We can't decide that now

This tactic is sometimes called *Not tonight, Josephine*, a phrase that early 19th century British satirists claimed Napoleon said to his over-passionate mistress and, later, wife. The other side appear to be lengthening the negotiation process to put pressure on you. You should counter with questions: "When will you be able to decide? What is stopping you from deciding now?" and point out the risks to them of delaying agreement: "That could make things difficult for us and you. If we don't have this contract signed by the end of this month, you will force us to reallocate the slot we have provisionally placed with you in our production schedule. This will mean we'll have to renegotiate the delivery dates." Find out what the real problem is and make clear what the consequences for them will be of stringing things out. Meet pressure with pressure.

We can no longer agree to that

Again, you are close to an agreement on everything and the other side puts it all under threat. They start saying that they have changed their mind on one or two carefully-traded matters that are vital to both sides. This move is sometimes called *the avocado*: soft on the outside (the beginning of the negotiation), hard on the inside (the end of the negotiation). To counter it, ask why they have changed their minds. Can they no longer do what they promised only a short time ago? What has changed to cause them to reverse their decision? Make them squirm. Make them feel that they, not you, are being unreasonable. Then outline the consequences if they try, at such a late stage, to unwrap the whole package.

As we keep saying...

This tactic is called the *Chinese water torture* or, for lovers of vinyl, *the broken record*: the other side keeps making the same unchanged demand, hoping, presumably, to wear you down through constant repetition. Ask questions to try and find out why they are so insistent. If that yields nothing useful, tell them bluntly that no amount of repetition will make you concede and that you may have to reconsider staying at the negotiation table.

Last year, Søren worked with a charity to help their consultants deal with a Danish version of Chinese water torture being applied by civil servants. These officials were under orders to reduce the financial assistance given by the Danish government to such charitable organisations. The charity helps those who cannot help themselves; the need for their services, and consequently their call upon government funds, has been increasing since the financial crisis hit. At a follow-up session with Søren, one of the consultants reported an extremely unpleasant meeting with two civil servants. They had put her under insistent pressure to replace some of her salaried staff with unpaid volunteers. This meeting took place just days before the charity was going to finalise its budget for the following year. A cut in government funding would mean redundancies. She said that she had been ready to give in to the officials' oft-repeated and unchanging demands when she heard Søren's voice.

This came as a surprise to Søren: "Really? What did I say?"

"Never give in to pressure," the charity consultant replied.

She recounted how she had asked for a time-out and left the officials alone in the meeting room for a few minutes. This had given her time to decide what to do. More importantly perhaps she had started, by her absence, to put some pressure on her tormentors. What were they thinking as they sat alone in that room? Did they look out through the window into the rest of the charity's office and wonder what effect their actions would have on the people they could see: real people, not a figure in a table in an appendix of a finance ministry report. Did they think of their own deadlines? Might they use their time more productively going to another charity and bullying some other person into giving up government support? This woman had asked for a break rather than give in to their demands. She might think of other ways of refusing to accept. Sure enough, when she came back into the room, she felt more in control and stronger. She had decided to dig her heels in and calmly battle it out with the officials. They soon saw that their time-pressure tactics were not working. She was using such tactics on them herself. They left to find easier victims of austerity elsewhere, having agreed to keep the government's financial support at the same level as before.

Just one more thing...

You are about to close the deal, or you have even reached agreement, when the other side says something like: "Just one more thing: could you give us a small discount...5% for the first batch of 2,000 units?" If you agree to the first "small" request, they will be encouraged to ask for more. Before you know it, you will have cut your margin to the bone. Lots of "small" concessions can add up to a very big one. And how do they show their gratitude when, at last, you refuse to give them any more: "Do you really want to risk the whole deal for such a small matter?" This *salami slicing*, as it is often dubbed, is a surprisingly common tactic in our experience. Maybe this is because too many people give in to such demands. Here is how Søren dealt with it in his days as an export sales manager.

He was negotiating with a big company that had a worldwide network of stores. The company had expressed an interest in one of Søren's company's products. The prospect's negotiating team would not reveal any of their packaging and delivery requirements until they had been given a price for the product. Søren quoted them a price ex-works per unit, unpacked. Once they had got the price and the negotiation was nearly finished, the buyers asked for *one more thing* and then another and another. All labels had to be printed on recycled paper, which for some peculiar reason is more expensive than regular paper.

Each product had to be packed in biodegradable cling film. And they did not accept delivery on euro pallets, only on their own pallets and stacked to a certain height. On its own, each special request would not have cost Søren's company much more; but together they would have turned a profitable deal into one where he would barely have broken even. The buyers waited to play this game until Søren had already, in his mind, opened the bottle of champagne to celebrate the done deal. And they added to the pressure by pretending that the price he had quoted was all-inclusive of their requirements. They were effectively accusing him of lying when he repeatedly denied this. Fortunately, Søren had put his offer in writing, so he was able to rebut their accusations (although that did not stop them arguing as to the meaning of *all-inclusive*). He also made it clear that if they wanted his company to follow their packaging and delivery requirements, they would have to pay for each and every one of them. In other words, he traded, rather than conceded. And he did not let the vision of the champagne bottle stop him from continuing to negotiate rather than give, right up until the moment when the contract was signed.

This story reminds us of the importance of keeping a record of what exactly has been promised and offered as the negotiation goes along. And summarising what has been agreed.

A variation of *salami slicing* is the *Trojan horse*. At some stage in the negotiation the other side ask you to provide just a small thing at no extra cost to them. It could be some training or some special packaging. Foolishly, you reluctantly agree. They then ask how much it will cost you to provide this. Even more foolishly, you tell them: "€12,000". They thank you for your generosity (and mark you down as an idiot). Right at the end of the negotiation, they say: "Just one small thing. We have decided that we don't need the training. I think you said it would cost you €14,000 to provide. Could you therefore knock €14,000 off the price? And then we'll have a deal."

Don't get angry, get even. If you allow this to happen, there is still an escape route. Tell them, with a big smile, that you admire their negotiating skills but are not going to fall for this ruse. You had made your offer of free training in good faith and in the hope that it would be accepted in the same spirit. Instead it has been used against you. There is no way that you will cut the price any further. "Do we have a deal?" Shamefaced and avoiding your eyes, they will invariably agree.

Sometimes it is best to be open and honest about the way you feel you are being mistreated and manipulated.

iii. Be reasonable! – Emotional pressure

There are two emotional-pressure tactics that you are likely to come across fairly frequently.

Poor me!

A salesman will tell the buyer how little they will be making on the deal. The stock response by a buyer to a supplier's initial price is that she can't afford to pay such a price. Big companies with vast incomes can be especially creative in explaining why their pockets are empty of all but loose change. This tactic is also known as *Mother Hubbard* (whose cupboard was bare) from an old nursery rhyme. Very occasionally somebody may be telling the truth but it is nearly always a feeble attempt to make you feel sorry for the other person, so that you will make concessions. If they have no money or won't benefit in some way from the deal, why are they meeting you? Ask a few questions about their apparently dire financial situation; you might learn something useful and it shows you are prepared to be sympathetic. But otherwise ignore their plea of poverty and carry on negotiating as normal.

Ignore him, I'm Mr Nice Guy

The old *good cop/bad cop* routine must still work sometimes. Otherwise why is it practised by negotiators the world over? The bad cop makes very extreme demands and behaves rudely. Finally, he exits the room slamming the door behind him or he just sits there scowling at you. The good cop apologises and suggests ways to make the bad cop happy. These ways always include concessions by you.

It can be hard to deal with, especially if you are in a foreign country. You may wonder if you have offended the angry guy by making some cross-cultural gaffe. But it is not normal in any of the countries we have worked in for a guest to be treated rudely, however many cultural mistakes the visitor may have made. You are almost certainly facing the good cop/bad cop tactic. Make a conscious effort to slow everything down. Pause before answering questions or responding to attacks. Ask for a break when you feel you are being pushed into a corner. Above all, focus on the facts and the issues. Do not get dragged by the bad cop into a stress-inducing argument that questions your morals or your intelligence. If the routine carries on for too long, you should openly acknowledge that you are beginning to doubt the wisdom of continuing to negotiate. Suggest that each side takes an extended break to discuss whether it is worth carrying on. Make it clear that you will leave if the abuse continues. Or you can do what both of us have done at least once when faced with this tactic: compliment the pair on their routine. "This is one of the best good cop/bad cop performances I have ever come across." In Richard's case, he was dealing with a nice HR woman in a Turkish law firm and the firm's managing partner. Their response was to laugh...and to carry on exactly as before. Richard left as soon as he could.

iv. You need us! – Power pressure

You need us more than we need you

Many salespeople fall victim to this line peddled by purchasing managers. Suppliers are forever being told that "the customer is always right... is king" (or in Japan "... is god."). The successful supplier should provide excellent customer service. But he should not assume that this means he is somehow in a weaker position than a buyer in a negotiation. Yes, he has to sell to survive. But a buyer has to buy or her business will die. You should assume she wants to buy from you because you have the particular product or service that she needs. She may be able to go elsewhere but there must be a reason why she has agreed to spend time negotiating with you. If you have done your preparation properly you will know why. You will not start making concessions out of a fear that if you don't, the buyer will do a deal with someone else. Go into the negotiation thinking that they need you as much as you need them.

You should pay for the status we give you

Negotiators who work for famous, highly-regarded companies and organisations will often make much of the value they are "giving away for free" by agreeing to form a business relationship with your company. If they work for a company that is regarded as the leader in its field and you are able to claim them as a client, supplier, or joint-venture or business partner, your sales or share price may get a significant boost. It's a powerful argument. But don't be fooled by it. Their company's high status will have already been priced into their offer to you. They are not giving that status away "for free". If you concede further, you are overpaying for their reputational value to you. Moreover, the people in a prestigious company would not consider doing business with you, if they thought that prestige could be put at risk by doing a deal with you. They must value you too.

v. My boss! Your competitor! – External pressure

Here are two old favourites. In both cases, the other side tries to put pressure on you by invoking an external being who can only be appeased or made to disappear by your making further concessions: the *phantom boss* and the *phantom competitor*. Other malign outside forces might be mentioned too: governments and their agencies, industry regulators, the media, financial markets, bankers...

My boss won't accept this

You think you have just reached agreement with the other party. Then he tells you that he just needs to confer with his boss. Of course, the boss is likely to want a few more concessions before the deal can be finalised.

If he is telling the truth, you have only yourself to blame for not discovering who the ultimate decision-maker is. Always establish, as early as possible, if you are talking to the right person. However, it may just be a tactic to get more concessions. Counter by checking if the person you have been negotiating with agrees that the deal you have just spent a lot of time agreeing is still agreeable to him. He is unlikely to say no. Then suggest that you meet his boss together. Offer to explain why you both think the deal is a good one. If he is bluffing, he will soon say that it may be best to leave his boss in peace. Anything to avoid your speaking to his boss. If he is not bluffing, make him your ally when you see the boss.

Your competitors can do better than that

Purchasing managers really should be taught never to say such things. It must be the oldest and least effective trick in the negotiator's manual. If that is the only argument that a buyer can use against a seller, she must be in a weak position indeed. It is also a wonderful opportunity for the seller to get some valuable information on his competition. If you are the seller, respond by asking questions:

> Which companies are you talking about? What exactly are they offering you? What is it about their offer that you don't like? What do you particularly like about our offer?

Those last two questions are the key ones. They remind the buyer that there must be a reason why he is sitting in a room with you rather than your competitor. The answers to them might also tell you where you score over your rival in the eyes of the buyer.

vi. 1.376 or 0.735? – Numeracy pressure

We said in Chapter 1 that the skilled negotiator should, ideally, have a head for numbers. However, not all of us are good at mathematics, especially when forced to do a series of quick calculations in our heads rather than with a calculator. Few will admit to this weakness, especially in a negotiation. This opens them up to being taken advantage of by those who love nothing better than throwing as many numbers as possible into the discussion.

Richard has a problem converting currencies quickly, a skill that can be crucial in the middle of an international negotiation. He has finally learned to stop pretending he is a wiz at number-crunching and insists on working things out slowly with his calculator. He may look a bit stupid. But better that than accepting a price in Turkish lira, say, that results in a loss once converted correctly into pounds. In fact, when Richard apologised a few years ago to a Turkish HR manager for his inability to remember which way round the lira-pound rate worked, she laughed and said that she could never remember the one that mattered most to her - the lira-dollar rate. They did the calculations together. Admission of weaknesses can sometimes lead to a more collaborative atmosphere and a better working relationship.

Another tactic sometimes used against the numerically-challenged we call *apples and oranges*. You must be careful that the other side does not try to confuse you by making comparisons between things that appear similar but which, in fact, are not. For example, a seller offers to increase the current discount by 50% in return for a 10% increase in the volume a buyer orders. To mathematical fools such as Richard this sounds like a generous offer: Wow; I get 50% if I give him 10%. It sounds as though he is getting a big cut in the price for not much increase in the order. But, of course, if the current discount is 4%, this offer only makes it 6%. And if the order is in tens of thousands of units, a 10% increase will make the overall order a lot more expensive. Use absolute numbers when responding to such confusing proposals:

> Your offer brings the unit price down by a further 60 cents to $28.20. In return you are asking us to increase the volume to 22,000 units. This would increase the overall price by$44,400. You would have to cut your price by a lot more before we could even consider such an increase in volume.

Percentages and ratios can be misleading.

Finally, if you are forced to discuss a measuring system you are not used to – e.g. the metric one for many US Americans – do not let the other side push you into making decisions based on those numbers without taking the time to ensure you have made the right calculations.

vii. Are you with me? – Linguistic pressure

If you go online and type in *negotiation dirty tricks*, you will find pages of sites that will list most of the tactics we have described above and many more. But not one that we have seen describes the dirty trick that is often towards the top of the list of an international negotiator whose first language is not English. English is the language of international business. Negotiations between, say, an Argentine and a Chinese will either be done through interpreters or conducted in English (or both). In such cases there will undoubtedly be misunderstandings and confusion because of language differences. But it is highly unlikely that anyone will use their language as a weapon with which to put pressure on the other side. Yet that is exactly what many native English speakers are perceived as doing when they negotiate with non-native English speakers.

Faced with people who speak English very fast and with an unfamiliar accent, and who use colourful idiomatic expressions and baffling words (such as *"baffling"*), many non-native speakers think that the native English speakers are trying to trick them into agreeing to things they do not truly understand.

Not long ago, a colleague, Gerard Bannon, conducted a survey on how non-native English speakers felt about using English, when doing business in the international arena. A total of 408 people from 26 countries responded. To the question, "Do native English speakers of English use their linguistic superiority to gain an advantage?" 242 people (59.3%) replied yes.

In fact, we believe only a tiny proportion of native English speakers consciously use their superior knowledge of English to put pressure on the non-native English speakers on the other side of the negotiation table. Indeed, we wondered whether we should include this pressure tactic in our list because it is so rarely used as a deliberate tactic. However, as Gerard's survey and our own experience show, many non-native English speakers believe that Brits, Americans, Irish people, Australians, New Zealanders and other native English speakers do deliberately use their better command of English to put pressure on them. And here, as so often when negotiating internationally, what people believe to be true is just as important as what is actually true.

We will come back to the use and misuse of English in the next two chapters and give advice to non-native English speakers on how to deal with this tactic, whether it is deliberate or not. Meanwhile, ask yourself what the title of this piece on linguistic pressure - "Are you with me?" - means. It has two meanings: "Do you understand?" and "Do you agree?". Now imagine that you are negotiating and somebody says to you: "Are you with me?". What are they asking you? The context will often tell you whether they are asking if you understand or if you agree. But not always; and almost never if you are not a confident English speaker.

We described the person who uses these pressure tactics as a "skilled negotiator". If he has been using them to put pressure on you, this seems perfectly legitimate to us. They are not really *dirty tricks*. However, if he is unskilled or plain stupid and continues to use these tactics even though you have shown that you will not yield to such pressure, you should consider whether it is wise to do business with him. You will have noted that we have used the word "pressure" in all our descriptions of these *dirty tricks*. We would have preferred to have entitled this section *Pressure Tactics*. But that is not so exciting, is it?

4.4 GerMedica and BTB – Getting to yes

Let's return to the negotiation between GerMedica and BTB. The third meeting between the two companies is taking place in and around BTB's headquarters in São Paulo. The two previous meetings and the various emails and phone calls between Ulrike and Anselmo were spent exchanging information, testing assumptions and making tentative proposals. Nothing has been finally agreed about anything. Ulrike has, at last, made it clear that GerMedica are looking for a third supplier of analytical scales. Initially this supplier will need to deliver ten standard scales to their Stuttgart site for testing over a six-month period. Should the test be successful, further orders will be placed for a mix of 90 standard and 25 bespoke machines for delivery to their German and US sites in the first year. From the second year, delivery will be solely to their new development lab in São Paulo, which has yet to be built. Ulrike has not specified what number of machines might be ordered for the second year. Anselmo has sent a revised proposal, based on this new information. He has not changed the basic price ex-works for a standard machine that he quoted after the first meeting In China. It is still $1,450. He has not given any prices for bespoke machines, or said if there would be any discount linked to the size of the first year's order.

Ulrike spends the morning touring BTB's plant and brand-new Research & Development building. She is allowed to talk to anyone she wishes to, with Anselmo acting as interpreter. She is impressed by the modern equipment and high standards of cleanliness, although perturbed at how close the whole complex is to a huge *favela*. Naturally, she uses the tour to extract more technical information from Anselmo and his colleagues.

Vitor Cunha, together with a professional interpreter, joins Ulrike and Anselmo for a delicious lunch at Senhor Cunha's favourite restaurant – *Bananeira* – in the nearby suburb of Morumbi. It lasts for three hours. You might think that this is merely an opportunity for both sides to strengthen the relationship. Perhaps Senhor Cunha and Frau Fröhlich will end up on first-name terms by the end of it. Certainly the Brazilians want to impress Ulrike and get to know her better over lunch, the normal occasion in Brazil to do serious business. But both sides know that this is the most important part not only of the day but of the whole negotiation.

Ulrike has done her homework. She learned during her last phone call with Anselmo that the ultimate decision-maker was not him but his boss. She had asked Anselmo what discount she could expect on the first year's order of 115 machines. When told 5% on the 90 standard machines only, she had said that this was nowhere near enough. Anselmo had countered by saying that Senhor Cunha would not accept a larger discount. She had responded by saying that in that case she would need to meet Senhor Cunha when she came to Sao Paulo. Anselmo told her that he had already arranged for this to happen. Ulrike later talked to a friend who had spent five years working in Brazil. The friend laughed when told of Anselmo's responses: "That's Brazil for you. The *patrão*...the *chefe*...he takes all the big decisions. It's very hierarchical there. It'll be a long lunch. Keep to water. No alcohol. You'll be doing the real negotiating with him." It was sound advice.

All three stages of the negotiation happen during the three-hour lunch. After Senhor Cunha discovers that he cannot persuade Senhora Ulrike to have a *Caipirinha* (she notices that both he and Anselmo have fruit juice), he suggests that Ulrike reports on what she observed during the morning and that Anselmo summarises, in Portuguese, what has been provisionally discussed and agreed so far. The interpreter gives simultaneous translation into German as Anselmo speaks. Ulrike is flattered that the Brazilians have taken the trouble to hire someone who can translate into and out of Portuguese, English and German. It also reinforces her impression that BTB care about the details (contrary, if she is honest, to her image of Brazilians).

Ulrike makes notes as Anselmo's summary is translated for her. She smiles at the number of times she hears the words in German for "We have agreed..." But she waits until Anselmo has finished before reminding the two men that "nothing is agreed until everything is agreed". She proposes, looking directly at Senhor Cunha, that both sides state what issues are still troubling them and on which points they are furthest from agreement. She then adds that she herself has the authority to sign any agreement but that she still has to see "a couple of your local competitors" before deciding who will be awarded the contract.

Now it is Senhor Cunha's turn to smile and admire her negotiation skills. In just a few words she has made redundant any pressure tactics he had thought of using on her. She is not in a hurry to sign. And the one big bargaining chip he thought he had – BTB as the only local supplier – may not be as powerful as he had been led to believe. He notes too that she has taken back control of the agenda.

Senhor Cunha diverts the conversation away from business for a while. He needs time to think and assumes the others need a mental break too. He asks Ulrike about Germany, a country he has never been to and whether she minds all the travelling she must have to do. He asks her for her first impressions of Brazil and how long she will be spending in the country. Ulrike laughs at the last question and teases the older man: "Senhor Cunha, is that a clever way of finding out how many of your competitors I will be seeing?" He laughs too and agrees that it is. He also suggests she calls him *Vitor* and takes the opportunity to ask her who she will be seeing. How will she be able to ensure that they can produce to GerMedica's standards and replace within hours any faulty machine?

Now it is Ulrike's turn to be impressed. He has asked the very questions she will be asking his competitor in southern Brazil and it would be foolish for her to pretend that she is seeing more than one other

Brazilian supplier. Senhor Cunha gets some valuable information from his artful "small talk" questions. He also notices with approval that she switches to calling him *Senhor Vitor*. The meeting is going well.

By the time they have reached coffee (and after a patriotic speech from Senhor Cunha on the superiority of the coffee grown in Minas Gerais), there are really only two major issues still to be resolved: what discount can BTB offer for the supply of different volumes of standard machines and what will they charge for bespoke ones? Ulrike tries to push for a discount for all machines. Senhor Cunha flatly refuses. She asks why. He tells her that the real costs of producing special, one-off scales are not known until the work has been done. BTB will have to take this uncertainty into account when quoting for each bespoke machine. Applying a universal discount to the special machine price takes the risk of BTB making a loss on such machines to an unacceptably high level. She says she will think about what he has said, noting that he cleverly proposed how to deal with the pricing of bespoke scales during his explanation.

As they leave the restaurant, Ulrike congratulates the interpreter on her excellent German and asks her how often she has to use it in her work. The interpreter thanks her and tells her, in German, that she has to use it more and more: German companies are investing heavily in Brazil. She adds that she spent all morning being briefed by Senhor Cunha on what they were likely to discuss at lunch. She could then make sure she knew the right technical words in German. Senhor Cunha asks the interpreter what she has told Ulrike. When she finishes telling him, he gives Ulrike a wink. They both know what it means: "You didn't expect us Brazilians to be so well-prepared or pay such attention to detail. Well, we in BTB, like you, believe such things are important. You can trust us."

Ulrike spends the rest of the afternoon hammering out a provisional agreement with Anselmo. When she says goodbye to him and Senhor Cunha, she does not say that they have a deal. But, as she tells her boss when she gets back to Stuttgart, it was the last words of the interpreter and Senhor Cunha's wink that finally made up her mind for her. BTB will be GerMedica Brazil's main supplier of analytical scales.

5

What should I say and how should I say it?

International negotiations nowadays are usually a mix of emailing, telephoning, meeting online and meeting in the same room. Much of the advice in this chapter assumes that you are talking and listening. Some of it also applies to writing. We have included a separate section on the many hazards and few benefits of conducting a negotiation by email.

We hope you have got used to reading about the negotiation between Anselmo Oliveira of BTB and Ulrike Fröhlich of GerMedica. We use imagined dialogues between them in this section. However neither of them would speak such accurate English. Nor, in fact, would native

English speakers. Ask any scriptwriter and he will tell you that natural spoken speech is full of grammatical mistakes and unfinished or mangled sentences. So, treat these dialogues as guidelines only.

5.1 Ask and listen

"Ask constantly and listen actively." This was the answer one of the authors gave to a course participant who had asked him what one piece of communication advice he would give to a novice negotiator. Was it cheating to give two answers? No; they are linked.

To be a skilled negotiator you have to build on your existing knowledge of those with whom you are negotiating. Test your assumptions about them, their needs and their aims throughout the negotiation. How? By asking questions. Constantly. This won't just mean that you will be better informed. Questioning, done well, gives you so much more. It shows the people with whom you are negotiating that you are genuinely interested in them. It gives you time to think, to observe reactions to your proposals and to assess what is important for the other side. It is a good way of introducing new ideas and ways around blocks to progress. Most important of all, the right kind of questioning at the right moment in a negotiation sends the right signal: this is a negotiation, not a fight; let's find an agreement which suits both sides. Research done by Professor Neil Rackham and the Huthwaite Research Group in the 1980s (see Chapter 1) support this contention. A skilled negotiator will spend a fifth of her time asking questions, twice the time of the average negotiator. The use of "her", by the way, is deliberate. Our experience of negotiating and teaching negotiation skills around the world for over 60 years between us has shown us that women usually ask more and better questions than men.

So, what type of questions should you ask? Well, that is an example of one type: the rhetorical question. This does not expect an answer from the listener and is best used either to begin a summary, to indicate the direction in which the negotiation might go (see "summarise" and "map and signpost" respectively below) or to introduce and highlight a key point in your argument:

Summarising: "So, Ms Fröhlich, what have we provisionally agreed so far?"

Signposting: "Shall we move on to the delivery schedule?"

Key point: "Can I just explain, Mr Oliveira, why reliability and accuracy are so important for us?"

I keep six honest serving-men
They taught me all I knew.
Their names are What and Why and When
And How and Where and Who.
Rudyard Kipling – British writer and poet

It is sometimes said that you should start any negotiation by asking open questions and then bring in more and more closed questions as the negotiation reaches its conclusion. There is a grain of truth in this. But only a grain. Open questions - those that begin with how, what, who, when, where and why and their many variants - will get the other side to give you information. You want such information before you get into the negotiation proper. But skilled negotiators will deploy open questions throughout a negotiation - to examine new facts or unexpected developments and to find creative ways around apparent blocks to progress. And closed questions - those that expect either a *yes* or *no* answer - can be very effective at any time to get agreement to something or to clarify a point. So, what should you do?

- Ask the right kind of open question at the right time to yield the maximum amount of information
- Ask closed questions that are likely to yield the answer "Yes"

The two types of open questions most likely to lead to new information are the exploratory ones that begin with "What if...?" and "How about...?". They are tentative suggestions of possible new options.

Anselmo: "What if we were to train two of your lab technicians to repair our machines?"

Ulrike: "How about seconding one of your technicians to our US site for a week at your cost?"

Open questions don't only give you greater insights into the other side's negotiating position. They give you time to think and to observe behaviour. They give you greater control and the impression (and often the reality) of movement:

Ulrike: "How long would it take BTB to design and produce a bespoke model with these modifications?"

Anselmo: "Once we have the spec...six weeks, maybe seven."

Ulrike: "What would you need to do to reduce that to four weeks?"

Anselmo: "Difficult to say. Not sure it's possible. I suppose we could add a third engineer to the design team. But that would increase the cost to you."

Ulrike: "By how much?"

Anselmo: "Roughly...20% for the design part of the project? I'd need to come back to you with an exact figure."

Notice the unspoken assumption in the second question that there must be a way to cut the time. If you ask such a question, you must give the other person time to answer. He has to make all sorts of calculations. He may well pause between sentences. The clever negotiator doesn't interrupt or push for a quick answer. Let the silences do the work for you.

In addition, see how the follow-up question – "By how much?" – has given Ulrike an estimate of the BTB's design costs.

Contrast that dialogue with the lack of movement and new information when using closed questions:

Ulrike: "Can BTB design and produce a bespoke model with these modifications in fewer than six weeks?"

Anselmo: "No. It may be difficult to do it in six anyway."

Ulrike: "Is there any way you can do it in under six?"

Anselmo: "Sorry, Ms Fröhlich, I don't think so."

Once someone has said "No" it's hard for them to say "Yes" to the same question. If you press them, they will become obstinate and even resentful: "Didn't you hear what I said?" and "Are you calling me a liar?" may be the unspoken reactions. So, avoid questions which permit a "No" answer.

This is illustrated hilariously by the actor, Samuel L Jackson, in the 1998 movie, *The Negotiator*. He plays an expert Chicago police negotiator who has taken hostages himself. Holding a gun and speaking over the phone to a colleague, Jackson gives him some advice:

Jackson: "Never say 'No' to a hostage taker. It's in the manual. Now, are you going to tell me 'No' again?"

Colleague: "No..."

Jackson: "Wrong answer! Never use 'No', 'Don't', 'Won't' or 'Can't'. It eliminates options. The only option it leaves is to kill someone."

Questions at the end of statements – "aren't you?", "don't you?" "is it?" – can be used to make sure you have understood correctly, to provide a platform of agreement from which to ask additional questions, or to push the other side towards a particular position favourable to you. These are known as check questions.

Ulrike: "You sell in a lot of countries, don't you, Mr Oliveira? So, presumably you can quote in different currencies, can't you? We would need you to quote in Euros. Is that okay?"

However, be careful with check questions like these when negotiating internationally. Many Asian cultures, for example, find such questions in English confusing. They can interpret them literally and logically. So, "You work in a lot of countries, don't you?" can be translated as "You do not work in a lot of countries" and, if not true, will generate "No" (meaning: we do work in a lot of countries), which is not the answer you were expecting. A way around this is to avoid using the negative ending, employ a rising tone with each statement and wait for the answer each time:

Ulrike: "You sell in a lot of countries, Mr Oliveira?"

Anselmo: "Yes."

Ulrike: "So, presumably you can quote in different currencies?"

Anselmo: "Er...yes."

Ulrike: "We would need you to quote in Euros. Is that okay?"

Even more confusing can be the technique of using negative check questions at the beginning of sentences: "Wouldn't you agree...?"and "Don't you think...?". British negotiators, in particular, love asking these types of questions. East Asian negotiators will often answer "Yes" to these, meaning "Yes, I would not agree" and "Yes, I do not think". The Brit, hearing "Yes", then deludes himself that his Chinese/Japanese/Korean counterpart agrees with him and finds out too late that he does not. Such negative leading questions do not work outside the UK culture anyway; they sound patronising and are an example of "saps", which weaken your arguments - see later in this chapter.

The most powerful and productive of Kipling's serving men is "why". You use it when probing for the other side's real needs and interests. You need to know these if you are going to find out where they will be willing to make concessions and where it will be much harder for them to do so. But "why" questions can sound and feel aggressive, even when prefaced by a signpost such as "May I ask?" or "I hope you don't mind my asking...". In some cultures it is even considered rude to ask a "why" question. The Japanese have two words for "why" but seldom employ them when negotiating. So, if you feel your "why" questions are making the other side too uncomfortable, note the discomfort - useful information in itself - and find other ways of getting the answers you require.

One substitute for the "why" approach is deductive questioning, using a mix of closed, check and open questions:

Ulrike: "Could you deliver an extra ten standard scales to our São Paolo site at a week's notice?"

Anselmo: "That would be hard for us to do."

Ulrike: "But you could do it, couldn't you?"

Anselmo: "Not with our current inventory policy."

Ulrike: "So, you could, if you changed the policy?"

Anselmo: "Yes, maybe. But it will increase our costs"

Ulrike: "How can we turn that from 'Yes, maybe' to 'Yes', Mr Oliveira?"

We said questioning and listening are linked. It is obvious. Why ask questions if you are not going to listen to the answer? But as we observe negotiations in the classroom and in the real world, we continue to be puzzled at how few people really do listen to the answers they get. At best, the average negotiator seems only interested in the content. But the good negotiator knows that she must listen to how things are said and exactly what words are used by the other side to make their points. She listens to the hesitations ("Do they really know the answer?" "Are they sure they need this?"). She listens to the vehemence with which arguments are made ("Is this passion real or feigned?"). She listens to the grammar being employed. We shall look later in this chapter at the difference between using the first and second conditional mood in English. But think what different messages are being sent when someone says "might" or "could" instead of "may" or "can"? And what do the degree modifiers in the following sentences really mean?

"That's a **pretty** steep increase."

"We would find that timetable **quite** tough to maintain."

"Those terms are **rather** more stringent than we would be prepared to accept."

As one officer in the USA's Central Intelligence Agency outlined in a then-secret paper in 1964[1], such qualifying words in a spy's report can be very dangerous if not quantified. One spymaster could understand "quite likely" to be 90% probable whilst another could think the probability to be 40%.

The use of these qualifiers when negotiating may not be dangerous but they can certainly - 100% probability - convey different information to different people. The good negotiator will note those degree modifiers in the sentences above and either immediately or later ask the probing question:

---

1 "Words of Estimative Probability" in *Studies of Intelligence* by Sherman Kent, published on the CIA website in 2007. This was later referred to by journalists writing about the intelligence reports on Saddam Hussein's alleged weapons of mass destruction.

"What exactly did you mean when you said 'pretty steep'/'quite tough'/ 'rather more stringent'?"

When listening, show that you are listening. It's flattering to the speaker. It encourages him to continue speaking, giving you more information and more time to think. Smile, nod, lean forward, make listening noises. Make the occasional note (even if it is, in fact, your shopping list). When the other side has finished speaking, let his words sink in. Show that you are really considering what he has just said (even if you are still thinking about your shopping). Long pauses such as this are also good calmers: if the other side has become angry and is accusing you of trying to cheat them in some way, let them voice that anger and let the subsequent silence absorb it.

David Ogilvy was one of the great advertising men of the 20th century. He left his native Scotland in 1938, went to the US and ten years later set up his New York-based agency, which was to become Ogilvy and Mather. His book – *Confessions of an Advertising Man* – was published in 1963 and became a must-read for all those entering the world of advertising. It is an entertaining and instructive book, full of stories of how he won (and sometimes lost) accounts. He was writing about the art of selling in the 1950s and 1960s but the point is still relevant to the skill of negotiating today. He wrote:

> There is one stratagem which seems to work in almost every case: get the prospect to do most of the talking. The more you listen, the wiser he thinks you are.

Ogilvy even once managed to secure an account while heavily intoxicated. Being too drunk to respond to the prospective client's points worked to his advantage!

In her recent bestseller, *Quiet – The Power of Introverts in a World That Can't Stop Talking* (2012), Susan Cain tells a story about the importance of questioning and listening when negotiating. She pretends to be talking about Laura, a young, shy Wall Street lawyer forced by her boss' absence on vacation to represent a South American manufacturing company about to default on a bank loan. In fact, we discover later that "Laura" is Cain herself. Cain faces nine grumpy US investment bankers across the table. She is intimidated by them and goes blank. She wishes she could disappear. Then she pulls herself together and does what comes naturally to her: she starts asking questions.

> Let's go back a step. What are your numbers based on?...What if we structured the loan this way?

At first, her questions are tentative. Then they become more forceful; she has done her homework and will not concede on the facts. Her questioning remains constructive though:

> Are you saying that's the only way to go? What if we took a different approach?

Cain, still calling herself Laura, then says this:

> Eventually her simple queries shifted the mood in the room, just as the negotiation textbooks say they will. The bankers stopped speechifying and dominance-posing...and they started having an actual conversation.

Cain eventually stopped being a lawyer and put her experience to good use for ten years as a negotiation skills trainer.

5.2 Check and summarise

The skilled negotiator spends around twice as much time as the average negotiator making sure he has understood what is being said. He doesn't just want to reach an agreement; he wants to reach a workable agreement. He wants to make sure that once the contract is being implemented neither side can say: "Ah, but our understanding of this clause is different." The average negotiator, often unconsciously, worries that checking understanding could reopen the discussion. But if it does, that shows there was no common understanding and hence further negotiation is needed.

In any international negotiation clarification is even more important. Linguistic and cultural misunderstandings bedevil almost any major cross-border negotiation. Books have been written just recounting them, as both authors know to their benefit.

Abdul Latif, the Kuwaiti owner of a large import-export firm in the Gulf, was negotiating with Helmut, a potential German supplier. The meeting was in Europe and Helmut was keen to get down to business. Abdul Latif presented his list of wishes but prefaced it by saying "I intend to buy from you." Helmut could not hide his delight. What could be a clearer buying signal than that? He swiftly listed what he could offer Abdul Latif and tried to move on to talking about delivery arrangements and terms of payment. Abdul Latif listened politely but then steered the conversation back to Helmut's company. He began by asking lots of questions about their history and range of products. He then wanted to know who else Helmut's firm was doing business with in the Arabian Gulf. Helmut initially did his best to answer the questions but became more and more irritated when he was asked for the names of his other customers and details of their orders. The meeting ended with both men feeling frustrated. There were a number of cultural misunderstandings that caused this frustration and we shall return to them in Chapter 6.

But the communication problem that caused the biggest trouble in this case was the use of "I intend" by Abdul Latif. Helmut let his emotions show when he gave his view of the negotiation to Richard later: "He said he intended to buy from me. He was lying. He was only thinking he might." Most other Europeans, certainly any native English speaker, would sympathise with Helmut. In English the verb to intend means "to have as one's strong purpose". For Helmut, it showed that Abdul Latif really wanted to buy his products. But that was not what Abdul Latif meant. He was using it as any sophisticated Arab businessman would: "I would really like to work with his company and I like his products. I wanted to express this positively by using the word 'intend'. But only Allah knows whether we can reach an agreement." So, what should Helmut have done? Clarify by asking a question. It is not normal for a potential German customer to begin a negotiation with the words "I intend to buy from you." This unexpected sentence should have put Helmut on full linguistic and cultural alert. A positive clarification question would have led to a useful discussion for both men:

Helmut: "I'm delighted to hear that. Can I ask: what do you mean when you say 'I intend to buy'?"

Clarification has to be done carefully though. The process, wrongly done, can lead to further misunderstanding, especially in cross-border negotiations. Asking a closed question such as "So, are you saying that you can only accept our fee if it remains unchanged for three years?" will often invite a "Yes", even if the listener has not understood a single word. This won't just be from the Japanese or Chinese who does not wish you to lose face (by saying "No" to you) or himself to lose face (by admitting he has no idea what you are talking about). Have a look at that question again and think how long it would take a native English speaker to work out what "only" and "unchanged" really mean in this context. Several seconds. And the good but unconfident non-native English speaker? He'll say "Yes" and hope to find out what he's really agreed to when he reads the record of the meeting.

Because that is what he really wants: a summary. Several summaries. The skilled negotiator summarises constantly to check understanding and to show that both sides are making progress. He makes sure his summaries are just that: a series of numbered vocal bullet-points, not a rambling repeat of what has been said in the last 20 minutes. He keeps his sentences short (aim for no more than seven words) and uncomplicated (subject-verb-object, if in English). He pauses between each sentence. He gives people time to absorb, process and understand.

Not only does summing up ensure greater clarity and fewer misunderstandings. It gives the summariser authority. If negotiating in a team, allocate the role of summariser/checker to one person, usually the team leader.

5.3 Map and signpost

Why should you always have an agenda for the negotiation meeting? Because it gives you an opportunity to confirm, at the start of the meeting, something that you have already agreed on. You summarise it (of course). This creates a positive atmosphere and a feeling that progress is being made. It also gives you the structure you will need to hold on to when the emotions rise and the discussion becomes stormy.

Ulrike: "You must be joking. $25,000! That's over ten times the price of the standard model! How can you possibly justify that?"

Anselmo: (after long pause) "May I suggest that we leave the price question for the moment and look at agenda item five - Volume - and in particular the split between standard models and bespoke ones?"

To switch metaphors, think of an agenda as the map to which both sides can refer as the negotiators explore this new country. It needs to have the main points along the route - the agenda items. You need to indicate when you are moving from one point to another. We call this a "signpost". We have used the word already in this chapter and there were two signposts used by Anselmo in the example above: "May I suggest that we leave...and look at..."

Most people use signposts without thinking. The clever negotiator employs them consciously: to change course when the road is blocked or to focus the attention of his angry travelling companion on a more attractive view.

The skilled negotiator also uses a special type of signpost to gain a subtle but crucial advantage. The Huthwaite researchers called it "behaviour labelling" because it is supposed to indicate the behaviour that the speaker wants both sides to adopt. An example of this can be shown by making small changes to the wording in the first signpost above:

You: "Can I make a suggestion? Why don't we leave the price question for the moment and ...?"

The questions "Can I make a suggestion?" followed by a pause, and then "Why don't we...?" are more cooperative than "May I suggest that...?" which feels more like a demand.

The Huthwaite team found that this kind of signposting was used five times more often by skilled negotiators than average ones. Whilst we agree with Huthwaite that this technique is effective, we don't agree with their analysis as to why it is effective. It works because, like other signposts, it gives structure to your utterances. This inspires confidence in you. You know what you are doing and where you are going. Moreover, as we have said before, genuine questions create a positive atmosphere, especially if they elicit the answer "yes", even if it is an unspoken "Yes".

Perhaps we should not continue with the travelling metaphor any further and move on to the next item (whilst using an over-elaborate signpost to do so).

5.4 Avoid saps

In medieval warfare, trenches were dug by soldiers when attacking walled towns. When a trench – called a sap, after the old Italian and French words for a spade – got to the wall, a tunnel was dug under it. The soldiers, called sappers, would then place a mine in the tunnel and collapse the wall (i.e. "undermine" it). The verb "to sap" means to weaken.

In negotiation, "saps" are words and phrases that undermine the speaker's position. By themselves, they don't destroy that position but cumulatively they can do so. There are three main types of sap:

- value assumptions
- range words
- overloaded arguments

When someone tells you that their offer is "fair", "reasonable" or "generous", how do you feel? Most of us are annoyed by such words. They imply that we are being unfair, unreasonable and ungenerous if we do not accept them. You may say to yourself: "I'll decide what is fair, not you." We call them "value assumptions". The shopkeepers in the souks of the Middle East will importune the passers-by with their "good price" and "special price". Some tourists are gullible enough to be persuaded that indeed they are paying less than average. But serious negotiators are not fooled. Using such language will lower their opinion of you. Huthwaite found that average negotiators were five times more likely to use value assumptions than skilled negotiators.

"About", "around", "round about", "in the order of", "approximately" are examples of "range words". Poor negotiators will often use them when giving figures. Here are three examples:

Seller: "We are looking at a price of about €150 per unit."

Contractor: "I reckon we can finish the project by around the end of October."

Advertisement on UK car sales website: "Price: £5,200 ono".

In the first example, the prospective buyer will listen only to what is good for him and assume that €150 is the maximum price and that the seller is prepared to accept a price below this. In the second one, the prospective user of the contractor's services will assume that the project will be finished no later than the end of October and start pushing for an end-date of mid-September. The final example is still commonly seen in advertisements placed by people in UK media. "Ono" stands for "or nearest offer". Any car buyer knows immediately that the price can be negotiated down from £5,200. In all cases, the seller should have had the confidence to say "...of €150...", "...at the end of October..." (note the change from "by" to "at") and "£5,200".

> Advocates often talk too much – and rarely realise how easy it is to make a good point start to seem like a weak point, just by going on for too long. (Anonymous British judge quoted in The *Observer* newspaper, April 2013)

The judge is referring to one of the most common and yet most harmful saps: the tendency of poor negotiators (and British barristers) to overload their arguments and talk too much. It may sound counter-intuitive: surely the more arguments you have to back up your position, the stronger your position? Not so. Say you give four reasons why you can't offer a volume discount. The experienced negotiator will politely listen to all four and then choose the one that is weakest and attack it. If she can find fault with that reason, your whole position is undermined. It is the sap that brings your wall down.

5.5 Speak conditionally

We started this chapter by saying that asking questions and listening actively are the key communication skills of the effective negotiator. We would argue that using the conditional mood is the next most important skill. Indeed, asking a question using the conditional mood is the most powerful negotiation communication tool of all:

Ulrike: "If we could reduce the payment terms to 30 days, what would you be prepared to do on the unit price for a standard model?"

Every offer you make must be expressed conditionally. You must trade, not give. "If" is a tiny word but is very powerful. It leads to creative thinking, to exploring, and to trading. If you don't hear "if" every few minutes during your negotiations, you are failing (to use another conditional).

The type of conditional you use – the first or the second – is important. Ulrike uses the second conditional in her question: "If we could reduce [past tense]..., what would...?" She uses the past tense and "would" to indicate that this is just an idea. It's tentative. She's exploring. In no way is she committed to reducing the payment terms. She just wants to see what might make Anselmo cut the unit price. The second conditional is the natural home of the negotiator.

What signal would Ulrike have sent to Anselmo if she had said:

If we can reduce [present tense] the payment terms to 30 days, what will you be prepared to do on the unit price for a standard model?

This time, using the first conditional, Ulrike sounds more certain about cutting the payment period. Anselmo does not feel under so much pressure to offer something in return. So, he won't.

Contrast the responses of two different sellers to the same request from a buyer:

Buyer: "We want staggered delivery over an 18-month period, starting in October."

Seller 1: "We **can** spread the delivery over 18 months but it **will** be hard to start in October. That's only three months away. However, we **can** do it, if the payment terms **are** changed."

Seller 2: "We **could** spread the delivery over 18 months but it **would** be hard to start in October. That's only three months away. However, we **could** do it, if the payment terms **were** changed.

The first seller is a poor negotiator. He is not trading. He has agreed to spread the delivery over 18 months without getting anything in return from the buyer. He has said that he is able to start delivering in October. The second seller does much better. He has not committed to anything. He is negotiating everything.

"Unless" is also used in conditionals:

Anselmo: "I'm sorry but we couldn't give you a bigger discount, unless you increased the volume to ten machines per month."

Ulrike: "I see. Would you be prepared to accept extending the payment period from 60 to 90 days?"

Anselmo: "Not unless you could pay in Reals and not Euros."

However, as with check and negative questions, the meaning of "unless" can be difficult for the non-native English speaker to grasp. Stick to the magic "if" in international negotiations.

So, the skilled negotiator keeps things open and tradable by using the second conditional. He also listens for "buying or concession signals". This is language and grammar that indicates that the speaker is already "buying" your product or your argument.

Ulrike: "If we choose BTB, we will expect your technical people to be on call 24/7. I'm not convinced that you are able to guarantee that, Mr Oliveira."

If you were Anselmo, you could put the champagne (or bottle of cachaça) on ice. Ulrike may seem to be raising objections to buying BTB's products. But she has used a first conditional and, unconsciously, revealed that she is already thinking she will buy from Anselmo. Much better (for Ulrike) if she had said: "if we were to choose...., we would expect... that you would be able..."

We have said earlier how useful it is to use such exploratory questions as "What if...?" and "How about...?". Be careful, though, not to use the first conditional:

Anselmo: "What if we send one of our technicians to Stuttgart and New Jersey to train your people? Or how about we deliver an extra machine for every batch of five you order?"

Anselmo is doing well in trying to find new options. But he has phrased it in such a way that it seems easy (and not costly) for BTB to do these things. It's a concession signal. Better to have said:

Anselmo: "What if we sent you/were to send you... Or how about we delivered..."

However, there is one warning that we have to give about using conditionals. If you are involved in a cross-border negotiation, in which one or both sides are not native English speakers (as is the case between Ulrike and Anselmo), the subtle difference between first and second conditionals is often not understood or simply not heard - can you hear the switch in tense from "send" or "deliver" to "sent" or "delivered"? Moreover, some languages do not distinguish between "when" and "if". There is also sometimes confusion between "could" (indicating uncertainty) and "should" (indicating strong advice or even an obligation). And many non-native English speakers mistakenly put "would"/"will" in the "if" part of the sentence. In the latter case, however, we would argue that the meaning and the message are still clear, provided you use "would" and not "will". That last sentence was also a conditional – a mix of second and first, using "provided" instead of "if". "Provided" and "as long as" are frequent and good substitutes for "if".

5.6 Sound strong and look confident

Go on almost any communication skills course anywhere in the world and you will hear about the "7%-38%-55% rule". This rule says that the meaning of any message is communicated 93% by the speaker's tone and body language and only 7% by the content. This is nonsense. It is a misinterpretation of two research papers written in 1967 by Professor Albert Mehrabian of UCLA in the USA. Mehrabian himself tries to put the record straight on his website:

> Total Liking = 7% Verbal Liking plus 38% Vocal Liking plus 55% Facial Liking. Please note that this and other equations regarding relative importance of verbal and non-verbal messages were derived from experiments dealing with communications of feelings and attitudes... Unless a communicator is talking about their feelings and attitudes, these equations are not applicable.

Anyway, Mehrabian's original studies were done in a very artificial environment and the equation is obtained by combining results from two studies in a manner that would not satisfy a mathematician.

However, voice and body language are important when negotiating. Both can have a large effect on the success or failure of your negotiating tactics. The problem is that these are things which most of us have little control over and find very hard to change. We are frequently asked at our negotiation seminars to run a "session on body language". What this usually means is: "Tell us how we can spot when someone is lying." Our participants are most interested in having a checklist of non-verbal mannerisms and tics that demonstrate discomfort, lack of candour and outright lying on the other side of the negotiation table. They are less keen on being told what they have to change in their own non-verbal behaviour. This is just as well. Telling someone not to put their hands in front of their mouths because this is an indicator of lying (which it can be) may cause amusement. But how easy is it for that person to stop doing something they have probably done since childhood? Not easy at all, and once in the heat of a real negotiation almost impossible. Much more important to spend time making sure that you are fully prepared for a negotiation and that you believe in your product or service. This will give you the inner confidence to enable you to have a positive body language throughout the negotiation.

A session on voice is much less sought after. We think this is because most people don't really believe voice tone and projection are that important. We would argue that these are vital and are easier to learn than changing the way you sit or what you are doing with your hands. At various stages during any negotiation you are going to have to present your position on one or more points. You are going to keep this short, of course, and only make one or two points to support your position. And you are going to speak in a persuasive way. How? If you are negotiating in English, you need to do three things:

- Vary your tone
- Enunciate your words
- Pause often

The last is the most important and makes it easier to do the first two. You can't learn to get this right by reading about it. You have to practise it. Prepare a two-minute presentation of your key points and record it. Try not to read what you have prepared: you will speak too fast and sound monotonous. Take time over your words and stress the key ones. Use questions to help you vary your intonation. Above all, pause. Pausing does so many positive things. For yourself, it gives you time to think and to breathe, which makes your voice stronger. For your listener, it is flattering ("He is having to think of the right words for me"), helps comprehension ("He is giving me time to absorb what he is saying") and builds confidence in you ("He is not in a rush. He thinks before he speaks"). It gives you gravitas, a quality which all the best negotiators have.

There is another factor to bear in mind: culture. Shaking the head means *No* to most people around the world but can mean *Yes* to an Indian, a Bulgarian, a Turk, a Greek or a southern Italian. Holding your hands over your mouth does usually mean that someone is probably not telling the truth (or the whole truth). But in Japan it is a sign that someone, very often a woman, is embarrassed either by what you have said or by what she is being forced to say (which may be an uncomfortable truth for you). Making a ring with your finger and thumb would be understood by your negotiating partner in northern and western

Europe as meaning *Okay* but is extremely rude in south-east Europe, Turkey, the Arab world and Latin America. We could go on.

Richard sometimes starts his courses by shaking hands with each participant, even if he has already done so when they first walked in. Some participants get a firm handshake and a direct look in their eyes, others a soft, limp handshake and a look away. And, finally, some people have their hands held for ten seconds or more. If the participants are men and women from the USA or northern/western Europe, Richard will then ask a man in the first group how he felt about the handshake. The participant usually looks puzzled and wonders why Richard has asked the question. He will say that Richard's greeting was "fine" or "normal". If pressed, he will say that it felt "strong", "confident" and "honest". The second group hate the greeting they got. Words like "weak", "not confident" and "can't be trusted" are used. The third group, the people who had the long handshake, take time to recover from the experience. If they are heterosexual men, they admit how uncomfortable they felt. If they are women, they say they felt threatened, even assaulted. But if we do this in Asia or Africa, the reactions can be very different.

Richard and a German colleague used to run sessions on *Working with your German Partners* at the German Chamber of Commerce in Tokyo. The participants were Japanese businesspeople working for companies such as BMW, BASF, Bosch and Bayer. Our German colleague, Peter, would go around the room, take a Japanese hand in a vice-like grip and wish the owner "Guten Morgen" with a smile and a stare. Richard would then ask the Japanese how they felt about Peter's greeting. "Rude" and "aggressive" were the almost universal responses. In Japan, as in much of east and south-east Asia, bowing is the norm. But they have adopted the Western-style handshake with Asian characteristics: gentle, soft, quick. And in the Middle East and Africa, it is very common for men when they greet each other, whether in the street or in the meeting room, to hold hands throughout the long "small talk" that follows.

What is the relevance of these different non-verbal behaviours to you as a negotiator? Is the negotiation going to fail because you gave an inappropriate non-verbal greeting or gesture? Probably not, if the other side are keen to do business with you. But you are making it harder to establish a warm, trusting relationship, if you make these mistakes. The first impressions you make on the other side in a negotiation are important. So, send positive signals: a firm handshake to someone who regards it as a sign of confidence and honesty, a softer handshake to someone who interprets this as a sign of warmth and politeness.

5.7 Use Offshore English

Offshore English was a term coined in the 1980s by Bill Reed, a colleague of Richard's, to describe the English that native English speakers ought to use when communicating with non-native English speakers. Others have called this International English, Global English or, with utter disregard for etymology and beauty, Globish. Whatever label you wish to use, the fact is that few US Americans, English-speaking Canadians, Brits, Australians, New Zealanders and other native English speakers know how to speak their own language when negotiating with people for whom English is a foreign or second language. Moreover, most of them are not aware that this is even a problem. Yet we know of cases where a failure to speak Offshore English has been the main reason why some British and American companies have lost contracts or not had them renewed. And both authors have seen how often a failure to communicate clearly in English has caused cross-border negotiations to falter or have a less than optimal result. So, what is this Offshore English and how should you speak it?

It is English spoken slowly with plenty of pauses. You use short sentences without subordinate clauses. Or if you use a subordinate clause, you pause for long enough so that it feels as though you are starting a new sentence. You use words and expressions that the non-native English speaker is likely to know. You enunciate clearly. You are a patient listener.

This sounds like an easy thing to do. In our experience, however, British, American, Australian and other native English-speaking business people and government officials, simply don't understand what we are talking about when we ask them to use Offshore English while negotiating internationally. The main problem is that few of them speak another language. They can't empathise with the difficulties the non-native English speaker is having. Moreover, they often don't know how their own language works. Richard blames the way English has been taught in English and Welsh schools since the 1970s for the failure of so many Brits to understand the foundations of the English language. He himself was educated in the late 1950s and the 1960s, first at an American school in Caracas, Venezuela, and then at four schools in England. He was taught English (and Latin) grammar. But his two children were not. His daughter, Katharine, is a fluent French speaker. She studied French at Edinburgh University and in Grenoble. She admits that she only understood how English grammar worked when she learned French grammar.

Richard was asked in 2010 by the London branch of a major Japanese bank to train their British staff to speak and write English in a way that could be understood by their Japanese and Continental European colleagues and clients. He recalls one of the first groups he taught. He was advising them to avoid using phrasal verbs. The British did not understand. He explained what a phrasal verb was: a verb plus a preposition or an adverb. He gave an example:

Can we put off the meeting? "Put off" is a phrasal verb.

A hand went up. It belonged to a young compliance officer.

"Richard. I'm lost. What is a preposition and an adverb? And if I'm honest with you, what is a verb?"

This man was no fool. He was doing a part-time EMBA at one of the UK's top business schools in the evenings. Yet he had no idea how his own language worked.

After teaching this group of adult British bankers what these grammatical terms meant, Richard asked them what word a non-native English speaker might understand better than "put off". They were silent. He suggested "postpone". He went on to explain that most non-native English speakers can understand English words and constructions derived from Latin and Norman French (e.g. "postpone") much more easily than those coming from the Germanic languages given to English by the Anglo-Saxons and Vikings (e.g. "put off"). Even Germans, he said, often find it easier to understand Latinate English words because much of the English they learned at school was the more formal, and hence Latinate, vocabulary found in written English. The compliance officer raised his hand again:

"So, Richard, you can speak to foreigners successfully because you learned Latin at school. Are you asking me to learn Latin too?"

Richard wasn't suggesting that. But he remains unsure what the answer is other than reforming the English education system.

By now, the fluent non-native English speaker is probably feeling very smug (a word that a Scandinavian might understand but an Italian almost certainly wouldn't; it means self-satisfied - a word that is itself half-German and half-French/Latin in origin!). However, such complacency is dangerous. The less confident non-native English speaker can have almost as many problems understanding the multilingual Scandinavian, Dutchman or Swiss as he does the American or Brit. Søren is Danish but speaks English like a native Brit. Most of the negotiation courses he runs are for non-native English speakers. He has learned to deliver them in Offshore English. And he does the same when negotiating for real in the international business arena.

When we learn a foreign language we love learning the colloquial phrases and slang that give flavour to our utterances. But the competent speaker of Offshore English at the international negotiation table learns to avoid such colourful expressions. One of the most common errors made by British and American negotiators is to employ lots of sporting idioms (men are especially guilty). All of the following have been heard by one or other of the authors during international negotiations. In every case, their use caused confusion and misunderstanding.

"Give me a ball-park figure." Give me an approximate number (US, from baseball)

"Those terms are par for the course." Those are the standard terms (from golf)

"It's time for you to step up to the plate." You need to take responsibility for doing something (US, from baseball)

"You're certainly playing hardball." You are tough negotiators (US, from baseball)

"You are giving us a full-court press." You are putting us under a lot of pressure (US, from basketball)

"That's right in our wheelhouse." That's our area of expertise (US, from baseball)

"That's a safe bet." That is certain to happen (from horseracing)

“You have moved the goalposts.” You have changed the rules, e.g. altered the specification (UK, from football/soccer)

“I won’t pull my punches.” Let me be frank (from boxing)

“We’re on a sticky wicket here.” We’re in a difficult situation (UK, from cricket)

These don’t only cause problems between native and non-native English speakers. Richard did not understand two of the US sporting expressions when he first heard them. He has had to deal with several Anglo-American misunderstandings. Once, during a meeting, a US American asked if an agenda item could be tabled. Richard and his British colleagues agreed and began discussing the item. The American looked surprised and said she thought it had been agreed to table it. It took a minute of confused explanation before everyone understood that for a US American this means to take it off the agenda, whilst for a British person it means to put it on the agenda.

You should also avoid using the many English words that look similar to words in other, usually Latin, languages but that have different meanings. These are called false friends. Take this example, which you might hear being said by a fluent English speaker when negotiating with a Frenchman:

What, **actually**, Jean-Marie, are the **benefits** to you if you take **this action**?

Jean-Marie will be confused. To him it may seem that he was asked:

What, **at this moment**, Jean-Marie, are the **profits** to you if you buy **this company’s shares**?

The context will almost certainly enable Jean-Marie to understand what has been said. But how, deep down, will he feel about the person on the other side of the table who uses such confusing language?

Richard’s previous company, Canning, asked over 400 clients from 26 different nationalities – all non-native English speakers – to complete a survey about using English in international business. 58% said they found native English speakers more difficult to understand than non-native speakers of the language. Almost exactly the same percentage believed that native speakers of English used English to give themselves an advantage. "You use English as a weapon to beat us" is a common complaint that we hear on our courses.

What then should the skilled international negotiator have said to Jean-Marie? Maybe:

What, **in fact**, Jean-Marie, are the **advantages** to you if you **do this**?

If you are still sceptical about the importance of speaking Offshore English when negotiating internationally, perhaps a true story from East Asia will convince you. One of Richard's colleagues was running courses in Seoul for Korean Airlines in the 1990s. One of the participants told him about a recent negotiation they had had with two European companies. The Koreans wanted to buy flight simulators. The final shortlist of potential suppliers had two company names on it, one British and one French. The negotiations were long and included practice on the simulators by the airline's senior pilots. Apparently it was a hard choice for the Koreans but in the end they decided to award the contract to the French company. The reason? During the negotiation and during the practice sessions both prospective suppliers had communicated in English, sometimes with interpreters, sometimes not. The Koreans - their negotiators, their pilots and their interpreters - had found it far easier to understand the English spoken by the French than that spoken by the British. Their pilots were going to have to be trained by the supplier in how to use the simulators. Such training was going to be done in English. They reasoned that it would be better to choose the French company, whose negotiators and trainers spoke clearer English than their British competitors. So, the British lost the contract, worth tens of millions of dollars, because they could not speak *Offshore English*.

5.8 Be silent

You may think it odd to end this piece on spoken communication with a demand that you don't speak. But silence is one of the most powerful forms of communication that the skilled negotiator can employ. You may not be speaking but that does not mean that you are not communicating. The words you have just spoken are still being processed inside your listener's head and will have greater force precisely because you are silent.

We have referred many times in this chapter to the power and uses of silence. We quoted with approval from Susan Cain's best-selling book *Quiet*. Note the title. To be a good listener you have to be able to remain attentively silent.

A long pause can do many jobs. It can add weight to your previous words and to the point you are about to make. It can flatter the other person. Best of all, it can put pressure on him to respond with new information or a better offer. He may interpret your silence, say, as a sign that the 2% discount he suggested is far too little, convince himself that he is in danger of losing the deal and propose 4%. As the US journalist and political commentator, Lance Morrow, said:

> Never forget the power of silence, that massively disconcerting pause which goes on and on and may at last induce an opponent to babble and backtrack nervously.

Pausing shows that you are patient and won't be rushed. Silence also gives you a chance to observe, to think and to react appropriately. It gives you control of the negotiation.

The Japanese and the Finns are masters at using silence to extract concessions. Richard got so used to this technique during negotiations in Japan, he began to time the silences. The longest pause came after he had proposed a price increase of 5% to a client who had benefited from a fixed price for the previous four years. A full 55 seconds elapsed before the client finally said "I agree". A few years later, in Espoo in Finland, Richard timed a silence at 20 seconds. Somehow, he managed to keep quiet.

5.9 Write clearly

Use email to ask for and send information, to state your position and to confirm what has already been agreed. But try, if you possibly can, to conduct the real bargaining face-to-face in the same room or via the growing number of ways we can see each other online.

That was not a quote. We say exactly those words in the next chapter when we look at how culture affects international negotiations. As we will explain, many people around the world find it difficult to negotiate effectively using just email. But even those who share a culture and language can find negotiation by email tricky. We will look now at the pros and cons of email negotiation that are universal. You may then want to read the Communication section of Chapter 6 to discover the cultural problems caused by email.

Before the arrival of email, experience and research had shown that negotiating only by telephone caused people to behave in a more aggressive manner than if they were in the same room. Using only email seems to exacerbate this[2].

Why is this? When negotiating with someone face-to-face, you can employ all the verbal and non-verbal methods of communicating. You can send signals with what you say, how you express your words - your tone, the speed of delivery, your voice volume - and how you use your body and eyes. Things that you are unaware of - flushed skin, enlarged or dilated pupils, a repeated gesture or tic - can be noted by an observant negotiating partner. And you, of course, are interpreting, consciously and unconsciously, what the other person is saying in exactly the same way. What do you lose when you negotiate by phone? Gone are all the visual clues to what the other person is really saying. Gone is your ability to communicate through gesture how you really feel. And email negotiation? Gone are the aural clues to meaning. Gone too is your ability to communicate your meaning by emphasising a key word, by switching from a rising tone to a falling one, by simply not speaking. You are left impoverished, almost powerless to communicate effectively. And what does powerlessness engender? Anger and mistrust. But we haven't finished. Imagine that you have to write and read emails in a foreign language. How powerless do you feel now?

Not convinced? How many times have you fired off an intemperate reply to an email, then re-read the email that so angered you and realised that you had completely misread it? All it requires for such misunderstanding is a misplaced "not", an overcomplicated sentence or the use of a word that has several meanings. But you can't retract your email. Battle is joined.

We are not saying that you should never use email when negotiating. That is totally impractical. But be aware of its many drawbacks and use it sparingly.

---

2 For a detailed look at the research see "Negotiation via email", a chapter by Noam Ebner, Assistant Professor, Creighton University School of Law - Werner Institute for Negotiation and Dispute Resolution, in *Negotiation Excellence: Successful Deal Making* (2nd edition, 2014), World Scientific Publishing, Singapore.

Let's assume that you must use email in your next negotiation. When should you use it? Despite what we have just said, there are times when email helps the negotiation process. Use it:

- to ask for and send data, drawings, plans, pictures and maps
- to confirm figures that were only spoken before
- to make a proposal or update a previous proposal
- to summarise what you believe has been agreed so far
- to confirm already agreed dates, times, locations and agendas of future calls or meetings

In other words, use email to provide information and confirm what has been agreed. Don't use it to state opinions, give reasons for proposing or rejecting something, criticize, praise, boast, tell jokes or amusing stories...in fact, anything that involves emotion.

If you absolutely must conduct a negotiation by email, here are some guidelines to help you get the best out of the medium and prevent it from disrupting the process:

- Meet or talk on the phone with the other side before you start negotiating. Even a quick phone call from the seller to check how many people should be copied in on his emailed proposal will make a big difference. Human contact is made. And it shows straight away that he is thinking of the customer's needs. It's in the buyer's interests to make an early phone call too. To the supplier's switchboard. She can learn a bit by listening to how the firm's staff deal with her
- Set the ground rules for using email as you go along. For example, agree who must always be copied in on emails. Suggest that people always reply to emails, even if it is only to say that they have received and read them. Propose that a time/date is given at the end of each email as to when a reply is expected
- Write well and clearly. Keep everything short – sentences, paragraphs. Use bullet points. Use a typeface that is easy to read and looks serious – e.g. Georgia, not Comic Sans. Remember that most emails are now read on smartphones, even when it would make more sense to read them on a tablet or laptop. How do you feel when you try and read a long and rambling email on a smartphone?
- Re-read all emails before sending them to make sure they are clear and are not likely to offend or cause confusion. Even better, get

a colleague to read them. Likewise, read all incoming emails, go away, come back and read them again. It's amazing how often a second read through can give a different impression and reveal new information
- Never send an immediate reply to an email, however banal it may be. Show respect for the other person by taking your time to consider what he has written
- Make sure the words in the subject box clearly indicate what the email is about. Complex negotiations using email and involving several people can go awry because people can't find a key fact or an amended proposal among the flood of emails they get every day. Keep the words in the subject box up to date. If you start a completely new subject, start a new email string

It is tempting to write the negotiated contract in the body of an email. This is fine if it really is a simple agreement with very few terms. But there have been a number of cases recently where statements made in emails have successfully been used in court to argue that a contract was agreed when those statements were made. Examples include single-word or short-phrase emails such as "Agreed", "Correct" and "I accept your proposal". It might be wise for all your emails to have an easily visible disclaimer along the lines of "Anything stated in this email does not constitute a contract." Any international negotiation should finish with a stand-alone written contract.

6

Who are those guys?

6.1 What do I need to know about culture?

When the authors first started running negotiation skills courses in the early 1980s, the main reference books in Europe were nearly all by US authors. The most influential and probably the most read was *Getting to Yes: Negotiating an agreement without giving in,* by Roger Fisher and William Ury, published in 1981. It remains a best-seller, though with substantial revisions. Fisher and Ury were members of the Harvard Negotiation Project, which we mentioned in Chapter 1. In those early days the assumption appeared to be that when negotiating, what applied in the USA applied everywhere. Lip service was paid to "international negotiation" but to your European authors some of the findings, which were being promoted as universal truths, did not tally with their experience at the negotiation table in western Europe nor, in Richard's case, in Africa and, later, Japan. So, we (separately) developed and delivered negotiation skills courses that took all that was good coming out of Harvard that could be applied internationally and added some findings of our own and of other Europeans. Chief among the latter was Gavin Kennedy, whose book *Everything is Negotiable* first came out in 1982. Kennedy remains one of our negotiation skills gurus but even he has never been sure that cultural differences play a significant part in explaining why cross-border negotiations so often fail (despite writing *Negotiate Anywhere,* published in 1985).

If the people running the Harvard Negotiation Project did indeed once think that the US way of negotiating was the only way, they don't any more. William Ury himself started and leads the *Global Negotiation Initiative.* Another current Harvard project is called the *China Negotiation Initiative.* Many negotiators no longer assume that what works in their own country will work anywhere. The internet and bookshops are full of advice on how to negotiate with the Chinese, the Indians and people of almost any country with a population above a million. Some of this advice is useful and useable. But only some. Much of it creates or reinforces stereotypical views of people, which are of no use to the foreign negotiator. How do we avoid falling into the stereotype trap?

The answer is by avoiding the Do's and Don'ts approach to cross-cultural negotiation training. Does it really matter if, while negotiating in Saudi Arabia, you hand over a document with your left hand, inadvertently show the sole of your shoe or refuse the cup of coffee you are offered? Those Saudis who have not travelled much outside the kingdom might consider you a bit ill-mannered but it is your communication style and overall behaviour that will be far more crucial to the success of the negotiation. Knowing the correct etiquette is always useful. But it is even more important to understand as much as possible about the attitudes and behavioural norms of the people with whom you are dealing. It's far more useful (and interesting) to learn why you should avoid refusing coffee when doing business in much of the Arab world than worry what would happen if you did so refuse. Coffee has been offered in the Middle East and North Africa to visitors as a sign of hospitality and friendship for centuries. To refuse it is an apparent rejection of that offer of friendship. Coffee originated in Ethiopia and Yemen (the word comes from the Yemeni *qahwa*). So, unless you are truly allergic to coffee, accept the first cup. If offered another, tip the cup gently from side to side (this means "No more, thanks"), and say what a pleasure it is to be drinking coffee so close to its original home. Ask what makes it different from coffee brewed elsewhere in the Arabian Peninsula. Don't worry if you then get a five-minute lecture on how it is made with saffron in one place and cloves in another. You have turned a potentially negative view of you into a positive one. How? By asking questions.

Talk of coffee may make our approach to culture still seem superficial. It isn't. You have to get into the mind of the negotiator from a different culture. What commonly-held beliefs and opinions in his society are likely to have influenced his behaviour? We like to go further: what are the historical, geographical, religious, philosophical, economic and political factors that have helped create those beliefs and opinions? Such an enquiring approach can then help you decide which behaviour and communication style to use to get the most positive results. For example, if you are negotiating with a group of Japanese managers from the same company, your exploration of Japanese culture will have told you how important it is for harmony to be preserved and for public embarrassment to be avoided. So, you are not surprised if the answers to your questions are unclear, evasive or even untrue. You do not show impatience or irritation. You note what you have been told and wait for the breaks in the meeting or for the evening meal to get clarity. At such times you can have one-to-one conversations during which the same person who told you a blatant lie in the group meeting tells you the cold truth. Why? Because there is no loss of face or disharmony when there are no witnesses to it.

You can also learn a lot about someone's national culture and hence how they are likely to behave as a negotiator by learning how they have been educated. It has been calculated that 70% of the Japanese primary school curriculum is spent learning Japanese and mathematics. The three Japanese writing systems – the 1,945 most-frequently used *kanji* characters, the 46 *hiragana* and 46 *katakana* syllabaries – and the requirement to learn English using the 52 *romaji* syllabary mean that the Japanese have had great memory training. Add in the fact that exams throughout their childhood and on to university are multiple-choice and you can see why the Japanese are likely to be impressed by facts and the smallest detail. Contrast that with the French negotiator, who could have spent two years preparing to get into one of the prestigious *grandes écoles* from which the cream of French business, government and politics are chosen. Much of that time will have been spent preparing and doing *colles* (or *khôles*) – oral examinations in a wide range of subjects. He, maybe with a couple of fellow students, will have spent an hour each time answering a professor's questions and debating with him and each other. A *colle* may involve giving a short presentation, using the standard French structure of thesis, counter-thesis and synthesis. All of this prepared our future French negotiator for the final oral exams to get into the *grande école* of his choice.

So, Toshiyuki Suzuki comes to the negotiating table having never had to take an oral examination in his life (sometimes not even if he studied a foreign language at university). He values charts, graphs, hundreds of PowerPoint slides and thick reports, and mistrusts those who are clever with words (there is a Japanese proverb: "Only a dead fish has an open mouth."). Jean-Paul Mercier had to do a lot of written exams too but in order to have the best of French higher education he had to learn how to present logically and argue persuasively. He values those who can do the same at the negotiation table. And if he thinks you are wrong, he will say so and explain why. He does not think about saving face; just as he didn't when competing alongside his fellow candidates in Paris all those years ago.

Why have we chosen to contrast the Japanese with the French? Because for over 10 years Richard worked with Renault and Nissan, trying to help the managers in both companies work effectively together in their Alliance. From the year 2000 onwards he and his colleagues in Canning witnessed first-hand the problems that can be caused when managers from two strong national and organisational cultures negotiate with each other. Renault did not take over Nissan in 1999, even though they bought a controlling share. The two companies remained and still are separate; hence the term "Alliance". Many meetings between them have, in effect, been negotiations. He has also seen how difficult it is for people from two such different cultures to work as one when negotiating with their suppliers. Yet the Alliance has been a success. So, it is clearly possible for these cultural differences to be bridged.

6.2 Negotiating the cultural minefield

What then should you as a skilled negotiator find out about another culture when preparing to negotiate outside your borders? We will answer this by looking at culture under four headings:

- Relationships
- Communication
- Time
- Truth

a. Relationships

You are about to start negotiations with a company in another country. You should have already asked the following questions: Is power shared among lots of people inside the company or is it concentrated at the top? Do people reach positions of power in the country because of who they are and the group they belong to – e.g. their class, race, family, sex, age, religion – or because of what they have achieved through their own efforts? Are the company's managers empowered to make decisions on their own or do they have to achieve a wide consensus first? The answers to these questions will tell you whether you are negotiating with the right people and how long it may take for them to decide whether to conclude a deal with you or somebody else.

In some cases the answers will also tell you whether you are placing yourself at a disadvantage by including someone on your negotiating team whom the other side is unlikely to respect or trust. When we say things like this in our seminars, some people look uncomfortable and others are downright hostile. We get accused of sexism – "Ah, so you are saying we must not send a woman to negotiate in Saudi Arabia." Of racism– "Are you seriously suggesting that an Indian will not want to negotiate with me because I am black?" Or of ageism – "Will the Japanese really disregard what I am saying because I am too young in their eyes?"

In fact, we are not saying any of these things. Some of the best and toughest women negotiators we have met have been Arab. The Saudis had huge respect for Margaret Thatcher as one of the most effective political leaders they had to negotiate with. There is indeed discrimination against darker-skinned people in India and the caste system reinforces this. But in our experience this racism does not appear to apply to foreigners. Richard was 38 when he first started doing business in Japan. His age proved no barrier to winning contracts. What mattered was that his British company had made him general manager of their Japanese subsidiary. His Japanese clients told him that he must be really good to be a boss at such a young age.

The things that can put you and your team at a disadvantage are perhaps less obvious. For example, all three countries named above are to a greater or lesser extent hierarchical (Japan, despite the stereotype, much less so than Saudi Arabia and India). What matters is not your sex, skin colour or age. If the business card that you present makes it clear that you are a senior person in your organisation, the assumption in the Arab World and India (and much of Latin America and East and South-east Asia) is that you are somebody who can make decisions. Your seniority also gives "face" – respect – to the other side. But if your business card does not show your management position, the assumption in these cultures is often that you are of no importance, even if you are, for example, a technical expert.

A Finnish company with which Richard was working had just opened a new representative office in Beijing. They were preparing to send a team out to China to negotiate a joint venture with a Chinese manufacturer. One of their new Chinese employees, a young woman engineer, was in Helsinki for some technical training. The leader of the Finnish team asked her to join their discussions. Perhaps she could give them some advice. She sat silently and listened. After some time one of the Finns asked her whether they should have business cards when they went to China. The woman looked startled. She said "Yes. You must. Please, can I see your card?" He apologised but said he had left his cards in a drawer in his office; he hardly ever used them. She looked even more surprised. The team leader gave her his card. She looked at it and frowned. "But your title is not here. Sorry but there is only your technical knowledge." Now, it was the turn of the Finns to look puzzled. They explained to her that the company only had five levels of management and most people were identified by their technical expertise, not by their management position. She smiled, as if understanding something for the first time, took out her business card and showed it to the Finns. It had Chinese on one side and English on the other. There were a lot more Chinese characters than English letters. They could read the English. It gave her name, her engineering qualification and her company address in Beijing. She turned it over and pointed to the Chinese: "This is my name, my qualification in mechanical engineering and university, and my title – senior manager – and the company address." There was a short Finnish silence. "But you are not a senior manager. We don't have such a title in this company." She kept smiling. "You are right, of course, but our customers...nobody...will meet me if I do not have a title." There was another Finnish silence, longer this time. "So, we need to have cards with titles for our meetings in China? But we don't have titles, most of us. What should we do? Invent them?"

The answer was yes. And so, they created the titles and asked their Beijing office to provide them with business cards bearing these titles in English and Chinese.

Different cultural attitudes to hierarchy and decision-making can make successful cross-border negotiation and post-contract cooperation very hard to achieve. In 1990 Volvo and Renault established a strategic alliance. They had already been working together in various ways over the previous 20 years. So, one might have expected this particular alliance to have been a success. It was a disastrous failure, ending in early 1994. It ultimately led to Sweden's flagship company having to sell its car division to Ford (it is now owned by China's Geely Automobile).

One study of this misalliance identified six factors that caused it to fail (Bruner and Robert Spekman, 1998). Two of these were "leadership style" and "cultural differences". In fact, the leaders of each company – Pehr Gyllenhammar, Volvo's Executive Chairman, and Raymond Lévy, Renault's CEO (who handed over to Louis Schweitzer in 1992) – were alike in many ways. They were strong, very bright, charismatic bosses, who dominated their boards and had similar visions of how the automobile industry was likely to develop, especially in Europe. They had little difficulty negotiating the alliance but once the deal was done, cultural differences between managers lower down in each company began to cause cracks to appear. One major problem was that whilst Lévy's leadership style suited Renault's very hierarchical corporate culture, Gyllenhammar's behaviour did not fit with Volvo's much more consensual culture and flat hierarchy. How then had he become head of the company? His father-in-law had appointed him, taking him from Skandia Insurance where he had been made CEO by his own father. He was thus in conflict with three strong cultural values in Sweden: the wish for consensus, the suspicion of anyone who considers themselves superior, and the dislike of nepotism. Raymond Lévy later told Bruner and Spekman of a crucial meeting during the negotiations:

> When we were working on the alliance proposal, we had a meeting of 200 of the top managers of Volvo and Renault. At the close of that meeting, Pehr Gyllenhammar said to his managers, "Those who aren't in agreement with this plan have one thing to do: jump ship." I thought that was wonderful. It indicated that Volvo had a powerful, strong man at its helm. I found later that this was deeply resented at Volvo as an expression of dictatorship.

We don't only know about this from Bruner and Spekman's excellent article. As said earlier, Richard worked with Renault and Nissan after they forged their strategic alliance in 1999. Unlike Gyllenhammar, who denied that cultural and language difficulties had caused any problems between Renault and Volvo, the bosses of Renault learned some painful lessons from the failed alliance. Lévy's successor at Renault, Louis Schweitzer, negotiated the deal with Nissan. He insisted that Renault introduce an intensive cross-cultural training and coaching programme for all those employees who would be working with their new Nissan partners. Nissan followed a couple of years later with similar training on how best to work with their colleagues in Renault.

Richard heard a number of stories from Renault managers of what had gone so badly wrong between Volvo and Renault ten years previously. For example, in the initial stages of that alliance a number of joint ventures and projects had had to be negotiated between the French and the Swedes. The French felt the Swedes showed no respect towards the senior Renault managers, openly criticising them during meetings and using their better English as a weapon to beat them with. They were also frustrated by the long time it took for the Swedes to make even the simplest decision.

Some of the Renault people had got the Swedish side of the story too. The Swedes in Volvo had found the senior French managers to be arrogant and their subordinates to be too deferential. They thought the French top-down decision-making process to be very strange, and mistrusted it. They couldn't believe that the leader of the French side could agree to anything important without seeking the views of others not in the room. They expected negotiations to be protracted, with many breaks between meetings so that others in the two companies could be consulted. The French viewed this as deliberate time-wasting, designed to put pressure on them. In turn, the Swedes complained of Renault engineers speaking French to each other during meetings and saw this as an attempt to exclude them from the negotiations. Richard's Renault informants said, with some exasperation, that they had only reverted to French to seek clarification as to what the Swedes were saying in their fluent English.

Many of the Renault managers who had survived the failed partnership with Volvo were in senior positions by the time they had to start negotiating and working with the Japanese in Nissan. The French, in fact, were surprised at how similar in some ways their new Japanese colleagues were to their old Swedish friends (some had indeed remained friends). If they thought the Swedes were obsessed with consensus-seeking, they would find the Japanese even more extreme. If they thought the Swedes took a long time to make a decision, they were going to have to learn to be yet more patient with the Japanese. And most surprising of all to the French, the Japanese in Nissan were less hierarchical than they were in Renault. But there were stark differences between the Japanese and the Swedes too, of course. Unlike the people in Volvo, many of the Japanese in Nissan could speak little English. Indeed many of the Japanese accused their new French partners of using English as a weapon, much to the delight of those old hands in Renault who had been bludgeoned by Swedish English. And unlike the Swedes, the Japanese hardly ever disagreed with Renault's senior French managers to their faces.

A few years ago Richard had the Managing Director of a medium-sized British company on one of his courses. This man's company made the mechanism in a vending machine that takes the customer's coins or notes and gives change. These days the mechanism would more usually respond to a credit card or signal from a mobile phone. The company was doing very well in Europe but had failed to break into the Japanese market, a country where there is one vending machine for every 23 people. There are even vending machines at the top of Mount Fuji. Apparently, the MD had been visiting Japan for over three years, trying to interest manufacturers in his products but without success. He nearly always got a meeting but usually only with a couple of junior managers. What should he do? Richard asked him how many people went with him on his sales trips.

> How many? You must be joking. You know how expensive Japan is. I go on my own.

Richard shook his head. "No wonder no-one wants to see you. It may say Managing Director on your business card and at the bottom of your emails, but the Japanese won't take you or your company seriously if you go alone. You need a bag carrier; someone who will give you and the Japanese 'face'. He will show, just by his presence, that you are important and, crucially, that you consider your prospective customer important too."

Three months later Richard was in Japan, negotiating contract renewals alongside his Japanese sales manager. By chance, he ran into the British MD on the ground floor of an office building in Tokyo. The MD was not alone: "Richard, meet my bag carrier!" It was his Marketing Director, who gave Richard a pained smile. "You were right. Nearly all the companies we approached this time agreed to see us, including ones who told me last time to bugger off." He was a straight-talking Englishman from Manchester. "Even better, we are seeing five or six people each time - senior people, technical guys, the decision-makers."

Richard reminded him that decision-making responsibility is spread among many people in Japanese companies. However, it was clear he had, at last, made significant progress. Six months and two visits to Japan later, his company had secured their first contract in Japan, worth nearly a million dollars. In many Asian countries, including China and South Korea, the size of your negotiating team and the seniority levels of its members are signals of how important you think the other side is and how serious you are about doing business together.

There are two other issues that we have put under the category of "relationships": the importance that many cultures give to establishing a personal relationship before doing business and the personal space between people that is considered normal within a society. The first is far more important to the international negotiator than the second, although we remain surprised at how much attention is devoted to the latter issue in books, research papers and courses.

A description of a government-level overseas aid negotiation should help us examine these two issues more closely. Two officials in a British Government delegation were sitting outside the office in Nairobi of a senior minister in the Kenyan Government. They were in the final stages of negotiating a multi-million pound mixed grant aid and loan deal with the Kenyan authorities. One of them, David, had flown out from London. The other, Martin, had recently arrived in Kenya to work at the British High Commission. As it happened, David had spent much of his childhood in Africa, whereas Martin, his senior colleague, was new to the continent. They were getting a little annoyed. The minister was keeping them waiting. People went in and out of the minister's office while the British watched the clock above his secretary's desk. It showed 2.30 pm, the time their meeting was supposed to have started, but it was, in fact, already past 3 o'clock. David got up and began chatting to the secretary, who seemed to have very little to do. He found out where she was from and gradually moved the conversation around to her boss. He was always surprised at how much useful information you could glean from people's subordinates. The minister had numerous properties around the country and was a major investor in a company that owned several tea estates around Kericho. He was trying to get a younger son into a British university. He loved football.

At last, the door of the minister's office opened and the minister himself, a very large member of the Luo tribe (to which Barack Obama's father belonged), came out to greet them. He was smiling broadly. Martin leaned across, shook his hand and then stood back. The minister frowned. David quickly took the minister's hand, introduced himself, and walked hand-in-hand with the minister into his vast office. The minister indicated a distant chair to Martin. David was commanded to sit on the sofa next to the minister, who placed a large hand on David's knee and kept it there. For the first 30 minutes, the minister and David sparred with each other over the terms and conditions of the proposed deal. Neither of them had any papers in front of them. Martin's interventions from afar were mostly ignored. Then the conversation switched to David's and the minister's childhood experiences in Africa. There was much laughter around the subject of British colonial rule. The minister briefly mentioned the problems he was having finding a university place for his son. David promised to see if he could help him. The minister's secretary brought in a copy of the draft agreement. Without looking at it, the minister summarised what he understood had been agreed by him and David – some minor changes to the loan repayment schedule and the interest rate terms. The secretary noted down what he said. As David and Martin left, the minister insisted that David visit his farm near Kisumu when he next came to Kenya, all the while holding David's hand. He nodded at Martin. A few minutes later, in the back of their official car, David breathed a sigh of relief. They had got what they wanted: tough controls on how the British aid money was spent and no change to the loan/grant ratio. Martin looked bemused.

What does this story teach us? Knowing the local cultural etiquette and reacting correctly to the signals being sent to you will always put you in a stronger position when negotiating across borders. David knew that African people tend to stand and sit much closer to each other than is the norm in the UK. They are much more tactile too and handshakes between men and between women can be long. Hands can be held throughout a conversation. He knew that withdrawing one's hand too quickly, as Martin had done, is interpreted as rude and unfriendly. And he also knew that people in Africa are not slaves to the clock and meetings seldom follow any fixed agenda.

However, we chose this story less to tell you about Kenyan etiquette but more because it illustrates a desire that is so little understood by many people in the rich countries of Europe and North America: the need to build a personal relationship first in order to do successful business. The story is based in the world of government-to-government financial assistance rather than that of business. But in much of the world establishing a strong relationship from the start of a negotiation is as important in business as it is in government. If the representatives of two companies can get to know and respect each other while negotiating a contract, the deal is likely to be one that will satisfy both sides. It will also be one that is more likely to survive all the strains that it will inevitably have to cope with as the two companies work together post-signature.

Many businesspeople from northern and western Europe and North America still find it hard to accept that they should spend time getting to know the people with whom they are negotiating. They separate their working lives from their private lives and feel that whether you like someone or not has no bearing on whether you can do business with them. There is a feeling too that getting to know your negotiating partner too well could lead you to agreeing a deal that is less favourable to your company than it could have been had you kept your distance. And there is the fear that getting too close to the other side can make you vulnerable to bribery. These are legitimate concerns and you need to be careful. But not so careful that you don't allow a relationship of trust to develop. In many, perhaps most, countries around the world, business has always been conducted in an environment where the rule of law is weak and courts are overly-influenced or even controlled by politicians, officials and rich businesspeople. In such an environment a person can only do business with someone in that country whom he trusts. Often there is no written contract between them. What is the point of having one when you cannot hope for fair arbitration in your country's courts? So, when the same businessman is negotiating with you, a foreigner, he wants to know if he can trust you. That does not mean he is happy to have no contract. In fact, he will almost certainly insist on having one and, perhaps to your surprise, will be willing to accept that its governing law should be that of your own country or a third country. Remember what we said at the end of Chapter 2. This is because he knows that such law can be relied on to give him better protection than his own country's commercial law. But, even so, all his upbringing and experience has taught him to do deals only with people he can trust not to cheat him. And if he is to trust you, he must get to know you.

b. Communication

David started to build a personal relationship with the minister by using the information he had got from the minister's secretary to lead the meeting into a discussion of the minister's interests and concerns outside his work. British people love this small talk. So do people from many other quite different cultures. They form an essential part of a negotiation. They are used to build relationships and also to get useful information that can be used in the negotiation proper.

However, you need to be careful. Richard has never forgotten a fee negotiation in Seoul in which, during the small talk, he praised the 5-star hotel he was staying in. He had hoped that the flattery and sign of his status would impress the Korean client. He felt very foolish when the fact that he had booked into an expensive hotel was used against him as a reason why his fees were "too high".

And Richard was once accused of being "dishonest" by a lawyer at Statoil in Stavanger for wishing to indulge in small talk. "You are not really interested in what I do outside work; so why do you Brits ask this kind of question?" Richard never had an opportunity to discover if this man took this view because he was a lawyer or because he was Norwegian. Probably the former, as other Norwegians have been more than happy to chat about matters outside work, though admittedly usually while naked in the sauna rather than when clothed in a meeting!

You will recall that the British MD of the coin-acceptor system was keen not to waste money. He agreed to invest more in cracking open the Japanese market by asking his Marketing Manager to go with him to Japan. However, to compensate for these extra costs, he insisted that they stayed in the cheapest "business hotels" which *gaijin* (foreigners) tend to avoid. These hotels have tiny rooms and only the most basic services. He did this to save money. But the decision helped him in his negotiations. Among themselves the Japanese will start a meeting with a lot of small talk but in meetings with *gaijin* they usually have to speak a foreign language, often English, and small talk is confined to a few standard questions – "How was your flight? Which hotel are you staying in? Is this your first visit to Japan?" The British MD took advantage of the second question to tell his hosts at every meeting that he and his colleague were staying in cheap business hotels in order to keep costs under control (he was a good student). He also told them that he had chosen such hotels because they were full of vending machines, supplying everything from breakfast to ear-plugs. So, he had been able to do some market research. He was lying. He had had no idea, until that trip, that such hotels were so reliant on vending machines to serve their customers. But he was a good enough negotiator to use this information in the small talk stage of the meetings to make a good impression on the Japanese.

You may remember the meeting between Helmut and Abdul Latif mentioned in Chapter 5. Helmut represented a German company negotiating a contract to supply its goods to Abdul Latif, owner of a Kuwaiti import-export agency. The German wanted to start negotiating as soon as possible, especially after Abdul Latif had said that he intended to buy some of his products. But the Kuwaiti insisted on asking lots of questions about the German company and its existing customers in the Arabian Gulf. Why was this? Because Arab businesspeople usually want to take time getting to know as much as possible about any future partner. They indulge in a lot of small talk, although they certainly don't consider the talk of small value; quite the opposite. Helmut grew suspicious when Abdul Latif asked him who else he was supplying in the Gulf. Maybe the Kuwaiti was trying to find out what prices the German company was charging elsewhere in the region. He probably was. Abdul Latif gave Richard a different reason though. He needed to know the names of Helmut's existing customers so that he could assess how well connected he was.

Dr. Jehad Al-Omari is a Jordanian businessman, author and friend of Richard's. They have run negotiation skills courses together in the UK and Abu Dhabi. Jehad describes what he calls the Arab world's "tribal ladder":

> I am acutely aware of the tribal ladder whenever I am doing business in the Middle East. Many people are appointed because of their tribal connections; not what they know, but who they know and are related to. My own access to them is often on a tribal basis. I grew up in Abu Dhabi; so I have many friends there. They will have their own tribal connections, which means I have a surrogate tribe there. I contact someone from a certain tribe and say: "I need to see so-and-so in the Ministry of Agriculture." He says: "Okay, I'll phone you back." He comes back and says: "I have a cousin in that Ministry. Go and see him." That is my tribal ladder.[1]

1 For more on doing business in the Arab World, we recommend you read Jehad's book – *Understanding the Arab Culture – A practical cross-cultural guide to working in the Arab World*, How To Books Ltd (2008)

Abdul Latif wanted to know if Helmut had a tribal ladder in the Arabian Gulf. If his ladder reached as far as the merchant princes and royal families of the region, Helmut would be someone he would want to do business with. Such is the power and importance of *small talk* in the Arab World and in so many other societies around the world.

We have been talking about just one aspect of cross-cultural communication that is important to the proficient international negotiator. We touched on a number of others in Chapter 5. For example, we described the handshake exercise that Richard often does on his courses. The central message of the exercise is contained in this assertion by Edward T Hall, a US anthropologist, and his wife Mildred Reed Hall from their book, *Understanding Cultural Differences: Germans, French and Americans,* published in 1989 by Intercultural Press:

> The essence of effective cross-cultural communication is more to do with releasing the right responses than with sending the right messages.

So, you may think that giving someone a firm handshake at the beginning of a meeting is sending your partner the message that you are confident and trustworthy. If your partner is, say, German or British, he will probably respond positively. He will interpret your handshake in the way you want it to be understood. But an Indian, Vietnamese or Japanese will almost certainly respond negatively. He will interpret your strong grip of his hand as aggressive. Are you going to try and dominate him in this negotiation?

When negotiating with people from her own culture, the skilled negotiator chooses her words carefully, says them in the most effective way and subconsciously adopts the appropriate non-verbal behaviour to accompany them. She knows what combination of all three will elicit the right response. But when negotiating outside her culture, the same words, tone and behaviour may release different and often quite negative responses. What must she do to make it much more likely that the responses she gets will be positive? She needs to know and understand the normal rules of communication in the culture she is dealing with. Then she can work out what changes she needs to make in her own communication style to elicit the right responses.

Edward Hall, the anthropologist quoted above, spent all his working life researching how people in different cultures think, behave and communicate. For those negotiating across borders, the most important concept that he developed was contextual communication. He divided people into high context communicators and low context communicators. Putting it very simply, if you vary your vocabulary, tone and behaviour according to the situation and the people you are dealing with (i.e. the context), you are a high context communicator. If you think it is best to say exactly what you think, whoever it is that you are talking to, you are a very low context communicator.

We all vary our communication to suit the context. You will speak differently to your boss than to your wife (unless she is your boss). An airline pilot will talk very differently to the air traffic controller than to his passengers (unless he works for Aeroflot). For a diplomat or the head of the US Federal Reserve, choosing your words carefully to suit the occasion or the audience is your raison d'être. Cultures tend to be either high context or low context and this strongly influences how people communicate within their culture. The Dutch, for example, pride themselves on being no-nonsense straight talkers. Most are indeed low context communicators. The Dutch businesspeople that we have had to negotiate with usually make it clear when a proposal or price is not acceptable, whether we are a supplier or a customer. But we have also worked with Dutch government negotiators who are highly skilled at using indirect, nuanced language to make their points without causing offence.

Many people mistakenly equate high context communication with being indirect and low context with being direct. It is true that high context communicators generally prefer to communicate implicitly. They employ understatement, allusions, euphemisms, irony, metaphors or humour to convey what they really think. Non-verbal signals and variations in tone need to be interpreted carefully. But this does not mean that high context communicators will always speak and behave in such a way. The key point is that they vary their communication according to the situation they are in. The most high context communicators in the world must be the Japanese, closely followed by the Chinese. Yet anyone who has worked in Japan will know that the same person who has been very polite to you in a group meeting can be very direct when there are only two of you. Indeed, one of the signals in Japan that tells you that you have been accepted into the in-group (*uchi* or home) is when the communication with you switches from indirect and implicit to direct and explicit. Likewise, anyone who has been part of a major negotiation with a Chinese company, especially a state-owned one, will have experienced the sudden switch from the indirect and considerate discussion of volume, delivery schedules, product design and quality control to the emotional and direct duelling over price, payment terms and penalty clauses. Very often a whole new Chinese team will be introduced to the negotiation just to argue with you about these key money matters. In such cases the language can be brutal and the volume high.

With high context communicators, the seniority, number and sex of the people you are negotiating with will all determine what words they will use and how they will use them. So will the location of any meeting: usually formal and indirect in the office environment or up-market restaurant, often much less formal and more direct when out at night in a bar (even before the alcohol takes effect). This, by the way, is why so much of the real problem-solving and bargaining takes place outside the formal "theatre" of the office meeting room in Tokyo, Shanghai or Seoul. Never refuse an invitation to go out in the evening with your negotiation partners in East Asia. It is the best possible signal that they want the negotiation to proceed and proceed more quickly.

We talked about the Renault-Nissan Alliance earlier. Yoshikazu Hanawa, President of Nissan during the negotiations with Renault in 1999 explains why he negotiated on his own, something almost unheard of in Japanese business:

> With many people around, it is difficult to tell each other the truth; that is why I decided to negotiate alone...I believe the process leading up to an alliance is all about telling the truth; dishonesty only makes the process longer. (Korine *et al.*, 2002)

If you regard yourself as a low context communicator, it's worth rereading Hanawa-san's words several times to get the full flavour of what it means to be a high context communicator. We will be looking at truth later in this chapter.

The problem in international negotiation occurs when a high context communication culture tries to communicate and behave in their normal way with those from other cultures, even with another high context one. The Japanese are horrified by the typical negotiating tactic of the Chinese we described above. If the context is as serious as the discussion of money, this, in Japanese thinking, requires the utmost diplomacy and careful use of words and tone. The Chinese, Japanese, Arabs, Indians and Russians are all regarded as high context communicators.

But they have very different rules on how to communicate in the same situation or context.

And what happens when a low context communication culture tries to do business with a high context one? Here is a real case on which Richard had to give advice recently.

A European company was building up a franchise chain in Asia. It already had 70 shops in China and was aiming to have 200 within a couple of years. It had negotiated a deal with a company in Beijing to be its master franchisee in China. As is usual, the franchise agreement listed exactly how the European company's products should be displayed and how the shops should be designed. The agreement also insisted that the Chinese had to accept any changes to the branding which the European company might make. The person who had negotiated the contract and dealt most closely with the Chinese in the first years had been transferred to a new job within the company. The Chinese venture had made a profit more quickly than forecast and she had established a close relationship with the people in Beijing. However, the European firm's management thought she had allowed the Chinese too much autonomy and had, to some extent, lost control. Not all the shops were sticking to the guidelines on layout, colour and product positioning. The master franchisee had got into the habit of ordering huge amounts without warning and with no regard to the Europeans' production and delivery schedule. So, the European board hired a new Sales Manager for their Asian markets. It was made clear to him that he needed to get the Chinese to stick to the agreement they had signed.

The new Sales Manager for Asia came from a European country whose people tend to be quite high context communicators. But he had spent much of his career in the USA, a country where low context communication is the norm in the office. He reckoned that what worked there should work anywhere. So, he started firing off emails that explained very directly what the Europeans expected from their Chinese franchisees and demanding that they fall into line with the agreement. These emails were not just sent to his main counterpart in Beijing; they went to all the franchisees. Many of the Chinese simply did not reply to his emails. Others responded by answering questions he had not asked but which suited their side of the story. The Sales Manager himself said; "The Chinese behaviour is similar to my children – pushing the limits, hearing what they like to hear, sudden memory loss." After a couple of months, the Chinese in Beijing made an official complaint to the

European board about the "rude communication" from the new Sales Manager. It was at this point that Richard was asked to help.

In fact, the Sales Manager had done many of the right things. His emails were clear, well-structured and written in simple English (just as we advised in the previous chapter). His arguments were logical and supported by spread sheets and diagrams. But where he had gone wrong was in openly criticising Chinese behaviour. He accused them of ignoring those aspects of the contract they did not like. Worse, the emails had been copied to lots of people both in Europe and in China. If he had sent the first email just to his Chinese counterpart in Beijing, his email might have had the desired effect. In China, you can speak your mind very directly when in a one-to-one meeting; there is no danger of loss of face. Likewise with an email: send it to just one person and you can say what you really think. But as soon as you put email addresses in the cc box, you are creating a group meeting; there is a real danger of embarrassment and anger. And please, never even think of blind copying (bcc) anyone. It is the quickest way to destroy trust in an international relationship.

So, how could the sales manager restore good relations with the Chinese and also get them to stick to the agreement? It was not easy but he did both. First, he went out to China and had a series of face-to-face meetings with the key people. He listened to their demands and ideas and explained his company's policy. Second, he sent an email to everyone apologising for his blunt communication style; he promised to do better in future. Finally, he decided to send emails to China only to one person at a time, unless the Chinese themselves requested for them to go to several people. Almost immediately he noticed a change for the better. People were responding quickly to his emails and, in most cases, answering his questions and agreeing to his requests. Within a couple of months the Europeans felt that they were back in control of the relationship.

As we have said earlier, much negotiation these days is conducted by email. Many contracts are signed without the two parties ever meeting. But email is a tool designed for low context communicators. Email does not allow you to indicate your true thoughts by varying the tone of your voice or doing something with your hands or face. Sentences are finished. Silences are not heard. And so only low context communicators – e.g. the Dutch, Danes and most US Americans – seem to be comfortable negotiating entirely by email.

High context communicators will try and make this inflexible medium work for them. They may use over-polite language and flattering words before they deliver the unpalatable message. They may use emoticons to try and tell you that they don't want you to get upset by their direct language. But in our experience such tactics only cause confusion and irritation. It's better to accept that email does not allow you to express yourself diplomatically or subtly. Use email to ask for and send information, to state your position and to confirm what has already been agreed. But try, if you possibly can, to conduct the real bargaining face-to-face in the same room or via the growing number of ways we can see each other online. Yes, that was the bit you read in the previous chapter. We are happy to repeat it; it is one of the most important pieces of advice we give you in this book.

c. Time

Let's go back to that negotiation in Nairobi between the two British aid officials and the Kenyan minister. You may recall that the meeting started over 30 minutes late. This had annoyed the more senior Brit, Martin. It probably confirmed his stereotype of Africans: disorganised, unpunctual time-wasters. The meeting, with its lack of any agenda, no doubt reinforced his view. He may even have thought the minister's behaviour was a deliberate "dirty trick", designed to put pressure on them. It possibly was; but more fool him for allowing himself to be put under pressure.

In Africa and much of the world outside northern Europe, North America and Japan, time is not linear. It is not something that should be cut up into discrete and sequential events. Edward Hall called people and cultures with such a relaxed attitude to time *polychronic;* others have used the term *synchronic*. They are very adept at doing several things at once. Punctuality is not considered so important that you ignore colleagues on your way to a meeting. Since living and working in France Richard has had to get used to meetings never starting on time. He was once mocked in Botswana for getting annoyed with a colleague who turned up late for a meeting: "In England, you have the clock. In Africa, we have the time." Agendas are seen as restrictive, hampering creative thought and the development of relationships. If you are from the other end of the scale - what Hall called *monochronic* and others call *sequential* – do not allow yourself to be put under pressure when negotiating by your liking for punctuality and order. Do what David did and make use of the extra time to get more information, deepen personal relationships or do totally unrelated work. As Richard is fond of saying:

"There are no straight paths in Africa". Or in many other parts of the world either.

There is another aspect of time that can cause problems when negotiating across borders. It is to do with pace. In some business cultures time really is money. Hence there is urgency to any negotiation. The USA is the usual example. In some hierarchical societies, for example France, Spain and Brazil, decision-making can be quick; only a few top managers are involved. So, as long as you are negotiating with those managers, negotiations can be swift. However, in those hierarchical cultures that place great importance on establishing a deep and long-lasting relationship – India, China, the Arab World – the pace of negotiation can be slow. They want to get to know their prospective new partners first. It is particularly slow if you are dealing with state-owned organisations in hierarchical cultures. People in countries at the other end of the hierarchical spectrum, flat and democratic, such as the Netherlands, Denmark and Sweden, also often like to take their time when negotiating. In their case, decision-making is slow because many people have to be consulted. Japanese companies are not as hierarchical as many believe and their decision-making process is glacially slow. This is because everyone who might possibly be involved in the outcome of any signed deal has to be consulted and persuaded of its merits beforehand. The problem occurs, of course, when people with differing ideas about the "normal" pace of negotiations try and negotiate. This was one of the causes of friction between Volvo and Renault in the early 1990s. It has been a constant issue between Nissan and Renault since 1999 (though the original negotiations were very swift – Nissan were weeks from bankruptcy).

There was the well-publicised case in the 1990s of the $3 billion contract between the Maharashtra state government in India and a subsidiary of the US company, Enron, to build a power plant near what is now Mumbai. A contract was signed in 1992 and the plant was supposed to have been built by 1997 to meet about 3% of India's energy needs. But the deal was cancelled in 1995 by the Indians because it had been concluded in *"unseemly haste"* and had been subject to *"fast track procedures."* Enron managed to renegotiate the terms of the deal despite mounting opposition in India to what was seen as a corrupt process that would have allowed Enron to receive over twice as much money per unit of power as Maharashtra state's electricity board could collect from its customers. The plant opened two years late and had still produced no electricity by the time Enron went bankrupt in 2001.

Corruption and political interference by three successive Indian governments undoubtedly contributed to this hugely expensive failure. But as one observer wrote in 2001:

> A company known for its hubris tried to accomplish too much, too quickly, playing fast and loose with the financial realities... (Parry, 2001)

Four years earlier, in February 1997, Rebecca Mark, then Chairman and CEO of Enron International, had declared that a new deal had been agreed and the project was back on track. Her interview with an Indian journalist shows her attitude to time and to Indian culture. Asked how she had got the deal cleared, she replied:

> I think what worked was that we never stopped talking. Our contract allowed us to arbitrate through legal international means, so we did.

And this was part of her response when asked what she thought she had done "right or wrong in India":

> People thought we didn't do it "the Indian way", whatever that means. We were extremely concerned with time, because time is money with us. People thought we were pushy and aggressive. But think of the massive bureaucracy we had to move. How do you move a bureaucracy that has done things one way its entire collective life? You have to be pushy and aggressive.[2]

d. Truth

If you have a different concept of truth from someone else, it is not easy to establish a business relationship with them based on mutual trust. Different people around the world have very different attitudes to truth and these differences can bedevil international negotiations.

The Dutch cross-cultural researcher and writer Fons Trompenaars came up with seven *value orientations*. One of them is *universalism v particularism*. Universalist cultures believe in absolute rules, which should be obeyed whatever the circumstances. Truth is fixed. Particularist cultures believe that loyalty to family, tribe, friends or colleagues is more important

2 The interview was published in *BusinessWeek* under the title: "You Have to be Pushy and Aggressive." *BusinessWeek*, February 24, 1997, http://www.businessweek.com/1997/08/b351586.htm.

than obeying abstract rules. Truth is relative. Rules can be bent to suit the circumstances. We prefer to use the terms *fixed-truth* for *universalist* and *relative-truth* for *particularist.*

North Americans, the peoples of northern, central and western Europe, Israelis, Australians and New Zealanders tend to belong to the *fixed-truth* category. They attach great importance to written contracts and often involve lawyers from the start of major negotiations. The goal of a negotiation is a signed contract. Such contracts are detailed; they are designed to anticipate all possible eventualities. If there is a problem post-signature, you refer to the contract for guidance. Bargaining ranges are narrow. People who move too far from their opening offer may be thought of as liars. *Fixed-truth* cultures are usually low-context. If people disagree with you or cannot accept your proposal, they will say "I disagree" and "that's not acceptable". The word *No* is used a lot. They distrust people who don't give straight answers and who appear to give conflicting messages. They expect proposals to be well-structured and clear. Arguments must be logical and based on facts. They are comfortable negotiating by email. They love agendas. They are irritated with relationship-building processes such as small talk, evening entertainment and gift-giving. Lavish banquets and expensive presents make them suspicious: *are we being bribed?*

Far more people and cultures belong to the *relative-truth* category. This is the mirror-image of the *fixed-truth* one. For them, establishing a relationship of trust is the main goal of any negotiation. Lawyers should be kept under control and are, ideally, absent from face-to-face negotiations. They will willingly sign contracts but they don't invest these paper documents with the same power as *fixed-truth* cultures do. Indeed they may want to spend more time agreeing a letter of intent or a statement of general principles than people from *fixed-truth* cultures would consider necessary. This is because such documents focus on what the two sides are trying to achieve by forming a business relationship. *Relative-truth* cultures expect any post-signature problems to be resolved by referring to these mutually-agreed goals. They expect you to be flexible and to be prepared to renegotiate the contract if circumstances change, especially if those changes are beyond either side's control. The bargaining range is wide. The haggling process is enjoyable. *Relative-truth* cultures are nearly always high-context. Preserving harmony and not losing face are far more important than telling the literal truth. Such statements as *I disagree* and *that's not acceptable* are rude, inconsiderate and arrogant. Are you really so all-knowing that you can say such things? Much better are euphemisms such as the Japanese *it is difficult* and *we will study carefully* (both of which effectively mean *no*). *Yes* may just mean *I understand what you are saying*. They are unhappy negotiating by email. Agendas are acceptable but must not stop the discussion going down interesting paths. Relationship-building is essential and may require many meetings to be held inside and outside the office before the negotiation can be concluded. Gift-giving is a sign of respect and a signal that you wish the relationship to be stronger and deeper. Asking for and doing favours is natural behaviour between friends. Beyond a certain point, bribery and corruption is regarded with just as much disgust in *relative-truth* cultures as in *fixed-truth* ones.

In truth (sorry), few people in *fixed-truth* cultures are as rigid in their behaviour and direct in their communication as we have painted them. British people, for example, belong firmly on the *fixed-truth* side. But they happily indulge in small talk and are relatively high-context communicators. In our experience, German businesspeople are as eager to establish long-term relationships when negotiating as anyone from *relative-truth* cultures. However, they tend to want to do that once the deal is signed!

Richard often recounts what happened when he asked a group of managers to define the word *contract*. It was in a chateau near Paris for Capgemini, the international, French-owned IT consultancy company. There were 16 people in the room: project and programme managers, all men aged around 30, from France, Italy, the Netherlands, Sweden, the UK and the USA. They had just finished role-playing a cross-border, post-contract negotiation with a client. It was just the kind of thing an employee of a company like theirs has to do a lot: renegotiate the contract because the client's needs have changed. The role-play had not gone well. Richard looked around the room and asked one of the US men a question: "Jack, what is a contract?" Jack clearly thought this was a dumb question: "It defines the deal. It's like the *Bible.*" The other Americans loudly concurred with this blasphemy. Richard caught the eye of Massimo from Rome. The Italian shook his head, grimaced and, making his hands form a grille in front of his face, said: "A contract is a prison!" One of the Frenchmen shrugged his shoulders and spoke for a couple of minutes. In summary, he said: "You have lots of clauses which can be interpreted in different ways." The lone Swede said he was still thinking about an answer. Meanwhile the three Dutchmen had been talking among themselves. One of them said: "We would call it an insurance document. You only refer to it if you have to." The British looked relieved that they didn't have to think of an answer and said they agreed with the Dutch. Same ages, same sex, same jobs, same company, but different cultures and different assumptions, in this case, as to the purpose, definition and importance of contracts. For some – Massimo in this case – contracts should not be waved in front of a client at the first sign of trouble; they can poison relationships and stop clients and suppliers looking for mutually-beneficial solutions. For others – such as Jack – they provide protection and comfort in a dangerous commercial world.

You need to identify what are the attitudes to contracts in the culture you are dealing with very early on. Otherwise the deal may never happen or post-contract problems never be solved satisfactorily.

Some of the people from *fixed-truth* cultures who we train and do business with can use racist language when referring to the moral code of people from *relative-truth* cultures. They seem to think that such people are not only untrustworthy but also intellectually inferior. This occurred in that meeting, referred to earlier, between Helmut (not his real name), from a German company, and Abdul Latif, owner of a Kuwaiti import-export agency. The two men started to discuss prices. Helmut showed Abdul Latif his price list and said he could only offer discounts above a certain volume. The Kuwaiti ignored this and pointed out that he could get the same items from other suppliers at 20% of the price the German was quoting. This was patently untrue. Helmut knew his market and no competitor, not even ones in Asia, could undercut him by more than 40%. His trust in Abdul Latif was immediately undermined: "How can I work with someone who lies to my face like that?" was one bitter comment, among many more openly racist ones, which he made later. Yet, the Kuwaiti remarked afterwards that he had just been signalling to the German that his prices were too high. By starting so low, Abdul Latif thought he was helping Helmut. The German could say to his colleagues that he had pushed the Kuwaiti back up to a price much closer to his own target. Abdul Latif added: "I would have accepted a base price for some of the products at around 10% below his list price."

This negotiation took place in Europe. If it had taken place in the Middle East, Helmut could have learned about the typical Arab bargaining range by visiting a local market or even a super-modern shopping mall. He would have seen that the range is very wide indeed. This is also true in Africa, much of Latin America and most of Asia. But the price on which both sides will finally agree may be no different in such regions than in Europe, North America and Japan, where the bargaining range tends to be far narrower.

In our negotiation workshops we run a number of very simple buyer-seller exercises known as *The Cards.* Two people are given a card each, one for the seller and one for the buyer. There are three or four slightly different instructions on each card. The people are asked to negotiate the purchase of a pen or a memory stick. The other participants are instructed to observe, to guess the instructions on the cards and to comment afterwards.

In the first of these exercises the instructions concern volume, colour and price. The volumes are identical and the colour not usually an issue, so the parties tend to concentrate very much on price. The seller's target price is $10, the buyer's is $8. Usually, a northern European seller will open on $12, in extreme cases on $15, and in most cases the pair settles on a price between $9 and $9.50.

However, on one course run by Søren for a major international company, the first exercise went a bit differently. The buyer was German and the seller Indian. Let's call them Klaus and Ashok.

Klaus: "So, what are these pens going to cost me?"

Ashok: "$100 per pen."

Klaus stared at Ashok, checked his card, stared at the Indian again and asked: "Are we doing the same exercise?"

The other participants started giggling and looked at Søren and then back at the negotiators. Ashok took this in his stride and asked: "What price were you looking for?"

Klaus' instruction said a target price of $8 per pen but, as he later admitted, the fact that Ashok had started at $100 had made him hesitate to suggest a price of $6 or $7, even though he thought Ashok was not playing the game seriously. "About $10", he replied.

Ashok: "I am sure we can work something out."

They did, and closed a deal at a price of $10, which was Ashok's target.

In the debriefing of the exercise one of the other participants asked Ashok: "How on earth could you suggest a price of $100 when your instruction said $10?" The Indian answered calmly, "I thought we were negotiating." The participant said, "But you moved $90 in one move!" Ashok answered, "Well, that may be so, but I got my target price, didn't I?"

Indian business people expect bargaining ranges to be very wide. An Indian buyer would have known that Ashok's opening price of $100 was completely ridiculous. He would have offered to pay, say, $1 per pen, knowing that this was far below the cost of producing a pen. Then the haggling would have started. Neither person would have considered the other untrustworthy simply because the opening bids were so far apart.

You may have been shocked by the contempt for Abdul Latif shown by Helmut who felt the Kuwaiti was a liar and cheat. We are not comfortable with such attitudes either but there is no point pretending that they don't exist. And they are not confined to the *fixed-truth* side of the scale. We have heard people from *relative-truth* cultures express disdain for the moral code and intellects of those *fixed-truth* people who regard following rules and regulations to be of greater importance than commitments to family and friends.

We say more about truth in Chapters 8 and 9.

6.3 Dealing with stereotypes

Many people on our courses feel uncomfortable when we start discussing the stereotypical images that nearly all of us have of other cultures. Some, usually those who feel the world has a negative image of their country, would prefer us not to raise the issue at all. *What has this got to do with negotiation skills?*, they will often ask. The answer is *a lot* and by the time we have finished, all agree.

According to Nigel Nicholson, Professor of Organisational Behaviour at London Business School, stereotyping is as old as the human race:

> To prosper in the clan, human beings had to become expert at making judicious alliances. They had to know whom to share food with, for instance - someone who would return the favour when the time came. They had to know what untrust-

> worthy individuals generally looked like too, because it would be foolish to deal with them. Thus, human beings became hardwired to stereotype people based on very small pieces of evidence, mainly their looks and a few readily-apparent behaviours... People naturally sort others into in-groups and out-groups – just by their looks and actions.[3]

We have not progressed very far on this matter since leaving our Stone Age caves. All of us have images of other cultures that are almost impossible to shift. Only if we live in a different culture to our own are we likely to change our stereotypical view of it. And there are many expatriates whose stereotypical images of different cultures are only confirmed by their experience of living in (but not inside) other countries. These stereotypes are nearly always formed in childhood, are seldom based on direct experience and are usually out of date. They are predominantly negative, something that is reinforced by the media in every country, whether consciously (e.g by *The Sun* and *Bild* newspapers in the UK and Germany respectively) or subconsciously. We may wish it to be different and some delude themselves that they don't judge others in this way but, as Professor Nicholson says, stereotyping is hardwired in us. So, we should stop pretending otherwise and work out how we can turn this human trait to our advantage when doing deals across borders.

As we hinted in Chapter 2, getting someone to talk about their own culture's Do's and Don'ts is a great entry point to building a strong relationship. People love telling you how things are done in their own culture. And once they are in full flow, you can ask them how they perceive your culture. Your hosts will take great delight in telling you, directly or indirectly. They will, of course, tell you that these are not their views but those of their compatriots. Don't believe them. If your hosts are the people you are negotiating with, listen carefully and note what they are saying. It could be more valuable information than your competitor's price quotation.

A Latvian logistics company was trying to break into the British market. They were already doing good business transporting goods across Russia, the Nordic region and eastern and central Europe. But they could not get any British company to consider them, despite tendering for a large number of contracts. They were confident their prices were lower than the competing bids from their German, Dutch and British

---

3 *How Hardwired is Human Behaviour?* Harvard Business Review, July-August 1998.

competitors. So, why were they not even getting to the shortlist and the negotiation proper? It was their country's image. Their website's home page had a map showing their location. The map showed Latvia in the middle, with the Baltic Sea to the west, Russia and Belarus to the east, Estonia to the north and Lithuania to the south. Ask British businesspeople what their image is of Latvia and some of them will mumble something about the country being "up there" and wonder whether it is "Baltic" or "Balkan".[4] Many will say "poor", "cold" and "Russia" (or "Soviet Union"). The Latvian company's website map reinforced this image. What British transport manager is going to place his valuable business with a company from a place he doesn't know and suspects of being impoverished and corrupt? So, Richard advised the Latvians to change their map. Latvia moved to the right-hand side, making it possible for Denmark and Sweden to appear on the left. Russia and Belarus somehow disappeared. So, now Latvia was part of Scandinavia, a region that connotes high quality, reliability and beautiful blonde women to the average British transport manager. The Latvians already had the third and could now add the first two to the image the British had of them. And they had one extra advantage over their new Scandinavian friends: the biggest negative image of Sweden and Denmark that the British have is that both countries are very expensive. So, the Latvians were able to say to the British: We are the company for you – Scandinavian-based and inexpensive. They were on several British companies' shortlists within weeks.

Ask our British and US American clients to give their stereotypical views of each other and we get pretty much the same responses – the loud, self-absorbed American and the cold, aloof Brit. Here is an example of how one senior British manager used the US image of Brits to his subsidiary's and, ultimately, his own considerable advantage.

The manager was European Sales Director of a major Connecticut-based multinational company. The French head of the European office, which was in the UK, felt that relations between some of his senior British staff, including the Sales Director, and the US head office needed improving. The British were failing to get what the Europeans wanted in internal company negotiations. Richard and a US colleague were asked to run a day's session on US business culture for the British. It had been agreed that the two consultants and the five British participants would have dinner together the night before. Richard asked if

4 We know because Richard asked British businesspeople exactly that question in early 2012.

two American managers from the same company, who were on secondment to the European office, could join them for dinner. He hoped that the two Americans could give their British colleagues some tips on US culture. During coffee, Richard asked the two American expatriates to go off into a corner and discuss their perception of British behaviour after 18 months of working in the UK. While they were doing this, the British were discussing how they perceived US working practices and behaviour. The Americans were first to report back. In summary, they said that the British:

- Always talked about problems, not solutions
- Focused on the past and not the future
- Sounded depressed, even when giving good news
- Did not respect their senior managers
- Were badly prepared at meetings

The British said that they felt that Americans:

- Were always over-optimistic
- Did not analyse problems properly in order to come up with workable solutions
- Came across as boastful and superficial
- Were too deferential to their superiors
- Did not listen to other points of view at meetings

Even Richard, who had done this exercise many times before with different nationalities, was astonished at how diametrically opposed the two sides were. During the subsequent discussion it became clear that it was mostly the different communication style of each side that had caused these perceptions. The European Sales Director then admitted that he was about to fly to the US to report to the board on the last quarter's sales and to negotiate an upward revision in his sales expenditure for the next half-year. In fact, he had brought his draft presentation with him. He was persuaded to show it to the others. It did not take long for the two American expats to start shaking their heads in exasperation. As one of them explained:

> This is so typically British. You spend 90% of your time explaining why you haven't achieved expected sales in the last quarter. It's all so negative. Nobody's listening by the time you get to your pitch for more money.

The Sales Director defended himself:

> But this is a sales report. I have to tell them what happened in the last quarter. And the figures don't look good.
>
> Sure. But only spend a minute on that. They have seen the figures already. They're history. Tell them how amazing sales are going to be if they give you the opportunity. And do it in a passionate way. None of this English understatement. Aim high.

The Americans were not there the next day but the British and the consultants spent much of it helping the Sales Director rewrite his presentation and prepare his arguments for a budget increase. They consciously decided to take the US stereotype of Brits - cold, unemotional, quiet, backward-looking, ironic - and make the Sales Director confound it. The board would know what to expect before he even walked through the door. After all, this was not the first time they would have heard him and his other British colleagues. They would have probably scribbled "boring Brit" on the agenda. So, he was going to go in and be the opposite of boring. He would present and negotiate in a way that would make the US board think: "Hey, this guy's different. He's one of us."

And that is what the European Sales Director did. His presentation was punchy, positive and forward-looking. It was full of charts with product income lines going up. He asked for 20% more money than he really needed to achieve an increase in sales, and countered every objection with a fact-backed focus on the benefit each extra investment would bring. The board loved it and gave him what he asked for. So impressed were they that 18 months later he was appointed CEO of the whole company (and was fired two years afterwards. But that's another story).

So, the next time you are negotiating with people from another culture, spend time finding out how they are likely to perceive you. If the image of your country's manufacturers is that they are old-fashioned and produce poor quality goods, and you are someone trying to sell products from that country, you should expect to face a tough negotiation on those clauses covering warranties and quality control. It doesn't matter how superbly engineered your own products are; you and they will be seen through the distorted image that others have of your culture.

A final word

You will recall that curiosity was one of the three character traits we believe can enable someone to become a skilled international negotiator. By showing a genuine and deep interest in the culture of the people you are dealing with, you become more likeable and more trustworthy. People will want to do business with you. And you, in turn, learn how best to do business with them.

7

What kind of negotiator am I?

7.1 Know thyself

When negotiators meet for the first time, there is always an element of uncertainty about the situation. We have just looked at how culture can be a complicating factor and can create uncertainty, or even anxiety, in a negotiation. If we could limit the complicating factors to culture, then it might be relatively easy to predict the behaviour we are likely to meet at the negotiation table. However, there is another aspect that will have an influence on a person's negotiation behaviour and complicates the negotiation process: the personality of the person you are dealing with and, more importantly, your own personality.

As we said in Chapters 1 and 2, it would be useful for you, if you had the time and opportunity, to try and assess the characters of the people on the other side of the negotiation table before you meet them. When you do finally meet them, you will make snap judgements of their personalities anyway, which will immediately influence how you negotiate with them. Even more useful to you, however, is to know how your own personality has shaped your negotiation style and what effect this style is likely to have on these with whom you are negotiating. This is tough. As Benjamin Franklin said in 1750:

> There are three things extremely hard: steel, a diamond, and to know one's self.

What is personality? It can be defined as the pattern of collective character, behavioural, temperamental, emotional and mental traits of a person. Each person is unique. However, there are some traits that are possessed by certain types of people. What these traits are and how they affect a person's negotiating style are what this chapter is about.

A possible influence on our style as a negotiator is whether we are extravert, introvert or somewhere between the two. The psychologist Carl Jung introduced these concepts. A Wikipedia entry defines the terms as follows: "Extraversion tends to be manifested in outgoing, talkative, energetic behaviour, whereas introversion is manifested in more reserved and solitary behaviour." Few of us are always introvert or extravered. Most have bits of both and our behaviour fluctuates. We need to imagine an extraversion-introversion continuum and try to identify our own and other people's place on this continuum, because this place will influence the way we talk with each other and resolve our differences – i.e. negotiate. Susan Cain's book *Quiet*, which we mentioned previously, should be read by every aspiring negotiator, especially US American ones. The strapline to the title is: *The Power of Introverts in a World That Can't Stop Talking.*

We used the words *negotiation style* just now. Style is the way we come across to others. It is the bundle of different behaviours that other people see and hear most frequently when we negotiate with them. Negotiating styles are relatively stable, personality-driven clusters of behaviours and reactions that arise in negotiating encounters. They are patterns that reappear through the mechanism of predispositions towards a particular way of behaving when we negotiate.

Can you change your negotiation style? We believe you can and should. One of the main messages of this book is that you need to adapt your style to suit the person you are dealing with, the culture they come from and the strategy that you have chosen. Your personality is partly inherited and partly learned. On the face of it, this would seem to make it difficult for you to change your behaviour and, hence, your negotiating style. How do you 'unlearn' something that is inherited? Moreover, how do you 'unlearn' what you spent all your childhood learning? If you grow up in a very competitive environment where the only thing that counts is to get results and be successful, this is likely to influence your behaviour when you negotiate. Similarly, if you are brought up to be nice and helpful, to share everything with others and not be greedy, then this will affect your behaviour as a negotiator.

Yes, it is difficult but not impossible (why do people go on negotiation skills courses?). As we said above, most of us have a mix of introverted and extraverted traits. If, for example, the negotiation requires you to be more extraverted, you will need to draw on those aspects of your personality that make you appear chatty and enthusiastic. The skilled international negotiator is a chameleon.

How do we identify the style of a negotiator? To answer this question, we will be looking at one model that we believe is of particular use to negotiators.

7.2 The dual concern model

You met the **dual concern model** in Chapter 4 (Figure 4.2) when we looked at negotiation strategies. It is inspired by the Managerial Grid model developed by the American psychologists Robert Blake and Jane Mouton in the 1960s. It is based on two fundamental aims:

1. To reach a result that satisfies my needs and interests
2. To create and maintain positive relations with the other party

Figure 7.1 The dual concern model

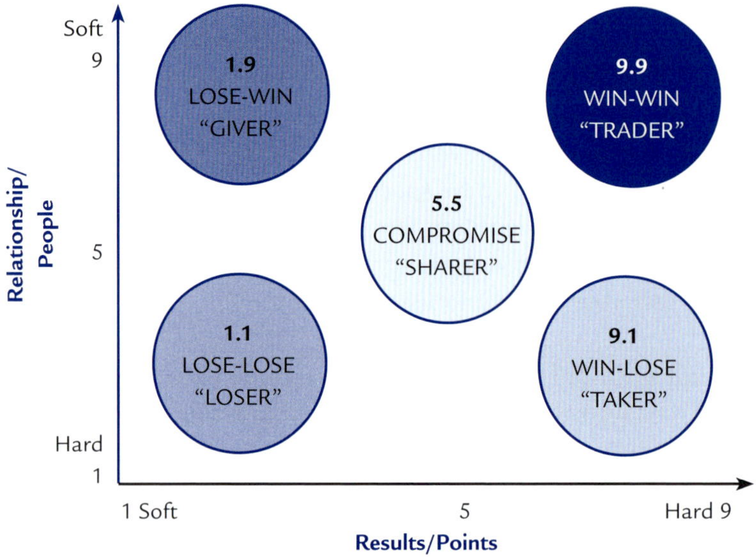

The model is two-dimensional - the horizontal axis plots *concern for own result/points* and the vertical axis plots *concern for relationship/people*. Both axes have nine points, so in principle there are eighty-one different combinations of styles, but as this is far too many for anyone to handle, we have reduced it to five dominant styles.

A questionnaire for the dual concern model

To identify your own style as a negotiator, you might like to complete this questionnaire, adapted from a generic model. It is divided into six categories - Decisions, Convictions, Enthusiasm, Conflict, Temper and Humour. Each category has five statements. Choose the statement that is most like you and give it a score of 5. Score 4 for the statement that is next most like you, then 3, 2 and, finally, 1 for the statement that is least like you. There is, of course, no point in you doing this if you are not totally honest with yourself.

Part 1: Decisions

— A1 Sound, creative decisions that result in understanding and agreement between me and my partners are very important to me.

— B1 I tend to accept my partners' decisions.

- C1 I place high value on maintaining good relations with my partners. The decision itself is often less important than making sure the relationship is positive.

- D1 I search for workable decisions from customers, suppliers and myself, even if those decisions are not perfect.

- E1 I aim to get decisions that give me what I want, and that commit my partners to that.

Part 2: Convictions

- A2 I prefer to accept the opinions, attitudes and ideas of my partners rather than push my own. It's important that they see that I agree with them.

- B2 I make sure I stand up for my ideas, opinions and attitudes, although these may not fit those of my partners. I know what I need.

- C2 I actively look for ideas, opinions and attitudes different from my own. I have clear convictions but respond to good ideas by changing my mind.

- D2 When ideas, opinions, or attitudes differ from my own, I try to find some middle ground between me and my partners.

- E2 I go along with the opinions, attitudes, and ideas of my partners and avoid taking sides.

Part 3: Enthusiasm

- A3 I am enthusiastic enough to get by. Demonstrating enthusiasm is not really a priority.

- B3 I offer positive suggestions because it keeps things moving along.

- C3 I know what I am trying to achieve and I will energetically pressure my partners into accepting what I want.

- D3 I direct my full energies into what I am doing and others respond enthusiastically.

- E3 I enthusiastically support, encourage, and compliment my partners on what they want to do.

Part 4: Conflict

- A4 When conflict arises, I try to be fair and find a suitable compromise.

- B4 When conflict arises, I try to identify sympathetically the reasons for it and to resolve the underlying causes.

- C4 When conflict arises I try not to get involved, and tend to stay neutral.

- D4 I don't mind when conflict arises, and I often use it to enhance my position.

- E4 I do whatever I can to avoid generating conflict, but when it does appear, I try to resolve it and to keep people happy.

Part 5: Temper

- A5 When things are not going right, I assertively defend my position, and come back with counter arguments.

- B5 Because of the disturbance that tensions can produce, I always react in a warm and friendly way.

- C5 When angry, I contain myself, although my impatience is sometimes visible.

- D5 When I am tense, I feel unsure which way to turn to avoid further pressure.

- E5 By remaining neutral all the time, I rarely get upset.

Part 6: Humour

- A6 My humour aims at maintaining friendly relations. When tensions do arise, it takes attention away from the serious side and makes sure everyone is happy.

- B6 My humour is intended to be persuasive in gaining acceptance for myself or my views.

- C6 My humour does not seem to have much effect on my partners.

- D6 I am not sure that humour has a place in serious business negotiations, but if I use humour, it is hard-hitting and is designed to strengthen my position.

- E6 My humour fits the situation, and gives perspective; I retain a sense of humour even under pressure.

Summary of personal rankings

Enter the 30 scores (six elements of five statements) into the table on the next page.

Add up the six scores in each vertical column and write the total in the space provided.

The highest possible score for any column is 30 (6 x 5) and the lowest possible score is 6 (6 x 1).

You can check your accuracy by adding the five sub-totals. The answer should be 90.

QUESTION	STYLE									
	1.1		1.9		5.5		9.1		9.9	
1. DECISIONS	B1		C1		D1		E1		A1	
2. CONVICTIONS	E2		A2		D2		B2		C2	
3. ENTHUSIASM	A3		E3		B3		C3		D3	
4. CONFLICT	C4		E4		A4		D4		B4	
5. TEMPER	E5		B5		D5		A5		C5	
6. HUMOUR	C6		A6		B6		D6		E6	
TOTALS										

The dual concern model (see Figure 7.1) is read in this way: The number before the dot shows the negotiator's concern for his/her own result, and the number after the dot shows his/her concern for the relationship. So if your highest score is 9.1, it indicates that you are significantly more concerned about your own result (the 9.) than the relationship (the .1). Look at the table and you will see that each column is headed by one of the five combinations of numbers: 1.1, 1.9, 5.5, 9.1 and 9.9.

To identify your preferred negotiation style, look at your highest and second highest scores. If the gap between these two scores is six or more points – e.g. 28 in the 9.9 column and 21 in the 5.5 column – then you are clearly in the 9.9 column and are a 'trader'. You are someone who tries to negotiate their way to an agreement by trading something for something. If the gap is five points or less, you need to include your third highest score to find out your likely style. If your highest score is in the 9.9 column, the second highest in the 5.5 column and the third highest in the 9.1 column, then you will probably adopt a negotiating style that fluctuates in the triangle 9.9, 5.5 and 9.1, as illustrated in Figure 7.2:

Figure 7.2 How to determine your own negotiation style

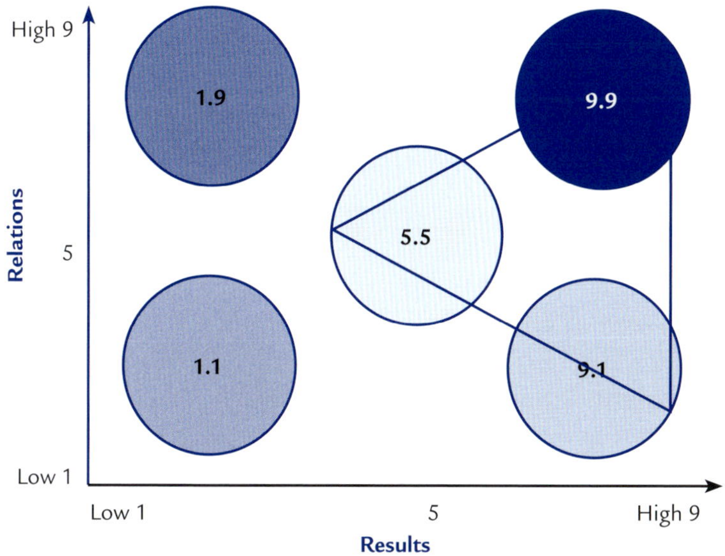

Why the fluctuating behaviour? Well, even though you have a clearly defined strategy to try to get the best possible agreement for both parties, sometimes the other negotiator may do or say something that makes you lose sight of that objective and instead make you concentrate on trying to end the negotiation as quickly as possible just to get out (1.9). If they behave in a way that really annoys you, then your objective may change to being one of wanting to punish them for their behaviour (9.1) rather than getting a good result for both sides.

The five styles and the corresponding negotiating strategies are explained as follows.

1.1 – LOSE-LOSE

This type of negotiator is truly an endangered species, and we do not meet them very often at the negotiation table and only rarely in training. Fundamentally, they cannot see the point in negotiating. When you do meet them, it is very difficult to find out exactly what their strategy is. That's because they don't have one. They may diplomatically avoid certain topics and may even contribute positively to the group dynamics, but as soon as there is conflict, they will retreat into their shells and miss many opportunities to achieve a satisfactory result for either side. They tend to lean heavily towards the introversion end of the spectrum.

1.1 LOSE-LOSE

Attitude to negotiating: LOSER

Negotiation strategy: DOESN'T EXIST

Very low concern for the result coupled with very low concern for the relationship

- Win or lose - who cares?
- Relationships and results leave me cold
- Indifferent about the problem and the people
- I don't talk about my needs, and I'm not interested in theirs
- Often perceived as being: passive, cold, low in assertiveness

This type of negotiator just does not want to be there.

1.9 – LOSE-WIN

This type thinks that no matter what the goal of the negotiation is, what is most important is to maintain a good relationship. If this means giving the other negotiator what she wants, then they will do that. That way they avoid conflict. If it means that they leave the negotiation having lost out on the deal, they are not too bothered. They get great satisfaction from solving other people's problems, and are very good at building relationships.

But they attach too much importance to the relationship, sometimes even in situations where there is no need for such a strong relationship. This makes them very vulnerable to exploitation by more competitive types, who will be tempted to get maximum benefit from a negotiation with such an accommodating negotiator.

This type of negotiator is normally very good company. They like giving and probably regard generosity as contagious. "If I give the other negotiator something, they will surely return the favour," they tell themselves. However, experience tells us that they are often disappointed in that respect, because the other negotiator may regard a gift (concession) as an indication that if they push harder, there will be more to be had. This type of negotiator could be said to be encouraging the other negotiator to be greedy.

They tend to lean towards the introversion end of the spectrum.

1.9 LOSE-WIN

Attitude to negotiating: GIVER

Negotiation strategy: CONCESSIONARY

Very low concern for the result coupled with very high concern for the relationship

- If you win and I am left with the scraps, that's fine by me
- The relationship is all that matters
- Very accommodating
- I hate conflict
- Often perceived as being: a push-over, over-sensitive, a nice person

This type of negotiator wants to be accepted and respected, and sees any conflict as a threat to the relationship. As a natural consequence, they rapidly put aside their own interests in order to get or keep a good relationship.

5.5 – COMPROMISE

This type of negotiator does not think it is possible or worth the trouble to achieve a win-win agreement. The objective is to find a quick solution that both parties can live with, and they prefer to "split the difference" to get a result. Unfortunately, this often means that both parties get a satisfactory result rather than a really good result. To us, compromising is the lazy option. It is very different from collaborating.

The compromisers of this world usually always try to find a formula or "fair" standard to minimise the distance between the positions of the parties. They tend to be happy with a result that does not cause loss of face to either party. Splitting the difference is a way of avoiding a confrontation with the other negotiator and is very tempting in situations where neither party has any BATNA-power. It is a typical development of what we call positional bargaining. As soon as the parties put down their markers by stating a position, it is tempting to go into haggling mode and gradually work towards some middle point between the two extremes.

A participant in one of Søren's workshops gave an example of a compromise. He explained that his girlfriend had wanted to paint a wall in their flat blue. He personally wanted the wall to be yellow, and after some discussion they agreed to mix the colours. When you mix blue and yellow, you get green, and they painted the wall green. "And we both really hate that colour!" he said. However, the positive aspect of this is that whenever they disagree on something he can now say: "Do we want another green wall?"

When time is tight or there is not very much at stake, it may be the best solution to compromise. But we very much agree with what the creators of the dual concern model have to say about compromising:

> Compromise is quite a different matter. It is selling out on a conviction. It means agreeing so as to be agreeable, even though sacrificing sound action; settling for what you can get rather than working to get what is sound in the light of the best available facts and data.
>
> Compromise can seem like flexibility, but they have little or nothing in common. Both involve adjustment and accommodation, backing and filling, twisting and turning, shifting and adapting. When these actions take place in the spirit of compromise, the motivation behind them is usually to avoid interpersonal emotions. Behaving in this manner is a reaction to disagreement, and means that effectiveness is being sacrificed. When such behavior takes place in the pursuit of flexibility, the motivation underlying it is usually to be more effective. Thus there are actions to adjust a difference to keep peace and actions to adjust to altered circumstances for better results. It is most important to distinguish between the two kinds. Flexibility for better results is likely to have a stamp of 9.9 on it; "flexibility" to avoid a clash of personalities is in the 5.5 area. One is enlivening and promotes creativity. The other is stultifying and leads to the perpetuation of status quo rigidities. (Blake and Mouton, 1969, pp 67-68)

5.5 COMPROMISE

Attitude to negotiating: SHARER

Negotiation strategy: SHARING

Moderate concern for the result coupled with reasonable concern for the relationship

- I win a little and you win a little
- I leave value on the table
- Not so easy to tell what I am hard/soft on
- I compromise to close a deal: no big win - no big loss
- Often perceived as being: impatient, fair, reasonable

This type tries to reach a compromise. They are moderately keen to meet their goals and keep the relationship on an even keel. Conflict has to be solved in a way where both parties achieve an acceptable result.

9.1 – WIN-LOSE

This type of negotiator sees a negotiation as a number of steps that are necessary in order to make sure that they achieve their goals, irrespective of how this might affect the relationship with the other side. In any conflict there has to be a winner and a loser. Winning boosts this negotiator's status, at least in his own eyes. It is a power-based attitude to negotiating where the person will use any means necessary to defend a position he or she sees as being the right one or simply just in order to win. This type of negotiator regards all negotiations as a zero-sum game: "More for the other negotiator means less for me".

Similar to their collaborative colleague, this type of negotiator enjoys the process of negotiation, but for different reasons. They see negotiating as a chance to win, as a kind of sports match. You will meet them everywhere, but they are truly in their element when there is a lot at stake, time is tight and there is a possibility of bluffing the other party. Their competitiveness can play such a dominant role that it affects the relationship with the other side negatively. They seem to focus almost instinctively on things that are quantifiable - such as money - and tend to neglect the non-quantifiable things that may otherwise contribute to generating great value.

9.1 WIN-LOSE

Attitude to negotiating: TAKER

Negotiation strategy: ANTAGONISTIC

High concern for the result coupled with very low concern for the relationship

- I win and you lose or we both lose
- Only the result (reward) counts
- Frankly, my dear, I don't give a damn (about you)
- More for me means less for you
- Often perceived as being: pushy, insensitive, inflexible, arrogant, a bully

They use all possible means to force others to accept their solution. The aim is more important than the relationship, and the fight is part of the game. Even though the game is about winning or losing, victory is more important than the potential rewards.

9.9 – WIN-WIN

The collaborative negotiator's attitude to conflicts is that a conflict is there to be solved in such a way that it does not affect the relationship negatively, but without sacrificing anything in terms of the result of the negotiation. In other words, this type of negotiator not only cares about his or her own needs and interests, they also take the other party's needs and interests into consideration and regard them as equally valid and important. When a conflict arises, this type of negotiator looks for an appropriate model for resolving the conflict and brings the situation back to normal. This attitude requires a similar approach from the other party, and requires time, energy and creativity.

The collaborative negotiator enjoys negotiating because they enjoy solving problems in an engaging and interactive way. Instinctively, they are good at getting under the surface of the conflict to identify the underlying interests of the parties, and they do their utmost to involve the other party in this process.

9.9 WIN-WIN

Attitude to negotiating: TRADER

Negotiation strategy: COLLABORATIVE

High concern for the result coupled with high concern for the relationship

- I win and you win (enough)
- We need to be gentle with each other but argue hard to get what we want (SOPHOP)
- Let's solve this problem together
- Don't rush
- I love saying "How about we...?" or "Why don't we...?"
- Often perceived as: confident, sensitive, creative, patient

The wise type. Both their own goals and the relationship are important. A strong relationship is seen as a way of reducing tensions between people. They identify conflicts as problems that have to be solved in a satisfactory way for both parties.

In 2013, Søren trained 551 negotiators across Europe. This questionnaire was completed by every single participant, and the distribution of the five styles was as follows:

1.1	7	1 %
1.9	45	8 %
5.5	115	21 %
9.1	36	7 %
9.9	304	55 %

The remaining eight per cent are the 44 respondents that had the same score in two or three categories e.g. a score of 24 for both 9.9 and 5.5.

Do those results mean that most people are either sharers or collaborators?

Few people are solely in one category. But if you were to ask a person you have done business with to describe your approach to negotiating, they would probably use several adjectives that would apply to no more than two of these five negotiation styles. But we have major doubts as to whether the majority would be a mix of compromisers and collaborators, despite what the results from Søren's questionnaire indicate.

How honest were Søren's respondents being with themselves? They were all on Søren's courses and most did not exhibit a win-win approach in the initial role-plays. Observation of and participation in negotiations in the real world tell us that most people are either predominantly result-oriented and don't care a lot about the relationship with the other side, or are relationship-oriented and care less about getting a great result for themselves . We see the first type of person doing well in the short-term but having considerable difficulty getting such favourable terms when a contract is up for renewal or when bidding for new business from an existing client. The relationship-focused negotiators may believe that they will win in the longer term by being accommodating at first. But we think they are fooling themselves. There are not many lines of business where you can sell cheap at the beginning and then just increase your prices. We can only think of drug-dealers, and then it is only because they build up a physical dependency in their customers.

Is it possible to change our style?

As the man said, yes we can. However, it is not an easy thing to do, because as human beings we are creatures of habit, and habits are very hard to change. The first requirement is for you to realise that there might be a need for a change in style. Then you need to decide on how you are going to achieve this. Not surprisingly, we would recommend that you get negotiation skills training. Many trainers use video feedback, and while many people do not particularly like seeing themselves in action at the negotiation table, it is an eye-opener. The camera is your friend, and like a true friend it does not lie to you. It shows you exactly how you come across to other people, and this gives you the possibility to evaluate your own performance.

8

Are we a team?

8.1 Why negotiate in a team?

The greater the complexity of the deal, the more likely it is that you will need to have several people involved in the negotiation. The extra people will normally be those with a particular expertise – e.g. technical, legal and financial. In international negotiations, you may wish to have a mix of head office and local staff; and you may require the services of an interpreter. Above all, conducting a long, complicated negotiation across borders is exhausting. Share the burden and you might get a better result.

As we have seen in Chapter 6, businesspeople from group-oriented cultures such as China, Korea and Japan expect negotiations to be conducted between teams, even when the matter being negotiated is simple and straightforward. You may recall the British Managing Director who was only taken seriously by prospective customers in Japan when he went with a "bag carrier" - in his case, the company's Marketing Director.

Whatever the reason for not conducting a negotiation single-handedly, you need to make sure the people in your team have clearly defined roles, which they stick to unless instructed otherwise. If you don't, you may be faced with a situation like the one Søren observed a few years ago. Luckily, it was in the training room and not during a real negotiation.

He was running a workshop in Germany with five men and one woman from the procurement department of a major international company. On the last day, the participants were divided into two teams for a negotiation exercise - three German men in one and the German woman, a Brit and an Indian in the other.

While preparing, each team chose a lead negotiator - the person who was going to do most of the talking and be responsible for including the others whenever appropriate. The culturally mixed team picked the native English speaker to lead them. When the teams finally started negotiating, the team led by the Brit presented their carefully-prepared proposal. As you might expect, this was politely but clearly rejected by the other team. Normally, when Søren ran this exercise, the two teams would then start trying to find common ground, moving gradually away from their original positions. But not this time.

The Indian participant started negotiating on his own. He went off in a direction that was clearly not in line with what his team had agreed beforehand. His British colleague - the appointed lead negotiator - was obviously furious. The teams decided to take a time-out to discuss progress. Søren followed the mixed team into their breakout room to see how they were going to sort out their differences. Once the door was closed, the British man vented his fury on his Indian teammate and sacked him from the team. The Indian accepted this with good grace.

When the teams met again, the British man apologised for his Indian colleague's behaviour in the first session and explained why he was no longer at the table. The all-German team looked somewhat surprised, but the parties carried on with the negotiation and managed to reach an agreement.

Why had the Indian gone "off-piste" and followed a different negotiation path than the one he had agreed only a few minutes earlier with his teammates? What could the British lead negotiator have done to stop his colleague deviating from their agreed strategy? The Indian said that he was simply trying to find a way to break the deadlock between the two sides. The Brit apologised for his loss of temper and said he should instead have tried to make his Indian colleague see the need for the team to keep to their plan. That's why a time-out had been called.

Both men learned a lot from this exercise. The Indian realised that he must not deviate from agreed plans when negotiating in a team. After all, without him and by keeping to their strategy, his two colleagues did manage to reach a satisfactory agreement. The British man took on board that if he did not control his emotions, they would control him. The major learning points that everyone took away were the need for discipline and presenting a united front when in a team negotiation and the importance of taking regular breaks to keep everyone on the team going in the same direction.

8.2 What difficulties do you face when negotiating in a team?

The biggest difficulty you face when negotiating in a team is what we have just described: making sure everyone on the team keeps to their assigned roles and the agreed strategy. Other problems include:

- the length of time it can take to get agreement beforehand as to aim, targets, strategy and tactics
- keeping to an agreed agenda
- people showing their disagreement and irritation openly, allowing the other side to play one person off against another
- teammates saying the wrong thing at the wrong time, unwittingly undermining their own side's bargaining power
- a lack of clarity as to who is responsible for what and whether the team can take decisions without reference to colleagues not present

8.3 What can we learn from hostage negotiations?

There is one kind of negotiation where doing it on your own is not only unwise, it could be life-threatening: negotiating for the release of hostages. In his excellent book *Negotiate and Win* (2004), the former chief hostage negotiator for the New York Police Department, the late Dominick Misino, explains that the ideal hostage negotiation team consists of five people: the commander, the primary negotiator, the backup or coach negotiator, the scribe and the floater. Each has his or her own role to play during negotiations. The *commander* makes the decisions. The *primary negotiator* negotiates. The *back-up* or *coach* offers suggestions and moves in when the primary negotiator needs a break. The *scribe* keeps track of what is going on. The *floater* runs errands.

Each person on the team corresponds to a different task common to all negotiations. Each task is different, requiring a different set of skills and even a different mind-set. All of these jobs are equally important. All come into play during a negotiation.

Misino goes on to explain the importance of defining the roles clearly before negotiating. He compares the composition of the team to the concept of separation of powers[1] in the government of a country such as the USA. Separation is critical to ensure objectivity in decision-making. And it can be a useful tactic. Separating the final decision-maker – the boss – from the negotiator gives the negotiator one more tool to work with. You can use it to build rapport with the other side: "You and I are working on this problem together, then we will deal with the boss".

However, it is not just a tactical thing. It keeps the negotiator from making a bad decision or a bad deal.

If there is a negotiation you cannot afford to lose, it is a negotiation involving human lives as in a hostage situation. Misino and his team resolved over 200 such incidents, including the hijacking of a Lufthansa flight in 1993, without losing a single life. Hostage takers are often desperate people who use this as a last resort to be heard, and if there is one thing we can learn from the hostage negotiation team it is the importance of **discipline**. Obviously, the hostage negotiator is the most important member of the team as he or she is responsible for defusing such a tense situation, but they cannot do their work if all the sup-

1 Charles-Louis de Secondat, Baron de La Brède et de Montesquieu, 1689-1755, generally referred to as simply Montesquieu, was a French social commentator and political thinker who lived during the Age of Enlightenment. He is famous for his model illustrating the need for a separation of powers. In this model, the state is divided into branches, each with separate and independent powers and areas of responsibility so that the powers of one branch are not in conflict with the powers associated with the other branches. The typical division of branches is into a legislature, an executive and a judiciary.

port functions are not in place. If the members of a team involved in a commercial negotiation could have the same discipline and stick to the function they have been assigned, then team negotiations would not be plagued with the problems that we listed above.

There are a couple of other lessons we can learn from Misino and the NYPD Hostage Negotiation Team, which are relevant to all commercial negotiations, not just one conducted by teams of people. The first is to show **respect** for the other side. Misino asks the question, "What do you call a hostage taker with a machine gun?" The answer is, "Sir!" He says that you cannot afford to put human lives at risk by disrespecting the hostage taker.

A second point is the need for **honesty**. Misino says that "the first principle, 'never lie'", ought to be obvious. This is as much practical as moral. Lies are counterproductive because they undermine the trust you're trying to establish during the negotiation. You have to assume that eventually the person is going to be able to find out the truth. If that happens and they realise you have lied, at best it demolishes the rapport between you. At worst, the other party may use it as a legitimate reason to end negotiations altogether.

> The thing about lies is that they are always tempting. They're seductive. They're almost impossible to resist sometimes, because you know, you just know, that if you say them you'll get what you want. Usually not, but boy it seems that way at the time. A lie is a quick fix to a complicated situation – and that's exactly why they're dangerous. (Misino, pp 48-49)

He goes on to give an example of a hostage situation in New York City where he was negotiating over a speakerphone so the whole team could hear what was going on. After lengthy discussions, the hostage taker said: "Look, I'll put down my gun and come out, but you have to promise me you're not going to handcuff me."

One of the department chiefs – in the role of commander of the team – nodded his head in agreement, mouthing the words "No handcuffs."

Misino explains that there is no way in the world that a person in that situation is not going to be handcuffed. They have just held others at gunpoint and, if he is not restrained, he may make a grab for a weapon once he is outside.

The whole team – including the chief – knew this; it would be an easy way out of a very dangerous situation. But it would be a lie. The chief kept urging Misino to promise the hostage taker that he would not be handcuffed. Misino told the hostage taker that he would be back in a minute and muted the phone. The department chief was a new guy; he and Misino had not worked together before. After some further heated discussion, he ordered Misino to tell the lie.

Misino picked up the phone and said: "Look, you're going to be cuffed. And you're going to be cuffed behind your back. That's the way it is. That's our policy. I can't change that."

"Okay," the hostage-taker replied. "Now I know I can trust you. I've been arrested before. I know how it goes. I just wanted to see if you were full of shit or not."

A few minutes later the man put his weapon down, came out and did not resist being handcuffed.

The chief obviously wanted some "personal time" with Misino afterwards. Why had Misino disobeyed a direct order?

Misino asked: "Are we talking chief to detective or you to me?"

"You to me", said the chief.

"Well, you didn't know what you were doing", Misino explained. "You saw a quick fix and thought that would solve everything. In this business, there is no quick fix. When something looks like one, that's exactly the time to stick to your guns."[2]

Misino explains that he had an advantage over the chief because he had been dealing with the hostage-taker for a while on the phone and had the entire context. He knew the guy was testing him. But it reinforces the point that if you are caught telling a lie, you will lose credibility with the other side.

The problem that commercial negotiators have with Misino's insistence on honesty is how you define the word "honesty". As we discussed in

2 An unfortunate idiomatic phrase to use in the circumstances! For non-native English readers it means "to maintain one's position or belief, despite opposition."

Chapter 6, people around the world have markedly different views as to what it means. Is a seller telling a lie when he quotes a price both sides know is absurdly high? Is a buyer lying when he says he can source the same product at 20% of the seller's price? Helmut from Germany thought so when told this by Abdul Latif and immediately began to mistrust him. But the Kuwaiti thought he was just giving a signal that Helmut needed to drop his price a bit. We believe that the commercial negotiator, especially one operating internationally, has to take into account how the other side is likely to interpret his words. If dealing with someone from a *fixed-truth* culture such as Germany or Sweden, it is best not to quote figures or make claims that the Germans or Swedes know to be untrue. Equally, when dealing with someone from a *relative-truth* culture such as China or India, realise that an opening price that is only fractionally different from your target price may cause the Chinese or Indians to mistrust you when they discover that you were not telling a lie!

There is another message from Misino's decision to disobey his boss. And it brings us back to team negotiations. Notice what he did when his boss, the team's commander, indicated that he should lie to the hostage-taker. He took a break by muting the phone. He did what we urge you to do should there be disagreement between members of a team during a commercial negotiation. In his case, he, the primary negotiator – the guy in charge of negotiating – disagreed with his team commander – the man who makes the final decisions. Strictly speaking, Misino was not following agreed procedure; he was not prepared to accept the decision of the person given the role of making decisions. So, he needed to discuss this with his commander out of earshot of the hostage taker. In the end, he still disobeyed him, and that can happen in a commercial negotiation too. But, at least, the disagreement was not audible to the hostage taker. And the same applies when you are negotiating a contract in a team. Keep your disagreements and dissension out of sight and sound of the other side as much as you can: take breaks.

Some of our clients say that it is much easier to ask for time-outs in the training room than in the real world of negotiations. We disagree. We know of several highly-experienced negotiators who insist on regular breaks during any negotiation, even if they are on their own. Richard can well remember the long and hard negotiations that he and his colleagues had with Renault in 2000 and, later, with Air France/KLM in 2005 before agreeing worldwide training contracts. There were teams of people on both sides of the table. In the final stage of the negotiations with Air France/KLM, for instance, there were just two people on the Canning side but nine in the airlines' team. It was an all-day meeting at Schiphol airport. Richard can't recall who proposed the first break but all were glad to take it and those that followed. Breaking away for intra-team discussions was particularly appreciated by the airlines, who were still learning how to negotiate together!

Time-outs also allow you to take what some Americans call a "bio-break". Many a deadlock in a negotiation has been broken by two men standing beside each other at the urinals.

8.4 What makes a negotiation team work effectively?

Team negotiations are challenging and complex, whether you are trying to stop someone killing people or attempting to reach a commercial deal. Developing a group of people into a team requires considerable skill, a desire on their part to get it to work and a lot of hard work to achieve good results.

Misino's ideal team to deal with a hostage-taker had five people in it, each with a specific role. We believe there is a limit to the number of people who can participate effectively at any one time in a commercial negotiation. In our experience, four is probably the maximum number of negotiators who should be involved in the negotiation process. The more people there are in a team, the greater the risk of a communication failure. Any additional people should only be there for one of two reasons: to contribute their specialist knowledge and expertise (and nothing more) or to give status or "face" to the meeting (and remain silent). Our four roles closely match four of those named by Misino. The missing one is an equivalent of his *floater.* Perhaps the technical expert in the commercial negotiation is the nearest match. These are our four roles (with the NYPD's equivalent labels, where different):

- a **leader** (*commander*), who focuses on the negotiation process. The leader proposes breaks when needed, summarises at regular intervals, tries to keep everyone to the agenda and takes the final decision for the team on what can be accepted and what cannot
- *a* **primary negotiator**, who asks questions, explores options, states objections, makes proposals and generally handles the communication with the other side

- an **observer and back-up negotiator** (*coach* or *back-up*), who notes how the other side is behaving and reacting, and may step in to the negotiation to give the primary negotiator time to think or recover
- a **recorder** (*scribe*), who is responsible for writing down any new information and everything that has been proposed and provisionally agreed. S/he may also summarise instead of the leader

If the team comprises only three members, the leader takes on the recorder role, and if only two, also assumes the role of back-up negotiator.

Functional roles are completely separate. It is generally not a good idea to make the corporate lawyer or finance director your primary negotiator. This is not to belittle them or their contribution to the negotiation's successful conclusion. But their functional roles make them better suited to the negotiation team roles of recorder or observer/back-up negotiator, adding relevant facts or arguments when required. The job of primary negotiator is best done by whoever got you to the table in the first place, usually someone in sales or purchasing .

8.5 What kind of people should you have in your negotiation team?

So, we have given you descriptions of the roles that need to be played in a commercial team negotiation. How do you identify the ideal person for these tasks? One possible answer is to consult Dr Meredith Belbin's studies of team roles.[3] These have been used for many years to identify people's behavioural strengths and weaknesses when working in teams.

Dr. Belbin says that a team is "not a bunch of people with job titles, but a congregation of individuals, each of whom has a role which is understood by other members. Members of a team seek out certain roles and they perform most effectively in the ones that are most natural to them. This knowledge can be used for:

- building productive working relationships
- selecting and developing high-performing teams
- raising self-awareness and personal effectiveness
- creating mutual trust and understanding"

3 Dr Meredith Belbin's work is described in numerous books. For further information go to www.belbin.com, where you can find a questionnaire to help you identify which role in a team would suit you most.

Let us take a look at how Belbin's nine-role framework may help you identify the right type of people for your negotiation team. Below is a general description of each of Belbin's roles and what we think are the pluses and minuses of having such a person in your team.

The Nine Roles

ROLE	GENERAL DESCRIPTION	SIGNIFICANCE IN NEGOTIATIONS
Shaper Primary negotiator, leader	Highly motivated with a lot of nervous energy and a great need for achievement: • Likes to challenge, lead and push others to action; can be headstrong and emotional in response to disappointment or frustration • Generally makes a good manager - generates action and thrives on pressure	*Action- oriented* + Dynamic + Doesn't give up easily - Argumentative - May offend others
Plant Keep out of the negotiation room but use when preparing	Innovator and inventor - can be highly creative: • Often enjoys working on his/her own away from other members of the team • Tends to be introverted and reacts strongly to criticism and praise • Great for generating new proposals and solving complex problems	*Thought-oriented* + Innovative - Not a good team player - Often a poor communicator - Tends to cut corners
Co-ordinator Leader	Has ability to pull a group together to work towards a shared goal: • Mature, trusting, and confident; delegates readily. Stays calm under pressure • Quick to spot an individual's talents and uses them to pursue group objectives • Useful to have in charge of a team because of diverse skills and personal characteristics	*People-oriented* + Mature + Confident + Good listening skills - May be seen as manipulative
Monitor evaluator Observer	Serious-minded and prudent: • Slow decider who prefers to think things over - usually has highly critical thinking ability • Makes shrewd judgements by taking into account all the factors • Great to have for analysing problems and evaluating ideas and suggestions	*Thought-oriented* + Analytical + Objective + Careful decision-maker

Resource investigator Primary negotiator	Good communicator both with other members of the group and with external organisations: • Natural negotiator, adept at exploring new opportunities • Good at finding out what resources are available and what can be done • Relaxed personality with a strong inquisitive sense and a readiness to see the possibilities of anything new • Very good at finding resources and heading negotiations	*People-oriented* + Innovative + Curious + Good at exploring + Good at developing contacts + Enthusiastic team member + Outgoing – May lose enthusiasm quickly – Sometimes overly optimistic
Implementer Primary negotiator, recorder	Well organised, enjoys routine and has a practical common-sense and self-discipline: • Systematic approach to tackling problems • Reliable and hardworking • Will do what needs to be done whether or not s/he will enjoy the task	*Action-oriented* + Gets things done + Turns ideas into plans and actions + Disciplined + Systematic + Efficient – May be inflexible – Does not like change
Team worker Leader, recorder, observer	Supportive member of the team: • Flexible and adaptable to different situations and people • Perceptive and diplomatic • Good listener • Avoids conflict • Good at allowing everyone in the group to contribute	*People-oriented* + Supportive + Flexible + Diplomatic + Perceptive – Not good at making decisions
Completer-finisher Recorder	Has a great capacity for follow-through and attention to detail, and seldom starts what s/he cannot finish: • Dislikes carelessness • Reluctant to delegate, prefers to tackle tasks him/herself • Good at tasks that involve close concentration and a close degree of accuracy	*Action-oriented* + Thorough + Attentive to detail + Concerned with deadlines + Perfectionist + Conscientious – May worry unnecessarily – Not good at delegating
Specialist	Proud of his or her technical skills and specialist knowledge: • Priority is to maintain professional standards and to promote own subject • Very committed	*Thought-oriented* + Contribution limited to own area of expertise – Usually not particularly interested in the expertise of others + Because of their knowledge they are indispensable members of the team when their particular expertise is needed

To make a negotiation team perform really well, each team member must be given clear responsibilities and, more importantly, perform their role(s) to the best of their ability. We have given you our opinion as to which type of person, according to Belbin's description, would make, say, the best primary negotiator in your team – a *shaper, resource investigator* or *implementer*. Not all would agree with our allocation and you may not have exactly the right person available. But we believe strongly that it is worth spending time thinking who would be best suited to take on each of the four roles. The right choice will enable you to reach an agreement much more smoothly.

9

Is that a bribe?

We believe that it is impossible to separate the way you behave in a negotiation from the person you are in other parts of life. There is only one you. You are either an ethical person or not.

Ethics are defined as a set of concepts and principles that guide us in determining whether a behaviour may be helpful or harmful, a kind of social standard for what is right or wrong in a particular situation.

If you are ever in a position where you begin to wonder whether you are behaving ethically yourself, you should ask yourself: "How would I like to be treated in this situation?" If your answer is "Not like this", then you need to change your approach and your tactics.

9.1 Bribery and corruption

If there are two matters which can ignite a heated discussion among our course participants, they are bribery and corruption. They are really one subject; bribery is one aspect of corruption. And we have fun testing the moral codes of all the participants. Everybody agrees that paying a decision-maker millions of dollars in cash to ensure that the payer's company wins a contract rather than a rival is a corrupt act. Sadly, not all would say that this is immoral behaviour and a significant minority are prepared to condone it if the "right" company (i.e. theirs) is the winner. What we find interesting is that there seems to be no link with culture here. Such views are expressed by some people on all points of the fixed-truth – relative-truth scale. The cultural differences occur when the corruption is not so obvious. When does a "commission" or "professional fee" become a bribe? At what level of expense does a gift turn into an attempt to influence a decision? At what point does doing someone "a favour" slip into gaining an unfair advantage? At government level, when does a "subsidy" become a blatant attempt to rig the market in a domestic company's favour?

You will recall that in the meeting with the Kenyan minister in Chapter 6, the UK aid official promised to help him secure a place at a British university for his son. We have asked our participants whether they consider this to be an example of corruption. The answers depend to some extent on how independent from government a country's universities are. Scandinavians, Finns, Germans, Dutch and US Americans usually consider the British man's offer of help to be corrupt. This view shocks almost everyone else. They applaud him for both deepening the personal relationship with the minister and gaining a loyal friend when the son becomes a businessman and politician in a few years' time (which, by the way, he did). Of course, David, the UK official, could not promise to find the son a university place. But he did write a letter to the vice-chancellor of the university to support the application, having got the agreement to do so from his bosses in the British Foreign and Commonwealth Office. In their opinion, such help was not corrupt and it impressed the Kenyan minister much more than any crude offer of a money bribe.

Another case, where corruption undoubtedly took place, splits the *fixed-truth* people from the *relative-truth* ones more clearly on what is acceptable when negotiating and implementing a contract. It concerns a joint venture between British and Chinese companies in the food and beverage industry. The two companies agreed to build a production and bottling plant near the Chinese company's head office in China. Despite the fact that the British firm had a majority stake in the joint venture, they accepted their Chinese partners' arguments that it would be better if most of the directors were drawn from the Chinese side, plus one representative appointed by the regional authority. In fact, the only British director permanently in China was the plant's Production Manager.

The British had insisted that the agreement contain detailed rules on budgeting and reporting procedures. Budgets had to be jointly agreed no less than two months before the new financial year. Annotated monthly management accounts and cash flow statements, drawn up according to British accounting rules,[1] had to be emailed to the UK no later than ten working days after the end of each month. Any unbudgeted capital expenditure above $5,000 had to be authorised by the Finance Directors of both companies. The negotiation was protracted but ended, as it usually does in China, with a banquet of many courses and much alcohol, accompanied by shouts of *ganbei!*[2]

For the first three months the Chinese kept to the agreed procedures. But then the management accounts began to arrive late and the cash flow statements not at all. When the management accounts for the seventh month arrived (two months late), the British noticed a sudden increase in depreciation, indicating capital expenditure far above the $5,000 threshold. The notes attached to the accounts made no mention of this. Emailed requests for an explanation from the Chinese Finance Director went unanswered. The Production Manager reported that no new machinery had been ordered. A British Quality Control Manager, on a visit to the plant, was asked to investigate. It was only when he had a one-to-one meeting with the plant's General Manager, who fortunately spoke good English, that he learned the truth. The two companies planned to expand production in Year 3 if sales hit the agreed targets in the first two years. Sales in the first six months had been much better than expected and the local Chinese management had decided to start the process of applying for permission to extend the factory. They knew that such decisions can take a long time in China and so wanted to give themselves an 18-month lead time. They also knew that they would have to pay a hefty bribe to ensure the decision was not needlessly delayed. The main reason for having a local government official on the board was to facilitate this. The official, of course, would take a slice of the payment for himself. The Chinese had not wanted to tell the British about this because they knew they would not approve. So, to save British face, they had shown the bribe

1 The contract was signed shortly before 2006 when the old Chinese accounting rules were almost entirely replaced by the International Financial Reporting Standards.
2 Ganbei means "Drink it all!" in Chinese, similar to the British "Cheers".

as depreciation in the accounts and assumed the British would be able to work out what had happened but pretend they had not.

When we use this story as a case study on our courses, the people from *relative truth* cultures have great difficulty seeing what the problem is. As far as they are concerned, the Chinese have behaved perfectly: they planned ahead to ensure a key part of the agreement could be implemented; they ensured that the bribe was kept to a minimum by having a government official on the board; they gave the British a way of avoiding having to admit to their own authorities that they were engaged in bribery. The *fixed truth* people take a very different line: the Chinese have not been honest with their partners; they have exposed the British to being sued for corruption; they have made it easier for other Chinese to demand bribes.

This is not a book on moral philosophy. Only you and your company can decide what to do if asked to pay a bribe or to take part in corrupt behaviour. This is a book on negotiation. So, the question is: what should you do during the negotiation process to avoid the kind of situation that the British drinks company faced nine months after the contract was signed? The first thing to do is obvious: find out what the attitude to bribery is in the culture you are dealing with. Transparency International's surveys are an excellent guide. Next, decide among your colleagues exactly what your company's policy is on corruption. We continue to be surprised at how few organisations have a clear policy (or perhaps they are not telling us even if they have one). Finally, and most importantly, probe as much as possible during the negotiations to find out what the other side's policy is.

Take the British drinks company. They were persuaded to accept a local government official as a board member. But they didn't question the appointment deeply enough: what exactly was this person on the board for? Was he there from the Chinese Communist Party to keep an eye on the *laowai*[3] or would he take a more active role? Should the joint venture pay him a director's fee? The Chinese side had insisted on a letter of intent, which included both companies' wish to expand production in

3 *Laowai* is Mandarin for *old foreigner.* It is not a derogatory term like *yang guizi* (*west ocean devil = European* in Mandarin) or *gweilo* (*ghost man = white man* in Cantonese). Many *laowai* make the mistake of referring to themselves as *gweilo* when with Chinese people, thinking that this makes them look clever. It doesn't. It makes them look ignorant and embarrasses their Chinese hosts. Conversely, many foreigners think *gaijin (outside person = non-Japanese* in Japanese) is a derogatory term in Japan. It once was but is not now.

Year 3, if sales targets were reached in the first two years. The British would have made life easier for themselves if they had asked what costs would be incurred to achieve this expansion. What investment (a word with many meanings) would be required? If the questioning had been deep and persistent enough, it is likely that the need to bribe government officials to get planning permission and import licences would have arisen. The British could then have agreed with the Chinese a common policy on bribery before the contract was signed. As we keep saying: ask questions.

So, you may ask, what did the Brits do when they discovered they were party to bribing Chinese government officials? They took advice in the UK. Their Finance Director then went out to China, sat down with her counterpart and redid the management accounts for Month 7. The two agreed that the accounts for Month 7 onwards would show the director from the local government office being paid a monthly fee for his valuable services. This solution may make you uncomfortable but whatever your opinion, the Finance Director's expensive trip to China could have been avoided if the right questions had been asked before the deal was agreed.

9.2 Gifts

And then there is the thorny subject of gift-giving. In many cultures from Latin America to East Asia it is customary for two negotiating teams to exchange gifts at several stages of a negotiation. Indeed, any readers from these cultures may wonder why the subject of gift-giving is raised in a chapter on ethics. For business people from North America, northern Europe, Australia and New Zealand in particular, however, the subject is the cause of much anxiety. They do give each other presents but usually only at the end of a long and complicated negotiation. But they often wonder whether giving a gift at any other time will be perceived as a bribe, both by the recipient and by the police.

So, we advise that any gift you give to the other side in a negotiation should be *MAPped:* modest, appropriate and proportionate.

Modest: An expensive present to someone with a *fixed-truth* perspective will make them uneasy: *is this a bribe?* They may be forced to refuse it because their company has a strict policy on not accepting gifts worth more than a certain amount. Even if there is no such policy and they accept the gift, they may resent having to buy something equally expensive which they may not be able to claim on their expenses (see proportionate).

We have been asked several times by business people from *relative-truth* cultures to define the words "modest" and "expensive". Søren's answer includes some facts about Denmark: a Danish employer can only give an employee a tax-free gift if the value is less than DKK 1,100 (about €150) and a gift to a customer or supplier is only 25% tax deductible. These rules are often greeted with incredulity by the questioner. What most surprises them is the fact that a Dane has to declare to the tax authorities any gift he receives.

Appropriate: This is vital. The gift that is tailored to the interests and likes of the recipient does not have to be expensive and yet will often be hugely appreciated. It shows that you have invested time and thought into the process. We have found that this is particularly appreciated by people from group-oriented cultures - East and South-east Asians, Arabs. One Chinese is as different in personality and interests from another Chinese as two Danes or Dutch are but their behaviour at meetings may make the individualist-minded Dane or Dutchman think "they're all the same". If you can acknowledge, by your gift, that you recognise the Chinese person's individuality, you will have started a friendship that can easily outlast any business relationship.

If you don't know the person at all, it is best to choose a gift that is connected with your own country. Many US companies insist that any gift must be consumable. So, if you come from France, Italy, Spain or any other wine-producing country, you have it easy (but not if you are negotiating with any culture that prohibits the consumption of alcohol). If you are still not sure what to give, just spend some time in the duty-free store at any major airport and observe what different nationalities buy. For example, at London's Heathrow Airport you will notice the Japanese buying shortbread, whisky and tea. They especially like anything in a metal box with a royal or Scottish-themed picture on it. A colleague of Richard's was once invited to the house of a client in Japan (a great and rare treat) and saw an empty box that had once contained a bottle of Glenfiddich whisky. It was placed next to the family shrine. He assumed it had been put there in his honour. He had given exactly the same make of whisky to his host when they had concluded a negotiation over ten years earlier.

Make sure your gift is wrapped beautifully and in the appropriate colour. Red is a lucky colour in China. Gold connotes wealth. Wrapping in a mixture of red and gold would be a perfect signal to your new Chinese business partner. But avoid white (death) and don't give anything that is a set of four (death again). In the Arab world, green and gold would be the best choice.

There are, of course, gifts that are culturally inappropriate. Richard had finished a course on the edge of the Arctic Circle for the Swedish side of the Sony-Ericsson joint venture (it became Sony Mobile Communications in 2012). A young Swede presented him with a superb Swedish hunting knife as a thank-you present from the group. Richard was touched but then had a troubling thought. He asked the Swedes what gift they normally gave when visiting Sony in Japan. There was some laughter. "The same knife we gave you," one said. "Sven here put his knife in his hand-luggage and it was taken from him by Arlanda airport security." Richard nodded. "Lucky Sven. If you give a knife to a Japanese person, you are asking him to commit suicide." The silence that followed really was stunned.

You need to consider when is an appropriate time in the negotiation to give a gift and who should receive it. As a general rule in a major negotiation the best times to give a gift are at the beginning, at any important milestone in the process and, always, at the end. If you want to give a gift to the other negotiating team, give it to their leader in front of everybody at the beginning of the meeting. If the gift is just for your main contact, we advise you not to give it to him in front of his colleagues. Do it separately, out of sight of everybody else. This is especially important in east and south-east Asia in our experience.

Proportionate: Deciding what gift to give to the other side in a negotiation can cause a lot of angst among those not used to it: we don't know what they are going to give us; so what do we give them? The answer is simple: ask your main contact on the other side what present he or she thinks would be appropriate for you to give them. What you are really asking is: How much money will you spend on the gift for us, so that we can match it? It is very important to avoid loss of face when the gifts are unwrapped in front of both teams. So, they must appear to be of similar value. By asking the other side for help, you are also ensuring you avoid the spiral in gift costs that can occur: one side gives something that is clearly of much less value than the gift they have just received and they immediately get some hapless junior to go out and buy something worth much more than the other side's gift. This is done in the mistaken belief that this will somehow even things out. It doesn't. The other side now feels it must reciprocate. It really does happen.

9.3 Lying

One of the most frequently asked questions in negotiation skills training is: "Is it okay to lie a little in a negotiation?" To which we always answer, "Yes, of course, provided you are willing to live with the consequences of your lie."

There are two ways of lying in a negotiation. There is *lying by commission,* where the negotiator tells the other side something she knows is not true, and there is *lying by omission,* where the negotiator omits certain facts or fails to correct a misconception.

The first we think foolish and short-sighted, especially if you are hoping to build a long-term relationship with the other side. If they discover you have lied and it has cost them in some way, not only will they not trust you in future, they will do their best to get their revenge when they can. They lose short-term and you lose long-term.

It is harder for us to be so definite in advising you never to lie by omission. You might argue that Ulrike lied by deliberately not telling Anselmo that her company were planning to set up a new R & D laboratory in São Paulo. She knew that giving him this information before he made his initial proposal would have tempted him to raise his price, thinking his company would be a monopoly supplier. However, her omission of this key fact seems justifiable to us: it was still confidential information after all. We would also argue, as we did earlier in the book, that Anselmo has only himself to blame if he did not ask Ulrike enough questions before sending his first proposal.

Certainly, the lie by omission that tricks the other side into signing an agreement without knowing all the relevant facts is not only unethical; it can often backfire on the liar. In a short video Søren sometimes uses in negotiation training, a car salesman fails to tell a buyer that the car engine is not working properly and may need expensive repairs. He waits until the buyer has signed the agreement. Such behaviour is, unfortunately, still all too common in the world of buying and selling second-hand cars. It has bred the expression "Would you buy a used car from this man?" But a lie like this only benefits the liar if he knows he will never see the buyer again and can be confident that the buyer will not head straight to his lawyer, the local media or his Facebook page.

We firmly believe that there is no right way to do a wrong thing, and while you may think that you only told a white lie, there is no guarantee that the other party will see it the same way, and it may have a serious impact on the future relationship with the other party. This does not mean that you need to be a boy scout to be a negotiator, but as the French poet Jean de la Fontaine said: "It is much easier to tell the simple truth than to fabricate an elaborate lie." It does not mean that we recommend that you tell the other party everything you know. Far from it. There are things they would like to know but have no need to know. We recommend that whenever you tell the other side something, tell them the truth. It has the great advantage that it is always the same.

A final word:

Quotation on the wall of a shop in Dublin:

> The secret of life is honesty and fair dealing. If you can fake that, you've got it made.
>
> Groucho Marx

It may have worked for Groucho Marx. It probably won't work for you!

10

What were we on about?

10.1 Back to 1921

We began this book by explaining where we had got the title from. We hoped that by the time you got here you would understand why we had chosen it. But people read books like this for many different reasons and extract whatever is of particular relevance to them. So, for those who still don't know why we picked *Why Doesn't He Use a Spoon?*, here is an explanation.

In July 1921 the Prime Minister of Great Britain, David Lloyd George, had a series of four one-to-one meetings in London with the Irish Nationalist leader, Eamon de Valera. A truce in what was later to be called the Irish War of Independence had just been agreed between the British and Irish. The official aim of the discussion between the two men was to find out "how the British Empire may be reconciled with Irish national aspirations." As we said at the beginning, there seemed to be little meeting of minds between them. De Valera made it clear that he and the majority of Irish people wanted complete independence from Britain for all of Ireland. Lloyd George countered by offering self-government, like Canada, Australia, New Zealand and South Africa, but for Ireland to remain part of the British Commonwealth. The Irish would still have to swear an oath of allegiance to the British monarch. De Valera rejected this, not even taking hold of the paper on which the offer was written. So far, so predictable.

Nobody knows what exactly was said between the two men in these meetings. Historians have had to rely on letters from each of them to their friends and colleagues and on second-hand accounts. One thing we do know is that De Valera did begin to search for ways to bridge the gap between them. For example, he proposed arbitration by a third country. The Prime Minister refused to consider this. And only days after the negotiations with Lloyd George had ended without any agreement, De Valera was trying to explain another option to his political colleagues. Typically for an ex-teacher of mathematics he used a Venn diagram to do so: five circles, representing Canada, Australia, New Zealand and South Africa, and Great Britain plus her empire, all inside another circle, representing the British Commonwealth, with Ireland as a circle outside but just touching the Commonwealth one. According to De Valera, Ireland would have an "external association" with the British Commonwealth. What this really meant was neither clear to the British nor to the Irish. But that is not the point. At least De Valera was trying to find a way through to an agreement. Lloyd George appears to have made no attempt to do so. He stuck to his original position. He did not try to be flexible nor to adapt to the person he was dealing with. He did not try and use a spoon instead of a fork.

We have blamed him rather than De Valera for the failure of their negotiation. This may seem unfair. But what evidence we have indicates that De Valera understood what Lloyd George did not: both sides had to find a creative solution that saved each side's face. There was very little substantive difference between the two men's positions. De Valera was, in fact, at that stage prepared to accept self-government rather than complete independence. As he wrote to the South African Prime Minister, Jan Smuts, on 31 July 1921: "The question of procedure and form, as distinguished from substance are very important...The British do not seem to realise this at all."

Lloyd George said negotiating with De Valera was like trying to pick up mercury with a fork. His choice of liquid was apt. De Valera had a mercurial personality (as, indeed, had Lloyd George). As the Irish leader's later actions showed, he was devious and volatile. Few, even among his closest associates, really trusted him. But for Lloyd George not to explore other options and, at least, try to adapt his style to his negotiating partner was a huge mistake.

10.2 Prepare, ask questions and adapt

And these are the main messages of this book on international commercial negotiation:

- Always look for creative solutions, rather than just sticking to your original position
- Prepare thoroughly and keep testing your assumptions by asking questions
- Adapt your negotiation strategy, your behaviour and your communication style to suit the situation and culture you are in and the people you are dealing with

The consequences for the ordinary negotiator of not being prepared to adapt can be serious but are seldom life-threatening. Lloyd George and De Valera's failure to reach agreement in July 1921 had momentous consequences and cost many lives. A treaty between the British and the Irish was signed in December 1921 but De Valera had refused to join his colleagues in the negotiations. He denounced the Irish signatories as traitors, even though what they had agreed to – self-government within the British Commonwealth – would probably have been acceptable to De Valera if presented in the right way and if he had negotiated it himself. One of the Irish signatories, Michael Collins, foresaw what happened next when he said "I may have signed my actual death warrant tonight." Six months later Ireland was broken apart by a murderous civil war and Collins was killed by his own countrymen, supporters of De Valera. Ireland did eventually become an independent republic in 1948 but without the "six counties" of Northern Ireland, which still remain part of the UK. This division of Ireland has continued to cost thousands of lives right down to the present day.

We cannot end on such a downbeat note. What happened to Ulrike and Anselmo? Did the relationship (the business one!) between their companies prosper and grow? We don't know, of course, because they were our inventions. We had thought of having a dramatic denouement – perhaps an email in two years' time from Anselmo to Ulrike, informing the new Head of Purchasing at GerMedica that BTB's factory had burned to the ground. Or an email from Ulrike to Anselmo cancelling the contract because of accusations in the media of "irregularities" in the tendering process. But we thought better of it. Instead, we wanted to illustrate, with the help of this relatively simple story, what to do and say to become a highly-skilled international negotiator: prepare, question and adapt. And have fun.

Bibliography

Adamson, Brent & Dickson, Matthew Challenger Sale – Taking Control of the Customer Conversation, New York: Pengiun, 2011

Al-Omari, Jehad Understanding the Arab Culture – A practical cross-cultural guide to working in the Arab world, London: Constable & Robinson, 2nd edition, 2009

Blake, Robert & Mouton, Jane The Managerial Grid: The Key to Leadership Excellence. Houston: Gulf Publishing Co, 1964

Cain, Susan Quiet – The Power of Introverts in a World That Can't Stop Talking, London: Pengiun, 2012

Carté, Penny & Fox, Chris Bridging the Culture Gap, London: Kogan Page, 2nd edition, 2008

Ebner, Noam "Negotiation via email", in *Negotiation Excellence: Successful Deal Making*, Singapore: World Scientific Publishing, 2nd edition, 2014

Fisher, Roger, Ury William & Patton Bruce Getting To Yes – Negotiating Agreement without Giving In, New York: Penguin Books, 2nd edition, 1991

Hall, Edward T. & Hall, Mildred Understanding Cultural Differences: Germans, French & Americans, Yarmouth Maine: Intercultural Press, 1989

Hilligsøe, Søren & Jakobsen, Henning Sejer (ed.) Negotiation – the Art of Reaching Agreement, Århus: Academica, 2009

Hofstede, Geert Culture's Consequences, Beverly Hills CA: Sage Publications, 1981

Hofstede, Geert & Hofstede Geert Jan Cultures and Organisations, Software of the Mind, New York: McGraw-Hill, 2nd edition, 2005

James, Geoffrey Business Without the Bullsh*t. 49 Secrets and Shortcuts You Need to Know, New York: Grand Central Publishing, 2014

Karass, Chester L. Give & Take, Darby, PA, Diane Publishing Company, 1974

Kennedy, Gavin Everything is Negotiable : How to Get a Better Deal, Upper Saddle River, New Jersey: Prentice-Hall, 1983

Kennedy, Gavin Negotiate Everywhere, London: Arrow Books, 1985

Kennedy, Gavin The New Negotiating Edge : The Behavioural Approach for Results and Relationships, London: Nicholas Brealey Publishing, 1998

Mattock, John & Ehrenborg, Jons How to be a better negotiator, London: Kogan Page, 1996

Misino, Dominick J. Negotiate and Win, New York: McGraw-Hill 2004

Ogilvy, David Confessions of an Advertising Man, New York: Atheneum, 1963

Rackham, Neil SPIN Selling, New York: McGraw-Hill, 1988

Rackham, Neil & Carlisle, John The Effective Negotiator, 1978
Part 1: The Behaviour of Successful Negotiators, Journal of European Industrial Training, Vol. 2, iss. 6, pp 6-11
Part 2: Planning for Negotiations", Journal of European Industrial Training, Vol. 2 Iss: 7, pp.2 - 5

Wheeler, Michael The Art of Negotiation: How to Improvise Agreement in a Chaotic World, London: Simon & Schuster, 2013

Zeldin, Theodore The French, first published 1983, Random House edition 2012

Information on different cultures

Culture Shock - a series of books on over 40 different countries, listed on www.expatriates.com/directory/books/cshockbooks/

Etiquette, Customs and Protocol Guides - a series of brief but good cultural guides on 87 countries, produced by Kwintessential www.kwintessential. co.uk/cross-cultural. The same people have published 46 *Doing Business in ...* country guides

CIA World Fact Book - www.cia.gov/cia/publications/factbook/index.html

ITIM International - www.geert-hofstede.com

Special Interest - Procurement:

Dominick, Chas. The Dominick Matrix (www.nextlevelpurchasing.com)

Kearney, A.T. The Purchasing Chessboard (available in pdf-format) from www.atkearneypas.com/knowledge/publications/2008/Purchasing_Chessboard.pdf

Kraljic, Peter The Kraljic Matrix, first described in an article in the Harvard Business Review, Sep-Oct 1983: "Purchasing Must Become Supply Management"

Index